THE
HISTORY
ATLAS OF
SOUTH
AMERICA

The Macmillan Continental History Atlases

The History Atlas of Africa
The History Atlas of Asia
The History Atlas of Europe
The History Atlas of North America
The History Atlas of South America

THE
HISTORY
ATLAS OF
SOUTH
AMERICA

Dr. Edwin Early
Dr. Elizabeth Baquedano
Dr. Rebecca Earle
Dr. Caroline Williams
Dr. Anthony McFarlane
Dr. Joseph Smith

MACMILLAN•USA

MACMILLAN USA

A Simon & Schuster Macmillan Company
1633 Broadway
New York, N.Y. 10019-6785

Library of Congress Cataloging-in-Publication Data

Early, Edwin.
    The Macmillan history atlas of South America / Edwin Early and Elizabeth Baquedano. with Caroline Williams ... [et al.].
        p.   cm.
    Includes bibliographical references and index.
    ISBN 0–02–862583–8 (hardcover)
    1. South America—Historical geography—Maps.   I. Baquedano, Elizabeth.   II. Williams, Caroline, 1962- I   II. Title.
IV. Title: History atlas of South America.   V. Title: Atlas of South America
G1701.S1 E4   1998   <G&M>
911'.8—DC21

                                                                98–11455
                                                                CIP
                                                                MAPS

Manufactured in the United States
10 9 8 7 6 5 4 3 2 1

INTRODUCTION

For the purpose of this atlas, South America consists of the geographical area extending from Mexico in the north to Argentina in the south and including Central America, the islands of the Caribbean, and the mainland of South America. Today these countries number more than twenty independent nations, each with its own individual characteristics and history. Maps and charts are a useful tool to exemplify both the unity and diversity of the region. They fix the location of important places in history and indicate social and economic trends. Indeed, from the fifteenth century onward maps and charts provided Europeans with the key to explore, exploit, and settle in the "New World" of South America.

In Part I, Elizabeth Baquedano covers a massive period of history stretching for more than 10,000 years. The first people to settle in the region were the descendants of hunter-gatherers from Asia who had crossed the land bridge of the Bering Strait, which divides Siberia and Alaska. Over many centuries these people steadily moved southward until they reached Mexico, Central America, and South America. In the process they also adapted to local conditions and established farming communities and tribal states. Some evolved into impressive civilizations, of which the Olmecs, Mayas, and Toltecs are the most famous. At the time Columbus embarked on his epic voyage of "discovery" in 1492, two impressive Indian empires were in existence—the Aztecs in Mexico, and the Incas in Peru.

The Spanish and Portuguese voyages of discovery were motivated primarily by the desire for material gain, especially gold and silver. As soon as the new lands were discovered the monarchs of Spain and Portugal laid immediate claim to them, and sought to monopolize all the benefits for themselves. The story of the conquest and the establishment of empire is discussed in Part II by Caroline Williams. The actual Spanish conquest itself was a remarkable military feat in that just a few hundred Spaniards defeated the Aztec and Inca empires so easily and quickly. In fact, the successes of both Cortés in Mexico and Pizarro in Peru, were greatly assisted by the cooperation of local Indian tribes. In return, however, the Indians suffered political subjection, economic exploitation, and religious persecution. The Europeans also brought epidemic diseases against which the Indians lacked immunity. The result was a serious decline in population and a shortfall in labor, which was partly met by European immigration and the introduction of black slaves forcibly transported from Africa. In the process, the population of Latin America became racially mixed and diverse.

The search for precious metals stimulated the Spaniards to explore further and press on to colonize Mexico, and Central and South America. With the king of Spain at its head, a system of colonial administration was developed to rule a vast empire extending from Oregon in North America to Chile and Argentina in South America. At the same time the Portuguese retained control of Brazil. They were initially less interested in empire-building than the Spaniards and concentrated on trade rather than colonization. The threat of foreign interlopers, however, persuaded the Portuguese to establish permanent settlements in Brazil and enforce their claim to that enormous country.

As Anthony McFarlane shows in Part III, by the middle of the eighteenth century the Spanish and Portuguese colonies had developed into distinctive economies and societies. The attempt, however, of the Bourbon kings to revive Spanish power and control over the empire was only partly successful and provoked opposition and popular revolt, notably in Peru and Colombia.

In Part IV Rebecca Earle analyzes the impact of the shock waves of the Napoleonic Wars in Europe after they reached the Americas in 1810. From Mexico to Argentina the creole elite sought to exploit the collapse of Spanish authority by organizing juntas to exercise local self-government. A period of major violence and disorder ensued in which internal rivalries hindered the struggle for political independence and temporarily aided the reimposition of Spanish rule. Two heroic military campaigns were fought—led in the north by Bolívar and in the south by San Martín . The Wars for Independence were eventually concluded in 1826. With the exception of the Caribbean islands of Cuba and Puerto Rico, Spain acknowledged the loss of its American empire. Portugal also suffered a similar fate when Brazil successfully declared its independence in 1822.

In Part V Edwin Early addresses the theme of transition from colony to independent state. The majority of countries initially proclaimed liberal constitutions and declared themselves to be republics. Internal rivalries between political parties, prominent families, and regions, however, created enduring friction and instability. Instead of democratically elected governments, political power was frequently seized and held for long periods by authoritarian rulers, *caudillos.* The most politically stable nation was Brazil, which retained monarchical rule for most of the nineteenth century. Political weakness made Latin America vulnerable to foreign designs, though this mostly took the form of economic penetration, especially by Britain. Mexico, however, suffered a considerable loss of national territory to the United States after being defeated in the Mexican-American War, 1846–1848. Territorial disputes in South America also resulted in the War of the Triple Alliance, 1865–1870, in which Paraguay was defeated by Argentina, Brazil, and Uruguay; and the War of the Pacific, 1879–1883, in which Chile was victorious against Bolivia and Peru.

The rise of "modern" Latin America is investigated by Edwin Early in Part VI. The years from 1870 to 1914 were a period of economic transformation in which Latin America became an efficient, low-cost producer of staple exports to the world economy. The whole region, but particularly Argentina, also experienced a massive influx of European immigration and foreign capital investment. The economic dislocations of World War I and the Great Depression of the 1930s underlined, however, the dangers of too much reliance upon exports and the smooth functioning of the world economy. Protest was evident in Mexico, where hostility toward foreign influence and a desire for economic and cultural independence led to the Mexican Revolution. There was also widespread popular resentment against the growing power of the United States and what was perceived as that country's determination to play a dominant role in the diplomatic affairs of the hemisphere. Argentina conspicuously refused to become an ally of the United States in both world wars. American diplomacy was, however, successful in forming closer links with the other leading South American nations, most notably Brazil.

In Part VII, Edwin Early examines some of the main features of contemporary Latin America. The desire for democracy has persisted, but the struggle for political freedom has often been ended by the imposition of authoritarian rule in the form of military dictatorship. The resort to political repression, however, has provoked counterviolence and the organization of national liberation movements, especially in Cuba and Central America. A root cause of political instability has been the economic poverty of the region. But the programs designed to advance industrial production and development have achieved only modest success at best. Progress has been hampered by explosive population growth, galloping inflation, and the fluctuating demand for Latin American staple products in the world economy. A variety of economic policies have been adopted, ranging from protectionism and import substitution to the abolition of controls on the import of capital and foreign goods. Regional trading blocs such as the North American Free Trade Area (NAFTA) and Mercosur have also been established and have made a promising beginning. Relations with the rest of the world, however, have not been neglected. The nations of Latin America are closely involved not only in discussions on international economic issues but also in participation in measures to improve the environment and to control the narcotics trade.

Joseph Smith

Contents

PART I: THE PRE-COLUMBIAN ERA

Despite many years of debate, the age and nature of the initial peopling of the New World remains essentially unresolved. Archaeologists agree that human beings probably crossed the Bering Land Bridge and through the "ice-free corridor," or along the Pacific coast by boat. Arguments are given for at least three distinct migrations over thousands of years. These occurred around 12,000 BC. However, recent research has concluded that this date might be as long ago as 40,000 BC. What has been commonly held is the view that man came over from Siberia, across the Bering Land Bridge into Alaska. However in the last four decades, due to advances in dating methods, linguistics, paleoenviron-

A prehistoric rock painting from Zamora in Ecuador shows a hunting scene where people pursue a snake or perhaps a large serpent.

ment reconstructions, and the finding of pre-Clovis sites, this view has been weakened. An earlier entry has been hypothesized, and an alternative entry route along the Pacific coast.

The commonly held view of the entrance to Alaska is via the Bering Strait; by walking either across the bridge which connected Siberia to Alaska or over the ice, or by rafting over.

There are also scholars who believe the entry into the American continent was along the Pacific Coast in view of the fact that there were well-spaced breaks in the chain of coastal glaciers, and the existence of refugia for plants and animals along the coast, which was richer than the corridor would have been. There is much confusion concerning when the bridge and corridor could have been exposed. As most of the ideas put forward are unverifiable it is possible that humans entered by boat, or by land to Alaska and/or by boat to the coast of North America, at any time in the last 40,000 to 60,000 years.

The most widely accepted earliest occupation in North America appears to be 15,000 BC and 14,000–12,000 BC in South America. This theory fits in well with the fully accepted Paleo-Indian culture, Clovis, that appears around this time. Clovis and Clovis-like fluted points are reported as surface finds from the Mexican states of Coahuila, Sonora, Durango, and Jalisco.

During his initial spread from North to South America, man must have passed through the narrow funnel of Mexico, but the date is still unknown. There is evidence that man reached southern Chile by 7000 BC, and finds from highland Peru indicate that man was present around 22,000 BC and that he was making stone tools by 13,000 BC. Excavations in Tlapacoya in the Basin of Mexico suggest that man may have been there 22,000 to 20,000 years ago.

The Pre-Columbian inhabitants of the Americas who developed most in political, economic, and cultural terms lived in three broad geographical regions: Mesoamerica, a large area running from central Mexico down to the fringes of present day Nicaragua; South America, particularly in parts of Peru,

Colombia, Ecuador, Bolivia, and Chile; and in the so-called Intermediate Area between the two. In these particular areas the political and cultural organization of the indigenous peoples far outstripped that of the many other Indian groupings living throughout the Americas, many of whom were nomads, hunter-gatherers, or residents in simple villages in diverse climatic regions.

Mesoamerica: From 1500 BC onward Mesoamerican societies depended primarily on plant cultivation for subsistence with corn as the major staple food. The only domesticated animals were the dog and the turkey, both of which were consumed as food. Hunting and fishing also provided a supplementary food supply in areas suitable for such activities.

By Old World standards technology in Mesoamerica was primitive. Metal was used only after AD 800, and was quite scarce until the arrival of the Spanish, unlike in South America, where metals were in use very early on.

Ceramics were produced for both utilitarian and ornamental purposes from 1500 BC onward. Elaborate ornaments were made of shell, bone, wood, and stone. Many headdresses were decorated with the feathers of colorful birds. Records of important political and ritual events, as well as myths and traditions, were documented in codices, painted books made of bark paper or deerskin.

Religion penetrated every aspect of Mesoamerican life. Gods often had to be fed with sacrificial offerings of human blood and hearts; likewise, self-sacrifice was an important religious practice. Blood was drawn from the earlobes, tongue, legs, and other bodily areas.

The Mesoamerican people worshiped various gods, and Huitzilopochtli, the Aztec tribal god, was offered mass sacrifices at certain times of year. Tlaloc also took his share of blood, and heads were offered up to the gods and placed in skull racks called *tzompantli*s. These two deities were worshiped at The Great Temple of the Aztecs. This building consisted of a pyramidal form with two shrines reached by steep stairways. Mesoamerican cities each had a single, enormous plaza with several buildings, each with its own set of temples. Ceremonial architecture was suited to rituals, conducted in and before the temples on the stairways and stepped facades of the pyramids. Rituals were watched by large crowds gathered in the plazas. Teotihuacán is the best example of a city built on a grid plan, with a series of plazas surrounded by pyramidal structures. The most impressive pyramids to be

A Maya carved stone relief showing a scene of sacrifice, from the ball court at El Tajín, Mexico.

seen in the Americas are here and are the so-called Pyramid of the Sun and Pyramid of the Moon. This city was one of the largest of the Americas, housing a population of perhaps 250,000 inhabitants. The city seemed to have reached the height of its power in the fifth century AD. After prospering for almost a millennium, it suffered a major social disaster in the eighth century AD, ending in total collapse.

The Intermediate Area: This area takes its name from its "intermediate" geographical position between the two areas of the pre-Columbian American "high cultures," Mesoamerica and Peru. It includes lower Central America, Pacific and Andean Colombia and Ecuador, and a portion of northwestern Venezuela. This area does not have impressive architecture or monumental art, but the ceramic art and jade work are important achievements.

South America: Knowledge of the ancient civilizations of South America is very uneven because most archaeological work has been concentrated in those areas, such as Peru, Colombia, and Chile, where one can expect to make spectacular finds of gold, silver, and copper objects as well as fine pottery, sculpture, and architecture. The last few years have seen work carried out in the Amazon region despite the difficulties of excavation there.

Because the environmental conditions in South America are so varied, the range of plants available, both wild and domesticated, is immense.

Manioc is a plant spread and cultivated by the tropical forest peoples from Brazil and as far north as Mexico. In the highlands the staple food is the potato, together with corn, which also grows at high altitudes. Other important food crops include beans, squash, peppers, and peanuts. In the lowlands the main crop is cotton, which has been cultivated since early times.

Along the coasts of both Ecuador and Peru the inhabitants developed irrigation agriculture in 2000 BC, and the sea was a valuable source of food. Approximately 4,000 meters above sea level, in the highlands, agriculture had also been developed in the *altiplano*, on the border between Peru and Bolivia.

The Peruvian area: The most advanced cultural development in South America took place in the central Andes and Pacific coast. This region is divided by most archaeologists into chronological periods that alternate between "horizons"—when an art style is found over a very wide area—and intermediate periods, when regional art styles indicate an absence of widespread movements.

The Initial Period (c. 1800–1200 BC) saw the building of ceremonial centers, and one of the most elaborate is La Galgada, situated in the Río Santa drainage basin.

During the Early Horizon (c. 1000–200 BC), there was a long period of regional development and technological experimentation, during which the Mochica (north coast) and Nazca (south coast) cultures flourished and produced their beautiful pottery styles.

The Middle Horizon (550–1000 AD) replaces the Early Intermediate Period. This period saw the rise of large urban settlements, especially that of the Huari-Tiahuanaco of the highlands. Huari-Tiahuanaco spread their empire-building process to the coast.

The Late Intermediate Period (1200–1300 AD): During this period a number of kingdoms (Chimú, Chancas, Huancas) flourished; one of the most notable ones was the Chimú of the north coast.

The Late Horizon (1300–1532 AD). The south highland kingdom in the late Intermediate Period, the Inca, with their capital at Cuzco, established an empire that eventually reached from southern Peru to northern Colombia. This period is known as the Late Horizon. The Inca empire stretched from Cuzco north to the Ecuador-Colombia border and south into central Chile and northwest Argentina.

Complex stone architecture begins in the third millennium BC in the central Andes. In general, stone architecture and sculpture are highland traits, and the use of sun-dried adobe bricks is confined to the coast.

Coastal people were renowned metallurgists, and made fine pottery and textiles.

The road system was very efficient and served many purposes. Observation posts, tollgates, and small posts for runners, called *chasqui* posts, were built beside the road at intervals of approximately every one or two miles. These posts were occupied by officials responsible for control of traffic of persons and goods. The Incas built over 25,000 kilometers of all-weather roads for men and llama caravans, from sea level to heights of about 5,500 meters. The roads allowed trade and exchange with several areas; for example, they obtained seashells (*lullu*) from Ecuador, and potatoes came from the highland area.

A reconstruction of an Early Classic period Maya temple at Tikal, showing a view of the North Acropolis.

Religion was the most powerful binding and permeative activity in the whole of South America. Every aspect of life revolved around religion in every culture in South America.

Information about religion comes from various sources: symbolic or religious architecture, art representations, burial practices, the contents that accompanied the deceased, the writings of the Spanish chroniclers, as well as analogies drawn with practices that persist today among the indigenous peoples.

In general, South and Central America had similar religious practices, with almost infinite variations, the most important supernatural forces being nature deities; water, sky, earth, mountains, and sea. Viracocha was the most important of the Andean gods, particularly for the members of the elite.

Judging by the depictions of ritual and sacrifice in pre-Columbian art, beheading was the most frequent of offertory practices. In Mesoamerica there was also a direct association between beheading, the ritual ball game, and agriculture. The losers of the ball game were beheaded, and the skulls were used as symbols of victory as well as life-sustaining qualities.

EARLY FARMERS AND TRIBAL PEOPLES

The domestication of plants and animals in the Andes includes both flora and fauna unique to this area as well as domesticates, which have a wider geographical spread. Particularly with plants, there exist varieties that have undergone such changes that they can no longer propagate unaided by man. Examples of these include corn, oca, and ulluco.

The first plants were taken into cultivation in the highlands between about 8000 and 6000 BC; these included chili pepper (*Capsicum*), ulluco (*Ullucus tuberosus*), beans (*Phaseolus vulgaris* and *Phaseolus lunatus*), and squash (*Cucurbita*). Between 6000 and 4000 BC corn (*Zea mays*) made its appearance. Reeds, which were important as construction material, appeared between 2500 and 1800 BC. On the coast, between 4200 and 2500 BC, other crops followed, such as avocados (*Persea americana*), peanuts (*Arachis hypogaea*), and yucca (*Manihot esculenta*). The cotton plant, of importance for clothing, was first cultivated around 2500 BC. Corn was considered a sacred plant, and for this reason was, and still is, cultivated wherever possible. It was also made into a beer, called *chicha*.

Corn (or maize) was first brought into domestic cultivation sometime between 1000 and 5000 BC. The later Inca, Maya, and Aztecs relied heavily on this plant as the major food source supporting their civilizations.

Llamas, alpacas, ducks, guinea pigs, and dogs were domesticated for their meat, and in some instances their wool and the loads they could carry. Their domestication took place some time between 5000 and 1800 BC.

Some of the more important sites for this period are Guitarrero cave, El Paraíso, La Paloma, Las Aldas, Chilca, Áspero, and Huaca Prieta in the Chicama Valley.

The development of agriculture is associated with the growth in sedentary life and the development of complex society. Agricultural systems based on terracing and irrigation are particularly linked to the establishment of hierarchical statelike structures.

In Mesoamerica, between 7000 and 6000 BC, cultivation was only just beginning. There was a time in the Tehuacán Valley when people ate seeds of wild grasses, maguey leaves, chili peppers, and

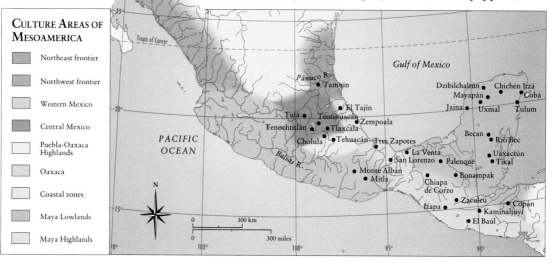

CULTURE AREAS OF MESOAMERICA

- Northeast frontier
- Northwest frontier
- Western Mexico
- Central Mexico
- Puebla-Oaxaca Highlands
- Oaxaca
- Coastal zones
- Maya Lowlands
- Maya Highlands

fragments of meat. At a later stage the diet was more varied, containing grasshoppers, snails, insects, game, and plants. The gathering of wild plants continued for a long time, but gradually some of the wild plants were brought into cultivation. People cultivated various foodstuffs in different regions: avocados and squashes in the El Riego region; and pumpkins, chilies, and bottle gourds in Tamaulipas.

Between 6000 and 4000 BC corn originated in Mexico, and it is very likely that it was transmitted to South America. Around 5000 and 3000 BC corn and beans became important cultigens in some areas. Not all the parts of Mesoamerica are dry and apt for corn cultivation. The tropical lowlands relied more on root crops and forest products. Along the coast, fishing was the most important source of food, together with shellfish collecting and hunting. Gathering continued with the gradual introduction of farming.

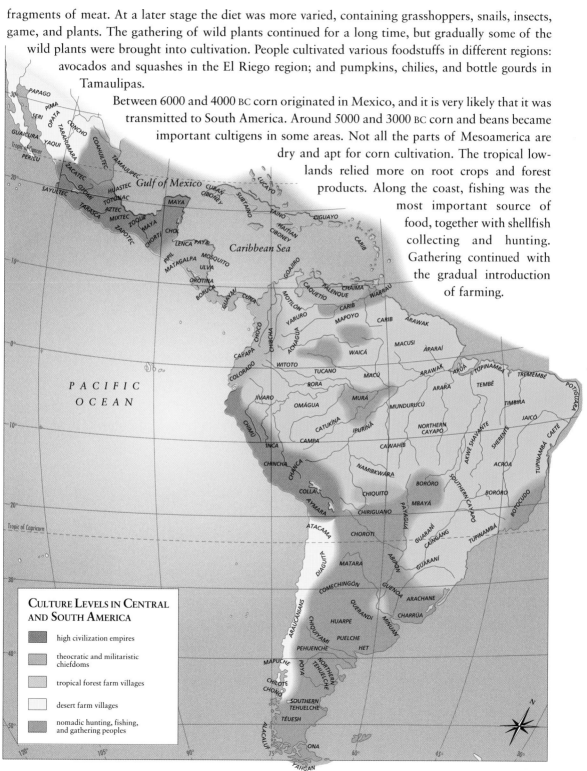

CULTURE LEVELS IN CENTRAL
AND SOUTH AMERICA

- high civilization empires
- theocratic and militaristic chiefdoms
- tropical forest farm villages
- desert farm villages
- nomadic hunting, fishing, and gathering peoples

OLMEC CIVILIZATION

Olmec civilization developed during a long occupation of the river valleys of the Gulf Coast region of Mexico. For a thousand years, small communities of egalitarian gatherers and farmers in this region slowly evolved into chiefdoms, and by 1200 BC complex political and religious institutions, and monumental architecture, began to be a part of the landscape.

Regional centers such as San Lorenzo and La Venta, which had evolved a chiefdom level of social hierarchy, politically organized the smaller communities within their territories. Archaeological investigations at the monumental sites of San Lorenzo and La Venta indicate that territorial control included a social system with political unity, similar religious practices and symbols, and extensive trade networks that linked centers within and beyond the Gulf Coast Olmec heartland. While cultural traits of the Olmec are present throughout Mesoamerica, it is uncertain if this is due to the physical presence of Olmec people from the Gulf Coast or because of trade and the diffusion of traits.

The Olmec exported animal and reptile skins, cacao beans, rubber, and ceramic pots and figurines throughout most of Mesoamerica. Some investigators have proposed that Olmec artisans may have traveled the long distance to western and central Mexico, and to Central America to provide specialized artistic services to the peoples in those regions. In turn, traders from those same areas, or returning Olmecs, brought highly sought-after materials for elite consumption such as feathers, shell, obsidian, bone, mineral coloring agents, jade and jadeite, and greenstone.

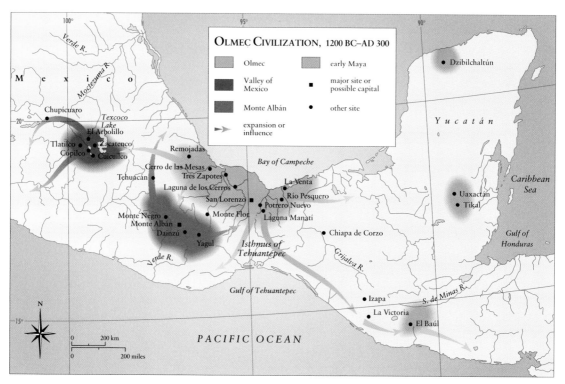

Most scholars have considered that there was a diffusion of Olmec cultural traits, objects, and beliefs throughout Mesoamerica, but not physical occupation. The Olmec cultural presence is characterized by two horizons: Horizon A or San Lorenzo, and Horizon B or La Venta. San Lorenzo Horizon A cultural markers are geographically widespread and distinctive, but limited to ceramic whiteware babies, three-dimensional stone sculpture, and carved ceramics, including bowls, birds, fish, and other animals. Horizon A cultural materials are noted in central Mexico at Tlatilco, Tiapocoya, and Las Bocas; in Oaxaca at San José Mogote; as far away as the states of Guerrero and Chiapas; and in Guatemala. Horizon B materials such as carved jade figurines and narrative three-dimensional stone sculpture had

This massive stone head of an Olmec ruler, dating from around 1200 BC, is intended to project power and grandeur. The carving weighs some 20 tons and is over 9 feet (3 meters) in height.

their inspiration from the Olmec of La Venta. Horizon A materials are lacking during this period, and Horizon B has a wider distribution than Horizon A, reaching as far as the Nicova region of Costa Rica and the Pacific piedmont of Guatemala, but also is found in the central Mexico states of Guerrero, Puebla, Chiapas, and Morelos.

Olmec art fully expresses a unified symbol complex in its ceramics, and sculpture, and those symbols are thought to have stemmed from a theocratically based belief system. Lifelike portraits of elite and other exceptional individuals are represented in a variety of materials, including stone and wood. Religious subject matter is also represented by using materials worked into three-dimensional sculptures and bas-reliefs. The Olmec were masters of the art of stone carving, and were able to create three-dimensional masterpieces from jade and other hard stones.

An important but unresolved question about Olmec civilization remains. Was Olmec civilization the Mother Culture of Mesoamerica, with Olmec cultural traits accepted and integrated in some form by the Maya and other civilizations that follow? Or were the Olmec no more than one of the many regional cultures during the Mesoamerican Pre-Classic period that contributed in varying degrees to later civilizations? There is no consensus among scholars concerning the answer to this question.

RISE OF THE MAYA

A ballcourt marker from the Mayan city of Chinkultic.

Maya civilization had its origins during the Late Pre-Classic (400 BC to AD 250) in the Highlands, and in the Pacific Coastal plain of Mesoamerica.

During the Late Pre-Classic (AD 250) in the Maya lowlands, additional complex societies began to emerge with social stratification, and monumental architecture. The Late Pre-Classic site of El Mirador, in the lowlands of Guatemala, has buildings far larger than those constructed by the Maya during the later Classic period, when Maya society reached its greatest extent. The core area of El Mirador, dedicated to civil and ceremonial buildings, is more than one and a half kilometers in length.

Based on a long development during the Pre-Classic, around AD 250 a flowering of Maya civilization began to take place. This period, called the Classic, is characterized by highly organized civic and religious ceremonies, military organization and tactics, art, markets, and the manufacturing of craft goods for local and long-distance trade, intellectual pursuits, and control of most civic and religious practices by a dynastic elite.

Population increase led to the concentration of power in the lowland Maya regions in the form of kingdoms with cities as their central focus. City-states occupied and began to control all viable lands, and warfare between those states was carried out to expand territory and gain wealth. For example, the defeat in AD 562 of Tikal, one of the largest cities in the southern lowlands by the allied states of Caracol and Calakmul, provided new wealth and power to those states, but also led to more warfare in the area by other Maya cities bent on expansion.

Similarly, cities such as Palenque, Toniná, Bonampak, Yaxchilán, and Piedras Negras flourished in the western lowlands and along the Usumacinta River. Archaeological excavations and analysis of written Maya texts from those sites provide a similar story of royal lineages, warfare, ritual sacrifice, trade, intense agricultural practices, and eventual weakening of royal authority that had been centralized in the king.

The ensuing depopulation of the southern lowlands during the Late Classic period may have been due to continual warfare,

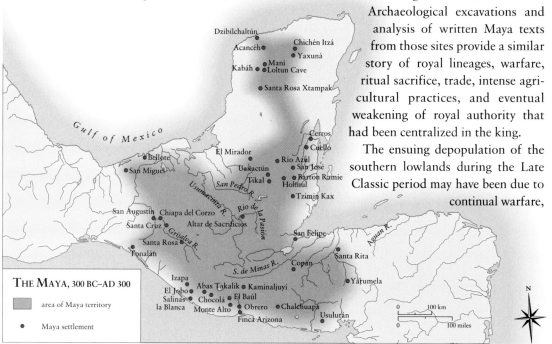

THE MAYA, 300 BC–AD 300

area of Maya territory

● Maya settlement

Dzibilchaltún
Acancéh
Chichén Itzá
Yaxuná
Maní
Kabáh ● Loltun Cave
Santa Rosa Xtampak
Gulf of Mexico
Cerros
Cuello
Bellote El Mirador Río Azul
San Miguel Uaxactún San José
Barton Ramie
San Pedro R. Tikal Holmúl
Usumacinta R. Tzimin Kax
Rio de la Pasión
San Augustín Chiapa del Corzo
Santa Cruz Altar de Sacrificios
Grijalva R. San Felipe
Aguan R.
Santa Rosa
Tonalá Santa Rita
S. de Minas R. Copán
Izapa Yarumela
El Jobo Abas Takalik Kaminaljuyú
Salinas ● Chocolá ● El Baúl
la Blanca Monte Alto ● Obrero ● Chalchuapá
Finca Arizona Usulután

0   100 km
0   100 miles

N

food shortages, and overuse of the environment, and a belief in an ideology rooted in a fatalistic religious dogma. This combination of factors probably eroded the political system, which was deeply rooted in kingship and its dynasties, and led to a division of political unity. For example, in the 400-year-old southeastern city of Copán around AD 800, archaeological and epigraphic evidence indicates that dynastic rule came to an end.

At the end of the Late Classic (AD 800) and during the Terminal Classic period the population of the southern lowlands moved slowly to more prosperous areas like Yucatán in the north, where Maya civilization was regenerated. The political structure of the Post-Classic (c. AD 1200) is characterized by governance of the state by an elite ruling council, and a social structure that reflected cultural influences from the highlands of Mexico. In northern Yucatán, large regions were under the control of city-states such as Chichén Itzá, and the influence of earlier cities such as Uxmal and Cobá was virtually eliminated. Ideally situated where it could control trade, Chichén Itzá became the most powerful capital in the area until its final defeat in AD 1221 by the physically smaller Mayapán. Control of the region by Mayapán ended in AD 1440 and the state was divided into smaller units.

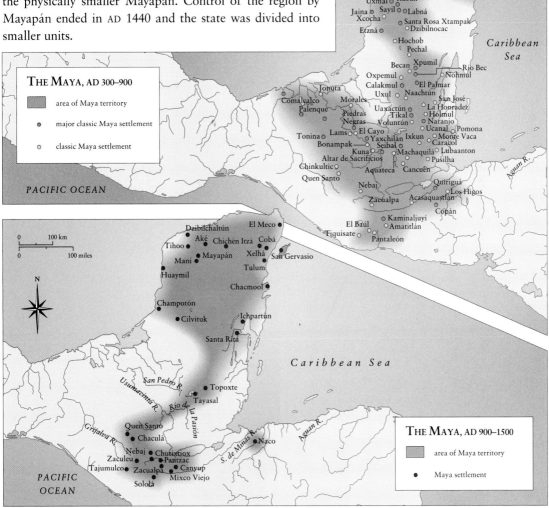

TOLTEC STATES

The Nahuatl word Toltecatl, which has been simplified to Toltec in English, basically refers to an inhabitant of Tula or Tollan, another Nahuatl word that literally means "place of reeds" but generally refers to an urban settlement. To the later Aztecs the term Toltec also described the skilled craftsmen, and all the legendary past glories were attributed to the Toltec era by the same Aztecs. However, Toltec architecture and art are not considered as impressive or aesthetically pleasing as those of other ancient Mesoamericans, and it is obvious that the Toltecs were not the skilled masters the Aztecs believed them to be.

Archaeology and ethnohistory have revealed that the Toltecs were a multi-ethnic group made up of people from north, northwest, and central Mexico who spoke Nahuatl, Otomi, and several other languages. The major immigrant groups among them were the Tolteca-Chichimeca, the Nahuatl and Otomi-speaking peasants of modest cultural attainments from the frontier zone north of Tula, and the Nonoalca, the highly civilized priests, merchants, and craftsmen, probably from Teotihuacán or the lowlands of southern Veracruz and Tabasco.

Tula, the Toltec heartland, lies north of the Basin of Mexico in the southern part of the modern Mexican state of Hidalgo. This location is farther north than any other ancient Mesoamerican

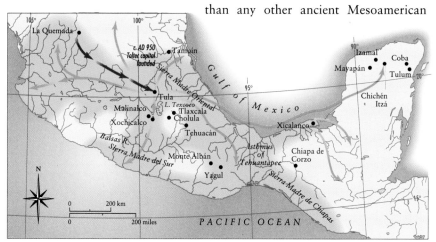

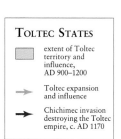

TOLTEC STATES

extent of Toltec territory and influence, AD 900–1200

Toltec expansion and influence

Chichimec invasion destroying the Toltec empire, c. AD 1170

city. The site is located on the highland river valley, which provided the inhabitants both rich alluvial soils and irrigation water for farming.

In central Mexican chronology, the Toltec period persisted between AD 900 and 1200, which corresponds to early Post-Classic period. Its relatively short period of expansion implies that the boundaries of the Toltec state must have shifted very rapidly, but at its peak the area is supposed to include much of central Mexico and adjacent areas to the north; specifically Hidalgo, the Basin of Mexico, the Toluca Valley, and parts of the Bajío and Morelos.

As a successor of the Mesoamerican traditions, Tula shows in its archaeological remains many traits inherited from Teotihuacán and other earlier Mesoamerican civilizations. Likewise, some new elements were invented by the Toltecs. Some of the common traits of Mesoamerican sites, such as a city laid out along a grid plan, pyramids with *talud-tablero* structures, ball courts, and *tzompantlis*, or skulls racks, can also be found in Tula. On the other hand, Chacmool sculptures, Atlantean figures, extensive use of columns as roof supports, and a *coatepantli* (serpent wall) are considered to have been the innovations of the Toltecs that affected both the contemporary and later civilizations in Post-Classic Mesoamerica, especially the Mayan city of Chichén Itzá and the Aztec culture.

The Toltec influence can be particularly seen at Chichén Itzá, a major contemporary Mayan city in Yucatán, in not only similar architectural features and motifs mentioned above, but also in their ethnohistory. The historical annals of the later period relate the existence of the same legendary hero called Quetzalcoatl in Nahuatl, or Kukulcan in Maya, both meaning "feathered serpent," who established the Toltec civilization and at the same time appeared as a great cultural hero in the Maya region.

The fall of Tula is thought to have been caused by diverse problems. It is believed that Toltecs, at the end of their empire, faced difficulties relating to subsistence and a poorly integrated social system along with external threats from enemies in different locations.

The Castillo built on the plaza at New Chichén Itzá. Dating from about 1400, the last phase of construction, this structure combines decorative features of both Toltec and Maya origins.

TEOTIHUACÁN—THE METROPOLIS

Mesoamerica was dominated by the power of the city of Teotihuacán for several hundred years. It was located 28 miles away from modern Mexico City.

Teotihuacán grew dramatically during the first few centuries after Christ, reaching a peak population well over 100,000 and perhaps in excess of 200,000 by the middle of the Classic period. This made it not only the largest city in the Americas, but among the half-dozen largest cities in the world at the time.

Around AD 200 more than 80 percent of the population of the Basin of Mexico lived in Teotihuacán. This concentration of regional population in Teotihuacán, together with the rigidity of its plan, has suggested the exercise of absolute political control to many scholars. It is likely that because the city enjoyed such an important place in religion, and because it was a very important economic center, it was attractive for people to live there.

Religious architecture dominated the city. The most imposing buildings were laid out along the so-called Avenue of the Dead. These included the largest pyramids to be seen in Mesoamerica, known as the Pyramid of the Sun and the Pyramid of the Moon. The latter guards the northern end of the central axis, the Avenue of the Dead. The Pyramid of the Sun is located east of the Avenue, and it faces west. The original buildings were built with the typical style of *talud* (talus) and *tablero* (entablature), or panel-and-slope wall profiles. At Teotihuacán the *tablero* always was larger than the *talud*. This style of architecture was introduced in about AD 200, and became almost ubiquitous during the next 500 years on the stepped pyramids that are typical of the city's religious architecture. This type of architecture can also be seen at the Great Temple of the Aztecs, the mecca of the Aztecs.

Teotihuacán spread its influence all over Mesoamerica but the site was abandoned and ravaged about AD 650. Next came the Toltecs, bridging the gap between the culture of Teotihuacán and that of the Aztecs.

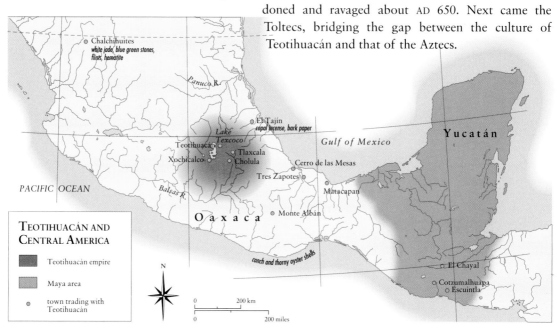

Chalchihuites
white jade, blue green stones, flints, hematite

Pánuco R.

El Tajín
copal incense, bark paper

Lake
Texcoco

Teotihuacán

Xochicalco

Tlaxcala
Cholula

Cerro de las Mesas

Tres Zapotes

Matacapan

Gulf of Mexico

Yucatán

PACIFIC OCEAN

Balsas R.

O a x a c a Monte Albán

conch and thorny oyster shells

El Chayal

Cotzumalhuapa
Escuintla

**TEOTIHUACÁN AND
CENTRAL AMERICA**

Teotihuacán empire

Maya area

town trading with
Teotihuacán

N

0   200 km

0   200 miles

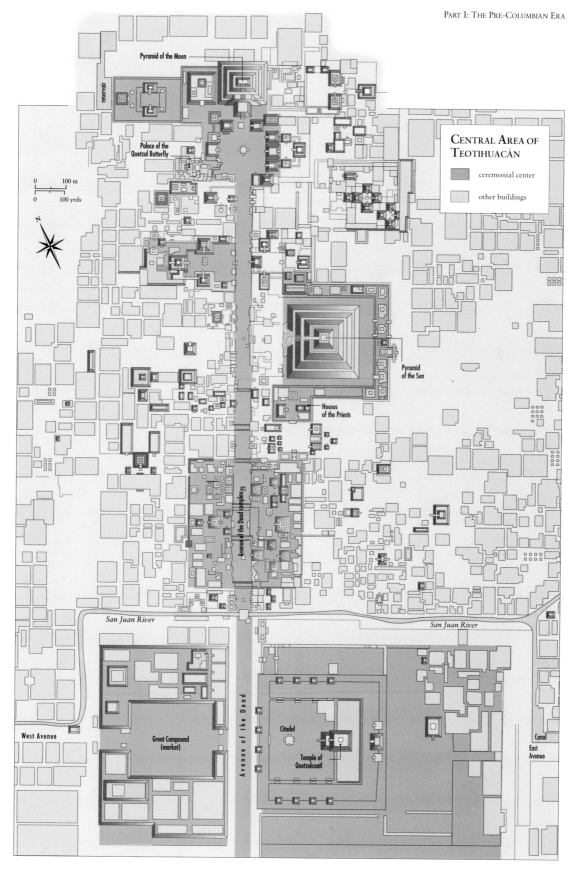

Pyramid of the Moon

reservoir

Palace of the
Quetzal Butterfly

**CENTRAL AREA OF
TEOTIHUACÁN**

ceremonial center

other buildings

0   100 m

0   100 yrds

N

Pyramid
of the Sun

Houses
of the Priests

Avenue of the Dead complex

San Juan River

San Juan River

West Avenue

Avenue of the Dead

Canal

East
Avenue

Great Compound
(market)

Citadel

Temple of
Quetzalcoatl

THE RISE OF THE AZTEC EMPIRE

The term "Aztec" refers to a generic name for the Nahuatl-speaking people of the Valley of Mexico at the time of the Spanish Conquest in 1519–1521. The Aztec culture thrived from the mid twelfth century to 1521 around its capital, Tenochtitlán (the modern Mexico City), which was founded by the Mexicas, a group of the Nahuatl-speaking people originated from the barbaric Chichimec tribes in the north of Mexico. Tenochtitlán was the last and one of the most powerful empires of the entire Mesoamerican history, which lasted for about 3,000 years. Especially during the last one hundred years before the Spanish conquest, the Aztec empire extended from the Gulf of Mexico to the Pacific Ocean, and from what is now north central Mexico to Guatemala.

Scholars divide Aztec history into three stages: the period of wandering (1168–1325), the period of consolidation in the Valley of Mexico (1325–1440), and the period of expansion and conquest (1440–1521). After the fall of Tula, the Chichimecs from the north started invading the central Valley of Mexico. The last group of Chichimecs are called the Aztecs or Mexicas. The period of peregrination began with the Aztecs' departure from Aztlan (the Place of Herons), their legendary homeland, in 1168. The geographical location of Aztlan is still unclear, but the place is thought to have been an island surrounded by reeds in the middle of a lagoon somewhere in the northwest of Mexico.

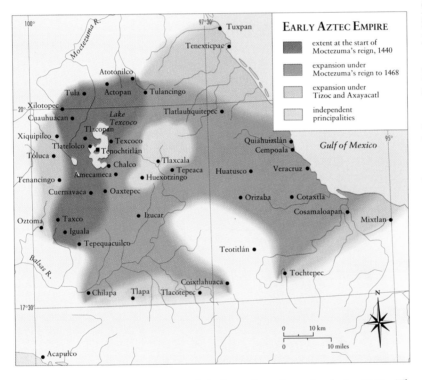

The period of consolidation started with the Aztecs' arrival in the Valley of Mexico in 1325, after two hundred years of nomadic life. Finally, in Texcoco Lake, they found a promised land, which was a small island where an eagle perched on a cactus devouring a serpent, predicted by Huitzilopochtli, their tribal deity. On that island they started building their capital, Tenochtitlán. Fighting in war as the mercenaries of the Tepanecs, and gaining power, the Aztec's first monarch was Acamapichtli in 1376.

The period of expansion began in 1440 when the fifth king, Moctezuma Ilhuicamina, ascended the throne. During this period the Aztec empire continued to increase its territory and to gain political power by means of alliances, tribute, and trade under the reigns of the successors, Axayacatl, Tizoc, Ahuitzotl, and Moctezuma Xocoyotzin. At the time of the Spanish Conquest, the Aztec influence reached as far as Guatemala, Belize, and western parts of Honduras and El Salvador.

The Aztec political-economic activities were controlled by their religion, based on the concept that the universe was maintained by the collaboration of gods and human beings. Human sacrifice was practiced on many occasions as an important ritual, offering human hearts to the solar deity in order to keep the sun in motion, and blood to the earth deity to nourish the soil. To the Aztecs, fighting in war was meant not only to gain territory and obtain tribute, but also to get captives for human sacrifice.

In planning Tenochtitlán, the Aztecs placed at the center the Great Temple, or the twin pyramid, dedicated to their two principal deities, Huitzilopochtli, the god of war, and Tlaloc, the god of rain. This structure provided the dual notion of the universe, in which the balance of two elements, such as gods and humans, heaven and earth, life and death, was considered to be crucial for maintaining the world. The Great Temple represented the fundamental elements to sustain the empire; war and agriculture, the sun and water. Moreover, the Aztecs conceived this pyramid as Coatepec, the mythical place of Huitzilopochtli's birth. Therefore, the Great Temple represented not only the physical center of the world but also the temporal axis connecting past and present.

A carefully carved head of an Aztec Eagle Warrior.

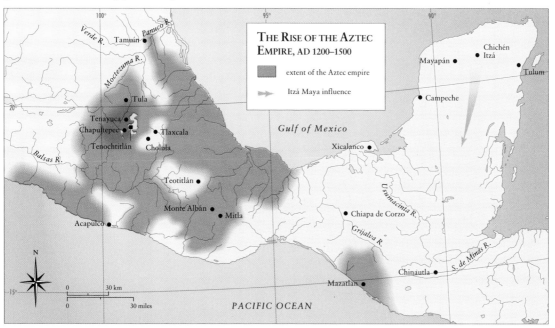

THE RISE OF THE AZTEC EMPIRE, AD 1200–1500

extent of the Aztec empire

Itzá Maya influence

Chimú Kingdom

A Moche culture stirrup spouted jar, at right, decorated with a fisherman and his pelican.

The Chimú culture arose out of the earlier Moche civilization, and was centered on the north coast of Peru. The Chimú culture lasted from c. AD 700 to 1470, and there are four phases recognized in its development: Early Chimú, Middle Chimú, Late Chimú, and Chimú Inca.

Spanish colonial documents carry fragmentary references to the kingdom of Chimor. There is also a myth of Naymlap, a legendary Chimú ruler who was said to have come from overseas,

together with an idol made of green stone. He established a dynasty of twelve kings, and his twelve grandsons are supposed to have founded twelve cities. Dynastic succession among the north coast rulers passed from brother to brother until the generation was exhausted, when it went to the next generation.

Chimú society was based on a dual social and administrative structure. A hierarchical state religion functioned, in which the rulers ensured the welfare of the state and people via their worship of and sacrifice to ancestors and deities.

The economic foundation of the state was based on irrigation agriculture and the exploitation

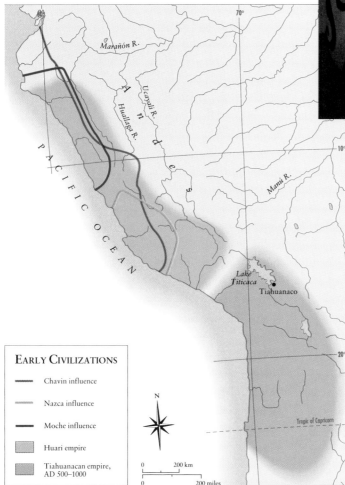

EARLY CIVILIZATIONS

━━━ Chavin influence

━━━ Nazca influence

━━━ Moche influence

▓ Huari empire

▓ Tiahuanacan empire, AD 500–1000

0   200 km

0   200 miles

of the resources of the sea. Principal crops consisted of corn, peanuts, beans, yucca, and peppers.

The Chimú had a well-defined style in art and architecture. The Chimú had other well-developed crafts, and other specialists who produced them were particularly known for their textiles and metalwork. The Incas, after their conquest of the north coast, brought a group of Chimú metalworkers over to their capital at Cuzco, where they established them in a special quarter to produce metalwork for the Inca state.

Although almost all of the adobe walls of Chan Chan are badly eroded or destroyed, many decorations can still be seen. They consist mostly of fish, bird, and human motifs. The site was abandoned around 1470 when the Chimú kingdom was incorporated into the expanding Inca empire.

The Chimú conquered the north coastal valleys from as far north as the area of the Sechura Desert, which separates the Lambayeque Valley from the Piura region, and as far south as Chillón. When the Incas defeated the Chimú, they replaced the Chimú ruler with his son and continued to use most of the established administrative structures and religious practices.

The Chimú capital was based at Chan Chan, in the Moche Valley. This large city measures some twenty square kilometers and is estimated to have had around 35,000 permanent residents. The central sector consisted of ten large rectangular compounds, which are thought to have been the residences of the successive Chimú rulers with their courts and administration. On the death of each king, this compound or citadel became his tomb, with his court continuing to attend to their master as they had in life. Many of the walls of these compounds were elaborately decorated with fish and birds modeled in mud plaster.

Some of the major dynastic and demographic changes that occurred over the period of Chimú domination of the north coast appear to have been associated with major climatological disasters, frequently triggered by El Niño events. This consists of a reversal of the gulf stream off the Peruvian coast, which results in the disappearance of much of the fish from these waters and tends to cause massive flooding in the coastal valleys.

CHIMÚ PRIOR TO INCA EXPANSION, AD 1000–1438

Chimú
Chincha
Chanca
Inca
Colla

THE INCA EMPIRE

Machu Picchu, an Inca fortress city built high in the Andes Mountains. This extraordinary city covers about five square miles (13 square kilometers) of terraces and buildings and was probably the last Inca stronghold at the end of the Spanish conquest period.

The Inca empire extended 2,050 miles from the northwest to the southeast of Andean South America and was about 200 miles in width. According to Inca legend, in AD 1458, under the Inca Pachacuti Yupanqui, it expanded from Cuzco Valley to include adjacent mountain regions north to Cajamarca and south to Lake Titicaca; further conquests were made by Inca Topa Yupanqui, who reigned c. 1471–1493, to include jungle areas from near Cuzco to as far as Ecuador. Subsequently, when Huayna Capac died, his two sons Atahualpa and Huascar fought for the leadership. In 1532, the Spaniards, led by Francisco Pizarro, landed in Peru during the civil war. Turning it to their advantage, they kidnapped the recently triumphant Atahualpa at Cajamarca and held him hostage while they consolidated their initial small conquest.

The Inca had no written histories, but accounts of their origins estimate their arrival in the Cuzco Valley around AD 1200 under Manco Capac, and their subsequent establishment in Cuzco and its environs through subjugation of other tribes during the reigns of the first eight Incas. The threat of the Chanca Federation to the northwest, and the successful defense of Cuzco against attack by the young Cusi Yupanqui, thereafter called Pachacutec (Cataclysm), resulted in the formation of alliances and military strength, which led to a rapidly expanding empire.

The Inca are unique in having successfully unified the vast area and differences of environment of the Andes in an empire, even for the short period of ninety years. Their technology was virtually that of the Bronze Age. There are widely differing estimates of Inca population at the time of the Spanish conquest. A conservative one would be about seven million people.

The empire was called Tawantinsuyu ("Land of the Four Quarters"), a name that was both symbolic and administrative: The empire was arranged around Cuzco, the "navel" in four great sectors oriented to the cardinal points. The Inca state was a strongly hierarchical society, with the Sapa Inca (emperor) at the head of a dual-structured pyramidal organization. The Sapa Inca shared his leadership role with a secondary lord. The primary kin of the Inca formed the class of aristocratic rulers (the council and provincial governors); the subsidiary kin were their assistants and servants; the native rulers often continued to rule their provinces, villages, or *ayllu;* all those not related to the Inca or native rulers were householders who served in the military, public works, and other governmental organizations and worked as agriculturalists on their allotted lands and those of the state and religion. They were arranged and organized into groups on a decimal system supervised by leaders.

The organizational genius of the Inca is illustrated by how they transformed earlier socioeconomic organizational forms from those of purely reciprocal arrangements into a complex state system based on the older system, highly modified. Thus, extravagant gifts were given by the Inca in exchange for work on produce. Security and guarantees were offered in exchange for acceptance of Inca sovereignty; colonists, who formerly extended the range of community access to goods by living in different ecological zones, became a new class of Inca culture bearers who kept non-Inca populations under subjugation. Pachacuti Inca changed the religious hierarchy so that the sun-god, the ancestor of the Inca themselves, became the principal deity, with the previously dominant Viracocha and Illapa, the creator and thunder gods respectively, relegated to secondary positions. This change reinforced the power of the Inca elite through divine right and the calendrical organization of the agricultural cycle, the success of which was vital to the maintenance of that power.

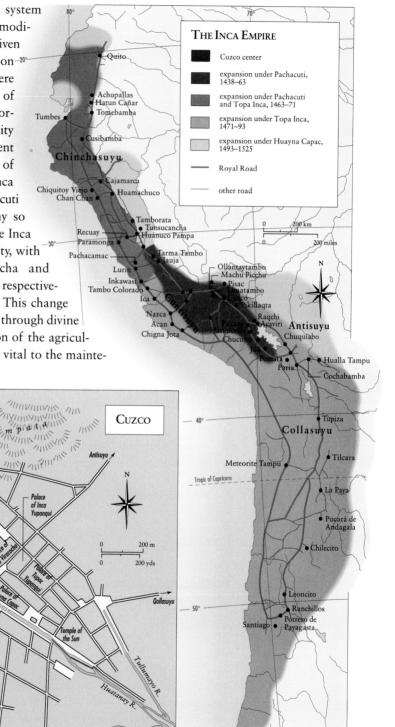

PART II: THE CLASH OF CIVILIZATIONS

This stone stele from Tikal shows a Maya ruler holding his chain of office with the head of the sun-god on his left arm.

The voyages of discovery were events of momentous importance in world history. Portuguese explorations in Africa and the Far East opened direct communication with previously little-known parts of the world and offered new possibilities for trade. The discovery of America, too, offered new resources and markets, but it also opened for both Spain and Portugal a vast new continent for colonization and settlement, and provided the opportunity for the creation of the first major European empires. For the indigenous inhabitants of the Americas first affected by the arrival of Europeans, the impact of conquest, of the clash of civilizations, was almost universally destructive. Conquest brought about the collapse of native power structures; it weakened, when it did not destroy, native religious practices. Exploitation and epidemic diseases previously unknown to the Americas led to serious population decline; and the introduction of money, new crops and livestock, and new working regimes disrupted native economies and settlement patterns. The arrival of white Europeans, the importation of African slaves, and the intermingling of both these groups with each other and with Indians, in the early days most usually women, also led to the emergence of new racial categories—the *mestizos* (Indian/white), *mulattos* (black/white), *zambos* (Indian/black), and all the gradations in between. Yet despite the initial devastation, the traffic was not all one way. Many indigenous crops, such as potatoes and corn, were introduced into the European diet, and the encounter with Indian civilizations forced upon Europe a reconsideration of long-accepted beliefs and attitudes. Nor was Indian culture completely crushed. While it is true that in certain areas, such as the islands of the Caribbean, native populations were wiped out by overwork, ill treatment, and especially diseases such as smallpox, measles, and influenza, in other areas Indian culture proved strong enough not only to survive the conquest but to continue to thrive to this day.

Trade, as well as a spirit of religious crusade against Islam, were the principal incentives to Iberian maritime activity in the late fifteenth century. Captains and crews of vessels seeking new routes to the sources of gold, spices, slaves, and other products in high demand in Europe all drew on a long tradition of seafaring in Atlantic and Mediterranean waters and on a large fund of experience of ship design and construction, map-making, and commercial practice, which had been growing since the fourteenth century, and which was to make this region ideally suited to taking the lead role in the process of overseas expansion. Although for a time Spain lagged behind Portugal in its maritime activities, all parts of the peninsula contributed to this common pool of knowledge and skills. Portugal had considerable experience of navigation and maritime technology, deriving from a long tradition of fishing and maritime trade with northern Europe, Italy, and other Mediterranean ports. The Catalans and Aragonese traded with North Africa and the eastern Mediterranean. The Basques had experience of deep-sea fishing in the Atlantic and were skilled shipbuilders and pilots. Castile had acquired greater maritime and commercial experience as a result of the growth of the wool trade with northern Europe. Other skills came into the peninsula from outside. Genoese sailors, for example, and the Genoese commercial communities of cities such as Lisbon and Seville (both of which were thriving maritime and commercial centers) also played a significant role; the latter, in particular, brought commercial contacts and capital that would prove invaluable to the conduct of overseas exploration and conquest in the late fifteenth and early sixteenth centuries.

Portuguese seafarers, however, were at the forefront of overseas exploration in the fifteenth century. Lured by the prospect of locating the source of the gold that was carried across the Sahara to the ports of North Africa, and by the desire to weaken Islam, from the 1440s Portuguese explorers began to establish *feitorias*, fortified trading posts, at strategic points along the African coast, where they exchanged European goods such as cloth for gold, slaves, and other products. No attempt was made to occupy these lands. Only in the Atlantic islands (the Azores, Madeira, and the Cape Verde Islands) did the Portuguese settle, for here the only profits to be made came from the export of cattle, wheat, and especially sugar, for which a settled population, partly consisting of slaves, was necessary. But in Africa and Asia and, until the mid-sixteenth century, in Brazil, Portugal sought principally to establish a chain of commercial entrepôts where trade could take place but that involved little inland penetration or settlement. Portugal had neither the resources nor the manpower to occupy new territory. In this sense, Portuguese expansion was to differ markedly from that of Castile; whereas Portugal aimed to create a trading empire, Castile was to opt for conquest and colonization.

Portuguese activities in the Atlantic, especially in Africa and the Canaries, were nevertheless sufficiently threatening to Castile to provoke rivalry and stimulate competing explorations in these waters. By 1479, both Portugal and Castile had agreed, in the Treaty of Alcaçovas, the first European treaty ever to deal with overseas possessions and in this sense a forerunner of the later and more important Treaty of Tordesillas (1494), to respect each other's spheres of influence. Castile agreed to recognize Portugal's claims to the Azores, Madeira, the Cape Verde Islands, and the African coast south of Cape Bojador in exchange for Portugal's respecting Castile's rights in the Canaries. The treaty was significant for several other reasons, too. For Portugal it opened a new era of exploration along the West African coast, as King João II (1481–1495) sought to strengthen his claim to lands that were now recognized as Portuguese.

For Castile, the acquisition of the Canaries paved the way to westward exploration and expansion and provided captains of Spanish vessels with a convenient port of call en route to the New World, where last-minute restocking and repairs could be carried out. For both Spain and Portugal, the occupation of the Atlantic islands was also to serve as an early experiment in colonization; many of the methods used in the settlement, exploitation, and government of the islands would later be transferred and adapted to the colonization of Spanish America and Brazil.

The Aztecs and the Incas are the best-known civilizations encountered by Iberians in the Americas, but they in fact constituted only a relatively small proportion of the total indigenous population inhabiting the region at the beginning of the sixteenth century. Ethnic and cultural groups too numerous to mention also inhabited these territories, ranging from primitive nomadic hunter-gatherers to sedentary societies characterized by quite complex forms of social and political organization—the Maya of Yucatán; the Chibchas or Muisca of Colombia; the Araucanians of southern Chile; the Guarani of Paraguay, northern Argentina, and southern Brazil; and the Chichimecs of northern Mexico, to name but a few. Although the size of the native population at the time of contact with Europeans remains a matter of debate, it is clear that the nature of the societies encountered greatly influenced not just the pace of conquest and settlement but also the ways in which each of the regions was to develop through the colonial period. It is no coincidence that the groups that fell most completely to Europeans were those that had been integrated into the Aztec and Inca empires; the degree of centralization of these more sophisticated civilizations meant that, once the native leadership structure had collapsed, the transfer of power to the Spanish was relatively swift. In the more peripheral regions, however, Spaniards found the process of conquest and colonization far more difficult. Nomadic and seminomadic groups who were not subservient to a central power were usually more resilient, and often extremely difficult to subdue. Not only did such tribes have to be conquered, or intimidated, one by one, but they also offered stiff resistance to Spanish efforts to resettle, exploit, and convert, in some cases, like that of the Araucanians, even mastering the use of Spanish weapons and horses to prolong their independence from Spanish rule. Despite the difficulties of taking and holding these peripheral areas, however, the largest, most advanced, and most rewarding regions had fallen to the Spanish within a little over a generation of Columbus's first landing in the Bahamas.

The extraordinary events surrounding the collapse of the Aztec and Inca empires have exercised the imaginations of historians for generations, but they can be satisfactorily explained. The Aztec and Inca empires were recent phenomena, both having been created over the hundred years or so prior to the arrival of the Europeans. The Incas' domain extended from northern Ecuador to central Chile; the Aztecs dominated most of Mexico, and their influence stretched as far south as present-day Guatemala, although there existed within the boundaries of the empire two large independent kingdoms that the imperial

"Carried away by love of gold, they become ravenous wolves instead of gentle lambs and heedless of royal instruction."
Peter Martyr, member of the Council of the Indies

armies had been unable or unwilling to defeat. Both empires had been created through the incorporation, by conquest or intimidation, of a wide variety of tribal groups and ethnic kingdoms. By the time of the arrival of the Europeans, the Aztecs and Incas were the dominant powers in their respective regions. The very success of the empires, however, created tensions that the Spanish were able to exploit. Both were plagued by internal discontent, deriving from the bitterness of subjugated groups who resented paying tributes to their imperial overlords; in the case of the Aztecs, the cost of conquest included the provision of victims for sacrifice to the bloodthirsty god Huitzilopochtli, upon whom the very survival of the universe was thought to depend. Many defeated tribes saw an alliance with the Spanish conquistadores as their best opportunity to reassert their autonomy from Aztec and Inca rule, and, in Mexico, they were encouraged by the cooperation offered to the invaders by the independent kingdom of Tlaxcala. Numerically, the Spanish were no match for the imperial armies; numbering in the hundreds (the force that Francisco Pizarro led to Cajamarca comprised only 168 men), they confronted determined, fanatical, and effective armies, fighting on home territory, and numbering in the tens of thousands. But the Spanish had several advantages in their favor. Indian weaponry was no match for the steel swords, lances, and firepower of their adversaries. The astonishment provoked by previously unknown Spanish horses also worked to the advantage of Europeans, as did Indian methods of warfare and the ritual that accompanied it. In Mexico, for example, where the Spaniards fought to kill, the Aztecs sought to capture victims for sacrifice. Most crucially, however, the Spanish were assisted by tens of thousands of Indian auxiliaries, who formed the bulk of the forces confronting the imperial armies; the conquests of Mexico and Peru soon took on the character of massive Indian

In this fanciful scene from the conquest of Mexico, the Aztec emperor Cuauhtemoc is captured by the Spanish.

uprisings against Inca and Aztec rule. Finally, European diseases, against which the Indians of America had no acquired immunity, particularly damaged the ability of both Aztecs and Incas to resist attack. In Mexico, smallpox struck the population of the Aztec capital Tenochtitlán just when Hernán Cortés was planning and launching the final assault on the city. The death from smallpox of the emperor Cuitlahua, Moctezuma's successor, struck a serious blow to the leadership structure when it was already in turmoil. In the city itself, which, with a population of over 200,000, was far larger than any European city of the time, the effects of smallpox were phenomenal: high rates of mortality, the trauma of an unknown disease, and the practicalities of treating the sick, weakened Aztec resistance. In the Andes, smallpox struck the population several years before the arrival of the Spanish, having spread along Indian trade routes from Panama, but its impact was no less serious. Among the Incas, smallpox caused the death of the emperor, Huayna Capac, in the mid 1520s, unleashing a divisive civil war over the succession between two of his sons, Huascar and Atahualpa. The war was just coming to an end as Pizarro marched his troops to Cajamarca, but the bitterness of its aftermath made a united effort against the invaders impossible. Indeed, one of the factions in the civil war, that of the defeated Huascar, actually cooperated with the Spanish, in the belief that they would restore the rightful branch of the royal family to the throne in Cuzco. The Spanish conquest, then, did not merely constitute the victory of small bands of Spaniards over strong and homogeneous empires. Without the assistance of tens of thousands of Indian allies, who willingly cooperated with the Spanish to wreak revenge on their imperial masters, and without the effects of epidemic diseases unknowingly imported by the conquerors, the Spaniards' success would have been neither as swift nor as complete.

Nevertheless, the determination of the conquistadores, in Mexico and the Andes as in other parts of the Americas, was another factor that made the conquest possible. Cortés was a special case. His tenacity and daring, which played an important role in the victory over the Aztecs, were the result of his persistent defiance of the governor of Cuba, Diego , who had given him strict instruction that his mission was to reconnoiter and trade, but on no account to attempt a conquest. In ignoring Velázquez's instructions and beginning the trek to the Aztec capital, Cortés was running the risk of facing a charge of treason on his return to the island. This made it imperative that he should succeed—he *had* to present the king with a prize valuable enough to save himself from serious embarrassment. Elsewhere in the Americas such conditions did not apply. But other conditions, equally if not more important, certainly did. Everywhere, for instance, conquistadores were driven by the prospect of gaining great wealth and social advancement, by the expectation that fortune and glory would be their reward for participation in exploration and conquest. They were also driven by a strong belief in their own superiority, as Christians and Europeans, over the Indian populations they encountered, a conviction that could only be reinforced by repeated victories against natives who engaged in practices that they found

> " . . . if the land had not been divided by the wars of Huascar and Atahualpa, we could not have entered or conquered it, unless over a thousand Spaniards had come simultaneously."
> *Francisco Pizarro*

utterly distasteful, such as human sacrifice. These were important characteristics of the mentality of the men who undertook the conquest and colonization of Central and South America, and they are directly attributable to the Reconquista, the centuries-long advance against the Muslims within the Iberian Peninsula itself, which was brought to a successful conclusion only with the fall of Granada in 1492, the year of Columbus's first voyage across the Atlantic. The values that had been formed during the years of the reconquest—that it was possible to improve one's standing in life through military service on behalf of the king and the Christian religion—were therefore deeply embedded in the psychology of the thousands of emigrants who made their way to the Indies in the years after Columbus, and strongly colored their behavior toward native peoples. Such attitudes were also shaped by more practical aspirations, however. The vast majority of the men upon whom the Spanish crown depended to expand its dominion over huge American territories were of humble origin— laborers, artisans, sailors, and so on. Another important group, though less well represented numerically, was the lesser gentry, the impoverished *hidalgos*. All these men aspired to be worth more, to *"valer más,"* to escape from lowly occupations, to acquire noble status. By the beginning of the sixteenth century only the Indies offered unlimited opportunities to such men.

Many of the practices and institutions employed in the colonization of the mainland were first tried out in the islands of the Caribbean, such as the *repartimiento*, later called *encomienda*. As conquest and settlement expanded into new areas, other institutions evolved to exploit native manpower. In Aztec Mexico and Inca Peru, Indians were accustomed to providing tribute and compulsory labor services, and institutions already in existence were adapted to meet the needs of the new ruling class. The *mita* system in the Andes and the *repartimiento* system in New Spain consisted of rotational labor drafts that channeled groups of workers for specified periods of time to a variety of activities, including agriculture, construction, mining, and textile production. Like the *encomienda,* the *mita/repartimiento* proved to be an essential tool of Spanish colonization, at least for the first century or so after the conquest. Indians mobilized through the *mita* system provided the manpower for the construction and maintenance of roads, public buildings, and the magnificent churches that replaced the old ceremonial centers. But continuing Indian population decline, coupled with the growth of the Spanish population, eventually undermined the utility of this system. In some areas, central New Spain for example, miners and *hacendados* (large estate owners) abandoned the *repartimiento* in favor of free wage labor, now the most effective means of securing an adequate and regular supply of workers. Many village Indians, as well as the landless, took advantage of the higher wages and better conditions offered to attract them to work on mines and *haciendas* (estates). On the estates, many became permanent residents. However, free laborers were often bound to their employers by mechanisms such as debt peonage, a system whereby loans were advanced against income to tie workers permanently to the enterprises in which they were employed.

> "The people of the city had to walk upon their dead . . . so great was their suffering that it was beyond our understanding how they could endure it."
> *Hernán Cortés*

EUROPEAN EXPLORERS

The "Catholic kings" Ferdinand and Isabella ride into Granada, reconquered from the Moors in 1492. That same year their investment in Christopher Columbus began to open new worlds for conquest and colonization.

In 1492, Ferdinand and Isabella were finally persuaded to support Columbus's plan to find a direct route to the Asian mainland by sailing westward across the Atlantic. In this endeavor they were motivated partly by rivalry with Portugal, but they had little to fear from this quarter. Unwilling to be diverted from his purpose of finding a route to the Orient around the tip of Africa, and convinced that Columbus had miscalculated the distance between Europe and Asia, the king of Portugal had already turned down his proposal. Castile, therefore, came to play the leading role in the exploration and colonization of the New World.

Columbus set sail from the port of Palos in southern Spain in August 1492, bound for the Canaries, from where, after final restocking and repairs, three vessels (*Niña, Pinta, Santa María*) departed in September. On October 12, 1492, land was sighted in the Indies, perhaps an island in the Bahamas. Until his death Columbus refused to believe that he had found something other than a sea passage to the mainland of Asia, but other European explorers soon became aware that far from being part of Asia, the Indies were a new and previously uncharted continent. By 1502, the Italian explorer Amerigo Vespucci, sailing on a Portuguese ship along the eastern coastline of South America, had concluded that this was a *mundus novus*, a new world, and in his honor, a map published in Europe in 1507 showed the discoveries as an independent continent and called it America.

Over the course of four voyages across the Atlantic, Columbus contributed enormously to the extension of geographical knowledge of the Americas and to Spain's claims to sovereignty over the newly discovered lands. But he was not alone. For his failings as governor of the Caribbean island of Hispaniola, combined with a growing realization of the sheer extent of the territories still to be explored, persuaded the Catholic monarchs to limit Columbus's jurisdiction over any future discoveries on the mainland by granting new licenses for expeditions to other Spanish captains. By 1499 expeditions by Alonso de Hojeda, Peralonso Niño, and Juan de la Cosa had explored the coast of Venezuela, engaging in trade with the local inhabitants. In 1501, following rumors of great wealth farther west, Rodrigo Bastidas and Juan de la Cosa conducted another expedition along the Colombian coast, reaching first the harbor of Cartagena and then the Gulf of Urabá (Darién). No attempt was made to settle the region until 1510, when Hojeda and Juan de Nicuesa made two separate but disastrous efforts to occupy the area. The most significant outcome of these abortive attempts at settlement was the establishment of the town of Santa María la

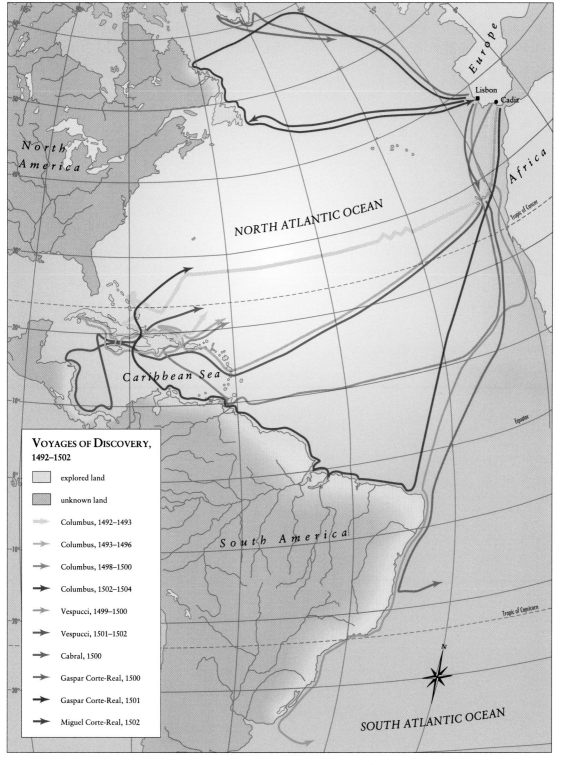

VOYAGES OF DISCOVERY,
1492–1502

	explored land
	unknown land
	Columbus, 1492–1493
	Columbus, 1493–1496
	Columbus, 1498–1500
	Columbus, 1502–1504
	Vespucci, 1499–1500
	Vespucci, 1501–1502
	Cabral, 1500
	Gaspar Corte-Real, 1500
	Gaspar Corte-Real, 1501
	Miguel Corte-Real, 1502

"All Christendom ought to feel joyful and make great celebrations and give solemn thanks to the Holy Trinity with many solemn prayers for the great exaltation which it will have, in the turning of so many people to our holy faith, and afterwards for material benefits, since not only Spain but all Christians will hence have refreshment and profit."
from a letter by *Christopher Columbus*

Antigua de Darién, which was to serve as the base for Vasco Núñez de Balboa's crossing of the isthmus in 1513, leading to the establishment of a new settlement at Panama by Pedrarias Dávila in 1519. This was the first Pacific coast settlement to be founded by the Spanish, and it became the principal base for explorations along the western coast of South America. Early interest in the Pacific coast of Colombia soon gave way to the potentially more lucrative prospects of more southern regions, evidence of the existence of a rich civilization leading to Francisco Pizarro and Diego de Almagro's conquest of Peru.

In Hispaniola, meanwhile, an additional stimulus to exploration was provided by the meager nature of local resources and by the need to replenish the labor supply. Indians on the island, unaccustomed to the new work regime imposed upon them and exposed to new diseases, were dying in large numbers at the same time that the demand for labor was increasing with the arrival of an ever-growing number of immigrants. The conquests of Puerto Rico by Juan Ponce de León (1508), Jamaica by Juan de Esquival (1509), and Cuba by Diego Velázquez (1511), all began in response to labor shortages. The islands proved unsatisfactory sources of labor, but Cuba was to become important in the 1510s; it was from here that Diego Velázquez, now governor of the island, launched the three expeditions that were to culminate in the conquest of Mexico—those of Francisco Hernández de Córdoba to Yucatán (1517), Juan de Grijalva to the Gulf of Mexico (1518), and Hernán Cortés (1519).

European voyagers meet new and exotic creatures as shown in this illustration of flying fish, by Théodore de Bry.

The weather, much more extreme than in Europe, held surprises for European visitors to the New World. In this engraving, both visitors and local people run for cover during a hurricane.

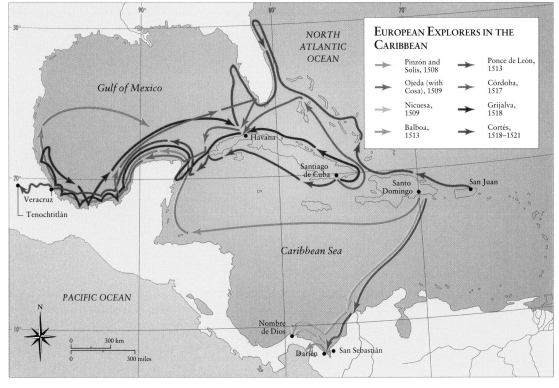

EUROPEAN EXPLORERS IN THE CARIBBEAN

- Pinzón and Solís, 1508
- Ojeda (with Cosa), 1509
- Nicuesa, 1509
- Balboa, 1513
- Ponce de León, 1513
- Córdoba, 1517
- Grijalva, 1518
- Cortés, 1518–1521

THE TREATY OF TORDESILLAS

Spain and Portugal agreed to a division of spheres of influence in the Indies long before the nature and extent of the new discoveries were understood. Upon Columbus's return from his first voyage, Ferdinand and Isabella sought from the papacy formal recognition that the newly discovered islands were Castilian possessions. In requesting recognition, the Catholic monarchs were following an earlier precedent set by the Portuguese, who sought and obtained a papal donation of rights of sovereignty over lands extending to the south of Cape Bojador, in Africa. Papal approval of Ferdinand and Isabella's request soon followed, in exchange for Castile agreeing to undertake the conversion of the native inhabitants to Catholicism, the only moral justification for conquest and occupation. By a series of papal bulls (the bulls of donation), Pope Alexander VI, himself a Spaniard, granted Castile dominion over all lands so far discovered and that might in future be discovered in the region explored by Columbus, thus legitimizing Castile's activities in the Indies and strengthening its case against any future challenge from Portugal. However, in order to avoid an immediate conflict with the Portuguese, the most famous of Alexander's bulls, *Inter caetera* (1493), drew an imaginary line of demarcation running north to south one hundred leagues to the west of the Cape Verde Islands: Castilian explorations were to be carried out to the west of the line, where their rights of sovereignty lay; Portugal's rights were to lie to the east. In this way, both Castile and Portugal were to be allocated a role in all future explorations and colonization in the New World.

However, a year later, following a protest from the king of Portugal, the Treaty of Tordesillas (1494) placed this boundary considerably farther west—Portugal's rights were now to stretch to a distance of 370 leagues west of the Cape Verde islands. The important point about Portugal's protest was not, however, that it wished for a larger share of any lands still to be discovered in the Americas, for no one was yet aware of the size of the South American landmass, but that King João II was concerned to push Castilian activities in the Atlantic as far west as possible in order to protect Portugal's interests in Africa and Portuguese explorations in search of a route to Asia. In 1487, Bartolomeu Dias had rounded the Cape of Good Hope, which at last opened the prospect of direct trade with India and the Orient in silks, spices, and other high-value products much sought after in Europe. Portugal had invested considerable time and effort in the search for a route to the Orient, and it wanted above all to protect itself from Castilian competition. The Treaty of Tordesillas, therefore, satisfied both parties, in the sense that both agreed that Castile was to be allowed to exploit the Western hemisphere, while Portugal would concentrate on Africa and Asia.

This imaginary boundary being drawn so soon after Columbus's return from Hispaniola granted Portugal dominion over the lands that came to be known as Brazil (the name deriving from the brazilwood trees, or dyewood trees, that grew abundantly along the coast and that produced a red tint used as a dye in Europe). But the Portuguese were quite unaware of the existence of these territories until 1500. In April of that year, Pedro Alvares Cabral, in command of a

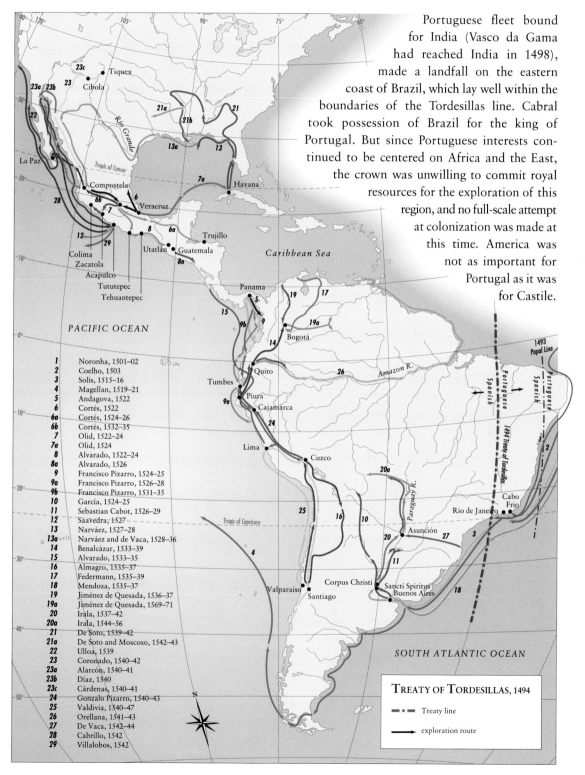

Portuguese fleet bound for India (Vasco da Gama had reached India in 1498), made a landfall on the eastern coast of Brazil, which lay well within the boundaries of the Tordesillas line. Cabral took possession of Brazil for the king of Portugal. But since Portuguese interests continued to be centered on Africa and the East, the crown was unwilling to commit royal resources for the exploration of this region, and no full-scale attempt at colonization was made at this time. America was not as important for Portugal as it was for Castile.

1	Noronha, 1501–02
2	Coelho, 1503
3	Solís, 1515–16
4	Magellan, 1519–21
5	Andagoya, 1522
6	Cortés, 1522
6a	Cortés, 1524–26
6b	Cortés, 1532–35
7	Olid, 1522–24
7a	Olid, 1524
8	Alvarado, 1522–24
8a	Alvarado, 1526
9	Francisco Pizarro, 1524–25
9a	Francisco Pizarro, 1526–28
9b	Francisco Pizarro, 1531–35
10	García, 1524–25
11	Sebastian Cabot, 1526–29
12	Saavedra, 1527
13	Narváez, 1527–28
13a	Narváez and de Vaca, 1528–36
14	Benalcázar, 1533–39
15	Alvarado, 1533–35
16	Almagro, 1535–37
17	Federmann, 1535–39
18	Mendoza, 1535–37
19	Jiménez de Quesada, 1536–37
19a	Jiménez de Quesada, 1569–71
20	Irala, 1537–42
20a	Irala, 1544–56
21	De Soto, 1539–42
21a	De Soto and Moscoso, 1542–43
22	Ulloa, 1539
23	Coronado, 1540–42
23a	Alarcón, 1540–41
23b	Díaz, 1540
23c	Cárdenas, 1540–41
24	Gonzalo Pizarro, 1540–43
25	Valdivia, 1540–47
26	Orellana, 1541–43
27	De Vaca, 1542–44
28	Cabrillo, 1542
29	Villalobos, 1542

PACIFIC OCEAN

Caribbean Sea

SOUTH ATLANTIC OCEAN

TREATY OF TORDESILLAS, 1494

– · – · – Treaty line

→ exploration route

PORTUGUESE SETTLEMENT

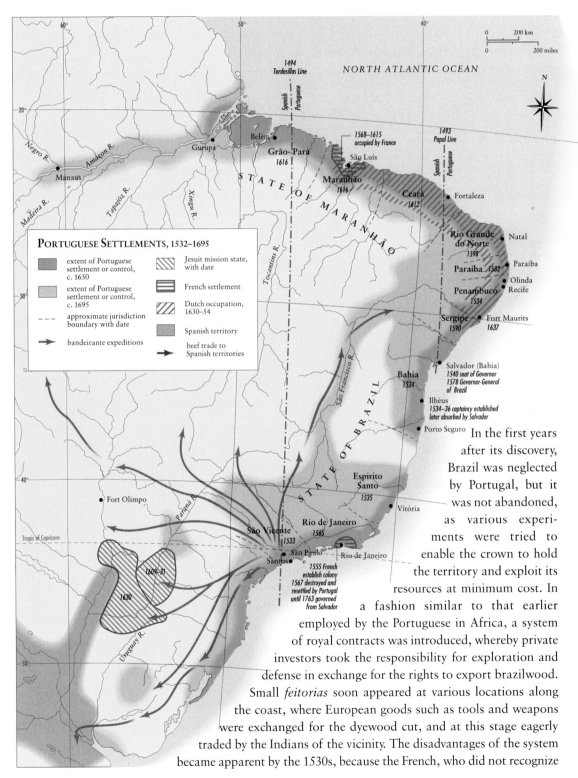

PORTUGUESE SETTLEMENTS, 1532–1695

extent of Portuguese settlement or control, c. 1650

extent of Portuguese settlement or control, c. 1695

approximate jurisdiction boundary with date

bandeirante expeditions

Jesuit mission state, with date

French settlement

Dutch occupation, 1630–54

Spanish territory

beef trade to Spanish territories

In the first years after its discovery, Brazil was neglected by Portugal, but it was not abandoned, as various experiments were tried to enable the crown to hold the territory and exploit its resources at minimum cost. In a fashion similar to that earlier employed by the Portuguese in Africa, a system of royal contracts was introduced, whereby private investors took the responsibility for exploration and defense in exchange for the rights to export brazilwood. Small *feitorias* soon appeared at various locations along the coast, where European goods such as tools and weapons were exchanged for the dyewood cut, and at this stage eagerly traded by the Indians of the vicinity. The disadvantages of the system became apparent by the 1530s, because the French, who did not recognize

Castilian and Portuguese rights of sovereignty, also sought to exploit Brazilian resources. The French attacked Portuguese forts, made alliances with local Indians, traded for dyewood, and generally threatened Portuguese interests. It became clear that unless Portugal made greater efforts to occupy Brazil, other Europeans would do so instead. In 1530, King João III dispatched an expedition to eliminate the French threat and establish a permanent settlement, leading to the foundation of São Vicente in 1532. But the Portuguese crown would still not commit the resources necessary for large-scale settlement, and continued to rely on private enterprise. Now the same system as had earlier been used to settle Madeira and the Azores was introduced in Brazil. This was the hereditary captaincy system. It involved the division of Brazilian territory into fifteen parallel strips (extending from the coast to the Tordesillas line), which were "donated" to *donatários,* or proprietors, who agreed to colonize, develop, and defend their territorial grants, at their own expense, in exchange for extensive powers over official appointments, taxation, and, crucially for the purpose of attracting colonists, land distribution. This experiment also proved of limited success. A few of the captaincies, such as those granted to Martin Alfonso de Sousa and his brother, did undergo some development through integration into the commercial structure of Europe, Portuguese and foreign investors providing the capital for the establishment of several sugar mills or *engenhos,* the basis for Brazil's principal export. But most others failed, either because they were simply never settled, or because they were badly managed.

By the mid-sixteenth century, the Portuguese crown, faced with the failure of the *donatários,* and also aware of the economic potential of the region should it be found to contain deposits of precious metals comparable with those of Peru, sought to redress the balance between the state and private initiative by limiting the prerogatives of individuals who had earlier been granted extensive powers. A governor-general was appointed (Tomé de Sousa, 1548) to impose a system of centralized control, and thus royal authority, over the donatary captaincies. But as no large urbanized societies comparable with those of Mexico and Peru were discovered in Brazil, Portuguese colonization remained limited to a few small towns and cities and a narrow strip along the coastline. Little attempt was made to promote the occupation of the interior; colonists were most attracted to the coastal areas, where the conditions were ideal for the cultivation of sugar, which found a ready market in Europe. Eventually, it was the need for native labor to sustain the sugar industry that stimulated exploration of the interior. The semi-sedentary Tupí groups who occupied much of the coastal region proved to be unsatisfactory workers; unaccustomed to the work regime imposed upon them, and susceptible to European diseases, Tupís either died in large numbers or fled. Slave hunters, the famous *bandeirantes,* pushed further and further into the interior in search of Indians to enslave, but they, too, proved unsatisfactory. From about the 1560s, planters increasingly turned to Africa to meet the labor requirements of Brazil. Brazil had begun the transition to slave labor that was to bring about a radical transformation of the region's population and culture.

> "This land is very pleasant, and full of an infinity of trees, very green and very tall, and they never shed their leaves, and all of them have a very soft aromatic odour and yield a great many fruits, many of them good-tasting and healthful to the body, and the fields bear abundant grass and flowers and very soft, good roots, so that at times the sweet scent of the grass and flowers and the taste of those fruits and roots is so wondrous that I could think myself close to paradise on earth."
> *Amerigo Vespucci*

CORTÉS AND THE AZTEC CONQUEST

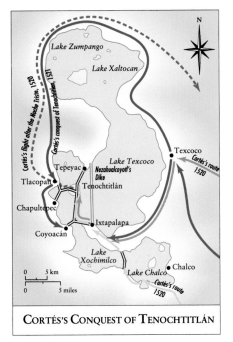

CORTÉS'S CONQUEST OF TENOCHTITLÁN

By the time of the Spanish conquest, the Aztec empire was showing signs of serious internal strain. Overstretched and only loosely held together, it was susceptible to internal dissension from subject peoples, often turning to rebellion over levels of tribute and victims offered in sacrifice to the god Huitzilopochtli. It also continued to tolerate, for reasons that are not entirely clear, the existence of independent kingdoms within the boundaries of the empire, of which the most important was Tlaxcala. The timing of Cortés's expedition could not have been worse for Moctezuma, or more propitious for the Spanish.

At first, only the Cempohualtecs, impressed by the weapons and horses of the newcomers, offered to assist Cortés—a difficult decision, for should the gamble fail, immediate and brutal reprisals would surely follow. The Cempohualtecs were no match for the Aztec warriors, but their material support was sufficient to enable Cortés and his small band of fellow conquistadores (the entire expedition consisted of approximately 600 men) to begin the march to the island city of Tenochtitlán, situated in the middle of Lake Texcoco. Other groups soon opted for collaboration with the numerically small but technologically advanced Spanish as the only means to defeat the Aztecs in battle. The Tlaxcalans, who had for many years succeeded in resisting

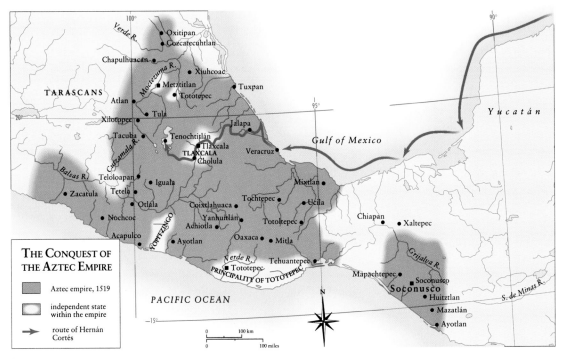

THE CONQUEST OF THE AZTEC EMPIRE

- Aztec empire, 1519
- independent state within the empire
- route of Hernán Cortés

the Aztecs but whose future was always in peril, were of particular importance: Their example, combined with Cortés's consummate diplomatic skills, persuaded many equally resentful groups to join forces with the conquerors against fellow Indians, giving the invaders the upper hand in an otherwise uneven confrontation.

The *tlatoani* (supreme leader), Moctezuma, had ample opportunity to eliminate the intruders before the key alliances had been negotiated, but, doubtful about their origins, confused about the intentions of white men who arrived on ships, rode horses, and carried firearms, or perhaps too complacent to fear an apparently insignificant enemy, he remained inactive as the Spanish traveled to the capital, and allowed them to enter Tenochtitlán, unharmed and without resistance, as his guests. His indecision proved fatal. Cortés, fearful for the safety of his men, and determined to deliver the Aztec empire to his king, made the decision to take Moctezuma captive, dealing a serious blow to the Aztec political and religious system. The uneasy atmosphere that resulted from the emperor's capture, however, could not last. When Cortés left Pedro de Alvarado in charge of Tenochtitlán while he traveled to Veracruz to deal with an expedition sent from Cuba, the latter ordered a massacre of Aztec warriors and nobles attending the festival of Toxcatl. The massacre dealt yet another blow to the political system, but at the same time it lifted all constraints and unleashed a violent reaction— a massive Aztec uprising, which resulted in the death of Moctezuma, inflicted heavy casualties on the Spanish, and forced their flight from the city. This was on June 20, 1520, the *Noche Triste*. The Aztecs, however, perhaps unaware of the determination, ruthlessness, and audacity of Hernán Cortés, even when the odds were clearly stacked against him, failed to follow up their attack, enabling the Spanish to return to Tlaxcala to regroup and recover.

There a new plan came into being. New allies were sought, and a naval force of brigantines was built to attack Tenochtitlán from the lake and cut off its supplies, all with the assistance of the Tlaxcalans. It was at this time that the Spanish gained a new and unexpected ally—smallpox. The impact of the epidemic was phenomenal. Moctezuma's successor, Cuitlahua, was one of the earliest victims, dealing yet another blow to the Aztec leadership structure just at the time when unity, and a new policy for dealing with subject tribes whose loyalty could no longer be counted on, was most required. The effects of the epidemic on the city's population also weakened its ability to resist the final assault. By 1521, Tenochtitlán had fallen.

This contemporary illustration shows the formal surrender of Cuauhtemoc, the last of the Aztec kings, to Hernán Cortés.

"I have read about the destruction of Jerusalem, but I do not think the mortality was greater than in Mexico."
Bernal Díaz del Castillo

PIZARRO: THE END OF THE INCAS

In this painting by Díaz Mori, the defiant Inca leader Atahualpa throws down the Bible presented to him by Friar Vicente at their meeting at Cajamarca. This led to rioting and his seizure and eventually his death.

One important consequence of Cortés's victory over the Aztecs was that it spurred new expeditions of exploration elsewhere in the New World. Only in the Andes, however, did the Spanish encounter a civilization comparable with Aztec Mexico. The Incas had been more successful than the Aztecs at integrating and controlling subjugated tribes, but their empire was also subject to widespread discontent, and not infrequently rebellion, over tribute demands and methods of control. But more significant for the progress of the conquest was the bitter war of succession which had raged in Peru from the mid 1520s, caused by the death from smallpox of the Sapa Inca (emperor), Huayna Capac, which was just coming to an end as Pizarro marched his men into the heart of the Inca empire.

The war of succession between the half-brothers Huascar and Atahualpa, a confrontation that ended with the latter's victory, left the Inca empire divided and in turmoil just at a time when unity was required to resist the Spanish conquest. In Peru, therefore, the conquistadores were able to capitalize not only on the resentment of the multiplicity of groups conquered by the Incas, but also on the bitterness engendered among a faction of the Inca ruling class itself by defeat at the hands of Atahualpa's armies. In the short term the hatreds caused by the civil war had the most negative effect on the Incas' response to the Spaniards. As Pizarro marched inland to Cajamarca to meet Atahualpa, no military action was taken against them. Since Atahualpa was surrounded by an army that had just emerged victorious from a civil war, he had no fear of a force of 168 men in alien territory. Even when the Spanish, with the example of Mexico to guide them, and taking advantage of the surprise provoked by their horses and weapons, captured the emperor, he remained more concerned about internal politics than he did about the invaders. In the expectation of eventual release, Atahualpa offered the Spaniards a large ransom, in gold and silver, and then proceeded to order the elimination of his brother Huascar, so as to prevent the latter's taking advantage of the situation to regain the throne. Atahualpa's decision only served to increase the animosity of Huascar's supporters. When the opportunity presented itself, after payment of the ransom and Huascar's execution, the losing faction in the civil war between the brothers chose to cooperate with the Spanish, now reinforced by new arrivals from Panama, to fight the remnants of Atahualpa's forces, and force their retreat to Ecuador. Instead of resisting the Spanish occupation, then, Huascar's supporters welcomed the Spanish as liberators, and believed that they would comply with their promise to reinstate the legitimate branch of the royal family to the throne in Cuzco. Manco Inca was indeed crowned puppet ruler, although the intention of the Spanish was not to support the claims of one Inca faction over another, but to facilitate the transition from Inca to Spanish rule.

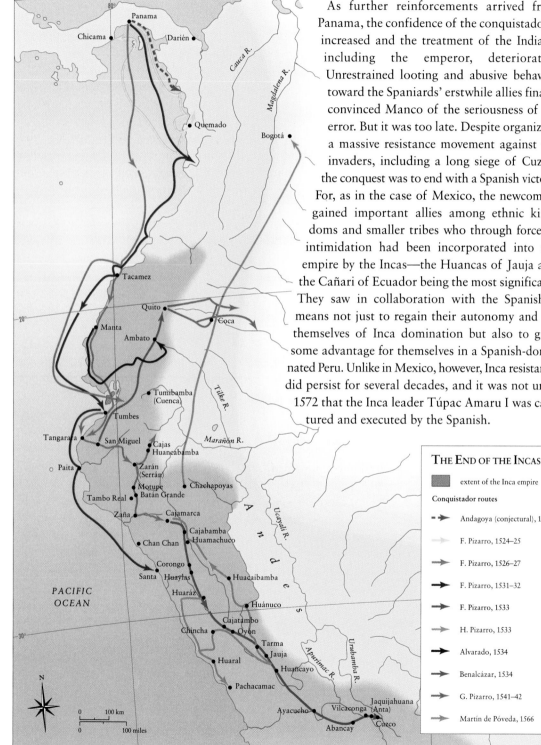

As further reinforcements arrived from Panama, the confidence of the conquistadores increased and the treatment of the Indians, including the emperor, deteriorated. Unrestrained looting and abusive behavior toward the Spaniards' erstwhile allies finally convinced Manco of the seriousness of his error. But it was too late. Despite organizing a massive resistance movement against the invaders, including a long siege of Cuzco, the conquest was to end with a Spanish victory. For, as in the case of Mexico, the newcomers gained important allies among ethnic kingdoms and smaller tribes who through force or intimidation had been incorporated into the empire by the Incas—the Huancas of Jauja and the Cañari of Ecuador being the most significant. They saw in collaboration with the Spanish a means not just to regain their autonomy and rid themselves of Inca domination but also to gain some advantage for themselves in a Spanish-dominated Peru. Unlike in Mexico, however, Inca resistance did persist for several decades, and it was not until 1572 that the Inca leader Túpac Amaru I was captured and executed by the Spanish.

THE END OF THE INCAS

extent of the Inca empire

Conquistador routes

Andagoya (conjectural), 1522

F. Pizarro, 1524–25

F. Pizarro, 1526–27

F. Pizarro, 1531–32

F. Pizarro, 1533

H. Pizarro, 1533

Alvarado, 1534

Benalcázar, 1534

G. Pizarro, 1541–42

Martín de Póveda, 1566

SPANISH SETTLEMENT

The chapel of La Conchita Coyoacan in Mexico City, amongst the earliest buildings from the colonial period, shows Moorish influences on its facade.

The defeat of the Aztecs and the Incas gave Castile control over the two most advanced civilizations of the New World, with large, fully sedentary, hierarchically organized populations already accustomed to providing tribute and labor. Although large parts of the continent remained to be explored and colonized, by 1540, Castile had established control over territories already far larger than the Iberian Peninsula itself and populations many times the size of that of Spain—at least, that is, until epidemic diseases brought about catastrophic demographic decline.

The enormous wealth that accrued to the first conquistadores, who took the lion's share of both the booty gained from conquest and of the rewards of a grateful monarch, served as a great incentive for further exploration and for large-scale immigration from the Iberian Peninsula—an estimated 250,000 people, mostly from Andalusia, Extremadura, and Castile, migrated to the New World between 1506 and 1600. No civilizations of the cultural and political complexity of the Aztecs and Incas were to be discovered elsewhere, but in the decades following the conquests of Mexico and Peru, new arrivals from the peninsula, hopeful that they too might improve their lot in America, extended Spanish domination over large areas of the continent. From Tenochtitlán, expeditions fanned out in all directions—to the territories that became the kingdom of New Galicia in the north, and to El Salvador, Guatemala, and Nicaragua in the south, where the explorers finally met up with expeditions sent northward from Panama. From the Andean region, new Spanish expeditions moved outward in all directions. Sebastián de Benalcázar, traveling northward through Ecuador, finally entered what became Colombian territory, founding Popayán (1536) and Cali (1537) before reaching Bogotá, the land of the Chibchas. There, his expedition encountered that of Gonzalo Jiménez de Quesada, who had penetrated the interior via the Magdalena River, and Nicolás Federmann, who led an expeditionary force from Venezuela. Other conquistadores moved south from Peru to Chile (Pedro de Valdivia founded Santiago in 1542) and northeastern Argentina. The exploration and settlement of the Río de la Plata region proceeded far more slowly, as the presence of hostile Indians, the absence of precious metals, and the failure of three early attempts at settlement meant that few Spaniards were prepared to venture here, preferring the more secure region of Paraguay.

Spanish settlement was not evenly distributed across the territory. The main purpose of Spanish emigrants to the New World was to grow wealthy enough to improve their social standing and to return to Spain as rich men. Precious metals and native labor were the surest and quickest routes to wealth in America, and colonists were therefore always more likely to congregate in those areas that offered both—principally the regions that fell within the boundaries of the Aztec and Inca Empires. The two capitals, Lima (newly founded to replace Cuzco) and Mexico City/Tenochtitlán, became the seats of the viceroys and the principal *audiencias* (tribunals), and the centers of trade between the colonies and the metropolis. Below Lima and Mexico City in importance came the capitals of the next largest pre-Columbian concentrations of populations—cities like Bogotá, Guatemala, and Quito. As precious metals were discovered in areas distant from the main cities, such as Potosí and Zacatecas, new population centers developed in the vicinity, and new foundations followed along the routes that linked these mining centers to the capitals, to the ports, and to the mother country beyond. On the whole, however, Spaniards showed less interest in those regions inhabited by nomadic or seminomadic tribes that were more difficult to subdue—except where precious metals had been discovered—and these were incorporated much more slowly into the empire. In some regions, Indians eluded the Spanish for the duration of the colonial period. In Argentina, for instance, it was left to the national governments of the late nineteenth century to extend white settlement to the southern reaches of the country still inhabited by hostile Indian groups.

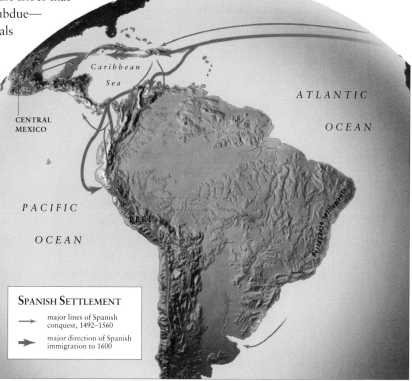

SPANISH SETTLEMENT

→ major lines of Spanish conquest, 1492–1560

➤ major direction of Spanish immigration to 1600

THE STAMP OF SPAIN

From 1501, when Nicolás de Ovando was appointed governor of Hispaniola and less than ten years after Columbus's first landing in the Indies, the Spanish crown began to assert its authority over the first discoverers and settlers and to make determined efforts to set up an effective system of government. Since the crown had no intention of allowing these newly acquired but very distant territories to slip from its grasp into the hands of the conquistadores, whose pretensions to nobility it feared, and since it was equally determined to draw revenue from the colonies, ensure the proper treatment and conversion of its Indian subjects, and keep other Europeans at bay, it was imperative that royal officials should follow hard on the heels of explorers and colonists.

By the last decades of the sixteenth century, a system of colonial government had been established that, with minor variations, would remain in place until the end of the eighteenth century. In Spain, the Council of the Indies was established in 1524 to oversee colonial affairs and report to and advise the king on matters relating to the empire. In America, a viceregal system, previously employed by the crown of Aragon to govern its possessions in the Mediterranean and Italy, was introduced. Spanish America was to be divided into two great viceroyalties, based in Mexico City and Lima—the Viceroyalty of New Spain and the Viceroyalty of Peru. The viceroys to whom the crown entrusted the governing of its territories were thus the two most important officials in the empire; they were charged with the implementation of royal policy, the supervision of the royal treasury and the ecclesiastical establishment, and the administration of justice. As the most direct representatives of the monarch in the Indies, they also carried with them some of the mystique of kingship. However, as the size of the territories to be governed was so vast, the viceroyalties were subdivided into smaller units, each of which fell under the jurisdiction of another institution imported from the peninsula, the *audiencia*. Ten were created in the sixteenth century, beginning with Santo Domingo in 1511, Mexico City in 1527, and Lima in 1543. Audiencias were supreme judicial tribunals consisting of a president and several *oidores* (judges), extremely influential individuals with the responsibility for ensuring the proper observance of the laws of the Indies. In addition to judicial functions, the tribunals also had administrative functions and, at times, executive functions. For example, the audiencias of Mexico City and Lima, the most prestigious of all, were responsible for advising the viceroy, and took on his government duties in case of absence or death; the lesser audiencias assumed similar functions in the absence of regional governors. Audiencia districts were further subdivided into smaller units—the *gobernaciones* (governorships), and, below them, *corregimientos* or, as they were known in New Spain, *alcaldías mayores*—small

AUDIENCIA SYSTEM, BEFORE 1550

THE STAMP OF SPAIN,
AFTER 1550

Spanish territory

boundary of viceroyalty

boundary of audiencia

1549 — date of foundation

■ audiencia capital

● major provincial center

under English control
or influence

under French control

under Dutch control

VICEROYALTY OF NEW SPAIN

NORTH ATLANTIC OCEAN

Audiencia of Nueva Galicia 1549

Monterrey
Durango
Saltillo
San Luis Potosí
Guadalajara
Guanajuato
Tampico
Mexico
Veracruz
Oaxaca
Campeche
Mérida

Gulf of Mexico

St. Augustine

Havana

Audiencia of Santo Domingo

Santiago 1511

Santo Domingo

Audiencia of Mexico 1529

Audiencia of Guatemala 1544

Guatemala

Granada

Caribbean Sea

Maracaibo

Santa Marta
Cartagena
Panamá

Coro
Caracas
Cumaná

Mérida

Audiencia of Panamá 1538, 1567

Audiencia of Santa Fé 1549

Cali
Bogotá
Popayán
Pasto
Quito
Guayaquil
Tumbes
Moyobamba
Cajamarca
Trujillo

Audiencia of Quito 1563

unexplored Spanish territory

VICEROYALTY

unexplored Spanish territory

OF PERU

Amazon

Equator

Audiencia of Lima 1542

Cuzco
Lima
Arequipa
Arica
Potosí

La Paz
La Plata

Audiencia of Charcas 1559

Salta
Tucumán

Asunción
Corrientes

Tropic of Capricorn

Mendoza
Valparaiso
Santiago
Córdoba
Buenos Aires

Concepción

Audiencia of Chile 1565, 1609

SOUTH ATLANTIC OCEAN

Tropic of Cancer

0   500 km

0   500 miles

rural districts headed by *corregidores* or *alcaldes mayores.* These were the administrators most closely in touch with the king's subjects. A further layer of government was introduced alongside these offices, consisting of treasury officials whose role was to supervise tax collection, customs revenues, and the payment of the *quinto* (the royal fifth, a tax on mining production).

The system was fully in place by the 1570s, although the number of districts did increase as new territories were incorporated into the empire and officials sent out to administer them. Some institutions, like the audiencias, also expanded in size as the business of government grew. The rationale behind the design was to build into government checks and balances to prevent too great a concentration of power in any single individual or institution. On the one hand, the diffusion of authority to which this gave rise frequently led to conflict between officials whose prerogatives overlapped; but on the other, it created space for royal officials to exercise some discretion in the application of laws detrimental to the interests of specific regions or groups.

IMPERIAL GOLD

African slaves at work in the mines of Hispaniola. The import of African slaves was in part driven by the Spanish desire to exploit all of the gold deposits within their new territories.

For Europeans, the discovery of the New World offered vast new territories for colonization and settlement, large new markets for trade, and access to a wide range of resources—cocoa, sugar, indigo, brazilwood, etc.—which found a ready market in Europe. From the very beginning of Spain's activities in the Caribbean, however, precious metals, especially gold, constituted the most potent incentive to exploration and settlement. The rapid exhaustion of the placer deposits of Hispaniola, combined with catastrophic population decline, spurred new expeditions to neighboring islands and the mainland beyond, where the search for the sources of the gold delivered up as booty to the conquerors continued unabated. Gold rush succeeded gold rush as each new region was incorporated into the Spanish domain. But despite some significant discoveries—Colombia became the region's principal gold producer—silver was to become the most important export of Spain's American possessions, outstripping gold in both volume and value from the 1540s onward. Early strikes were made in central Mexico in the 1530s, but the greatest producers were the silver mines of Zacatecas (and later Guanajuato) in northern Mexico and, especially, Potosí in Upper Peru—both of which were discovered in 1545–1546. These great silver mines were the jewels in the Spanish crown, the *quinto* tax—equivalent to one-fifth of mining production—becoming a crucially important source of royal revenues for the whole of the colonial period, and one that was protected by a system of convoys and a tight commercial monopoly intended to ensure that Spain alone should enjoy the profits of empire. The mining industry was, however, despite its peaks and troughs, of even greater significance for the colonies themselves. In the short term, the output of the mines financed the trade in imports from Europe—of the foodstuffs, equipment, and clothing that enabled the colonists to sustain a European lifestyle; in the longer term, it served as the principal stimulus to economic activity in other sectors. New settlements sprang up across a wide area to supply the mining centers with foodstuffs and livestock; new industries were developed to supply essential textiles, clothing, and tools, so that in time the colonies themselves became increasingly self-sufficient, threatening the ties with the metropolis.

In Brazil, on the other hand, precious metals were of little significance to the development of the colony, at least until the last decade of the seventeenth century, when expeditions launched from São Paulo made a series of gold strikes in the region that now constitutes the state of Minas Gerais. The finds were important—by the 1750s gold production in this region reached an annual average of fifteen tons—and their impact on Brazilian development, and on Portugal (the crown, like that of Spain, taking taxes equivalent to one-fifth of production), was similar to that of the silver strikes in Spanish America a century and a half earlier. Lured by the prospect of great wealth, prospectors from the coastal region soon made their way inland, to be followed later by migrants from Portugal itself, and even from the Atlantic islands. Thousands of slaves

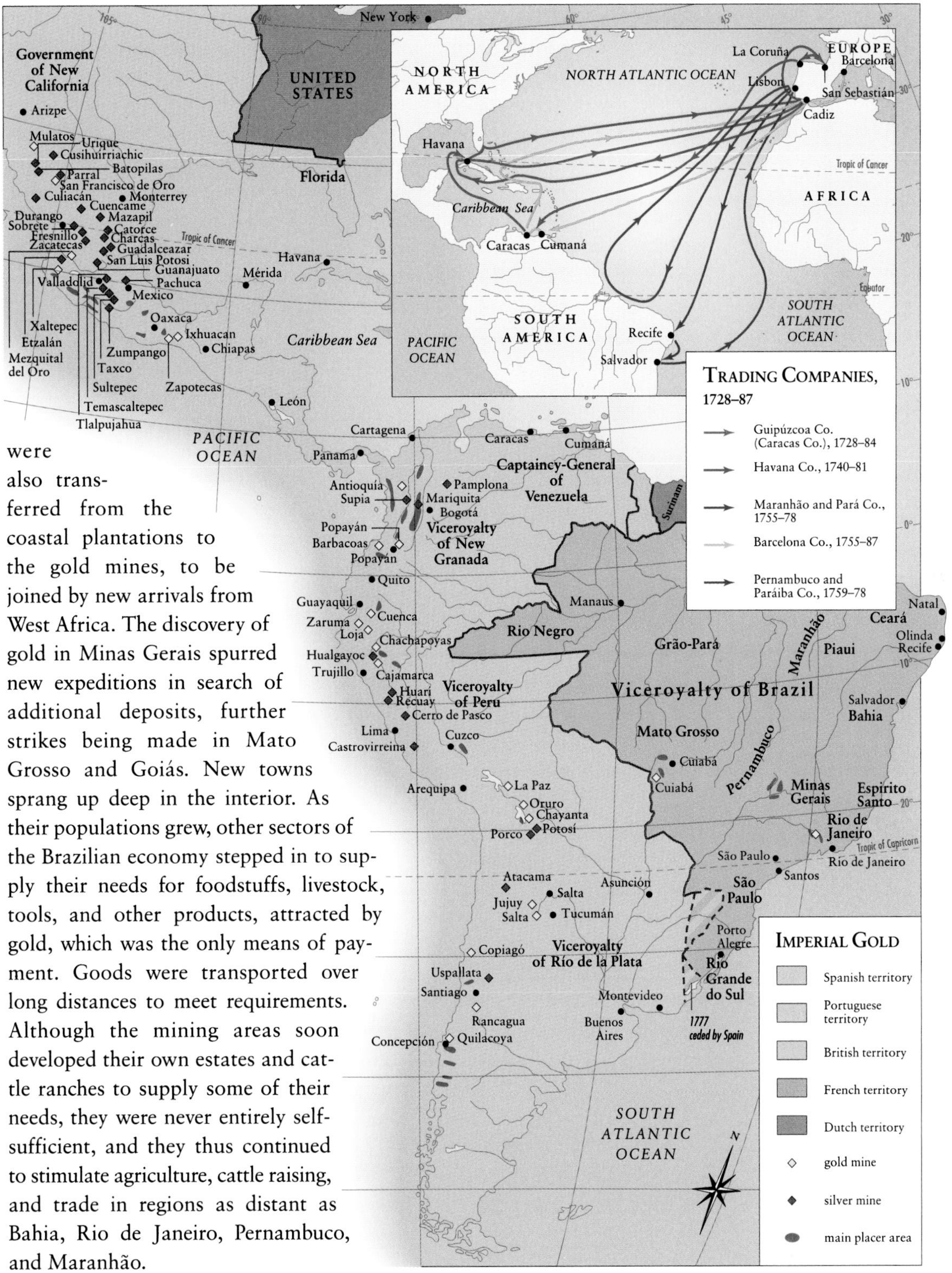
IMPERIAL GOLD
Spanish territory
Portuguese territory
British territory
French territory
Dutch territory
gold mine
silver mine
main placer area
TRADING COMPANIES, 1728–87
Guipúzcoa Co. (Caracas Co.), 1728–84
Havana Co., 1740–81
Maranhão and Pará Co., 1755–78
Barcelona Co., 1755–87
Pernambuco and Paráiba Co., 1759–78
NORTH AMERICA
NORTH ATLANTIC OCEAN
EUROPE
La Coruña
Barcelona
Lisbon
San Sebastián
Cadiz
Havana
Caribbean Sea
Caracas
Cumaná
AFRICA
Tropic of Cancer
Equator
SOUTH AMERICA
PACIFIC OCEAN
Recife
Salvador
SOUTH ATLANTIC OCEAN
New York
UNITED STATES
Florida
Government of New California
Arizpe
Mulatos
Urique
Cusihuirriachic
Batopilas
Parral
San Francisco de Oro
Culiacán
Monterrey
Cuencame
Durango
Mazapil
Sobrete
Catorce
Fresnillo
Charcas
Zacatecas
Guadalceazar
San Luis Potosi
Guanajuato
Valladolid
Pachuca
Mexico
Mérida
Havana
Xaltepec
Oaxaca
Etzalán
Ixhuacan
Chiapas
Mezquital del Oro
Zumpango
Taxco
Sultepec
Zapotecas
Temascaltepec
Tlalpujahua
Caribbean Sea
León
PACIFIC OCEAN
Cartagena
Panama
Caracas
Cumaná
Captaincy-General of Venezuela
Surinam
Antioquía
Supia
Pamplona
Mariquita
Bogotá
Popayán
Barbacoas
Viceroyalty of New Granada
Quito
Guayaquil
Cuenca
Zaruma
Loja
Chachapoyas
Hualgayoc
Trujillo
Cajamarca
Huari
Recuay
Viceroyalty of Peru
Cerro de Pasco
Lima
Castrovirreina
Cuzco
Manaus
Rio Negro
Grão-Pará
Maranhão
Natal
Ceará
Piaui
Olinda
Recife
Viceroyalty of Brazil
Salvador
Bahia
Mato Grosso
Cuiabá
Pernambuco
Minas Gerais
Espirito Santo
Arequipa
La Paz
Oruro
Chayanta
Potosí
Porco
Rio de Janeiro
Tropic of Capricorn
São Paulo
Santos
Atacama
Asunción
Salta
Jujuy
Tucumán
São Paulo
Porto Alegre
Copiagó
Viceroyalty of Río de la Plata
Rio Grande do Sul
Uspallata
Santiago
Montevideo
Rancagua
Buenos Aires
1777 ceded by Spain
Concepción
Quilacoya
SOUTH ATLANTIC OCEAN
N

were also transferred from the coastal plantations to the gold mines, to be joined by new arrivals from West Africa. The discovery of gold in Minas Gerais spurred new expeditions in search of additional deposits, further strikes being made in Mato Grosso and Goiás. New towns sprang up deep in the interior. As their populations grew, other sectors of the Brazilian economy stepped in to supply their needs for foodstuffs, livestock, tools, and other products, attracted by gold, which was the only means of payment. Goods were transported over long distances to meet requirements. Although the mining areas soon developed their own estates and cattle ranches to supply some of their needs, they were never entirely self-sufficient, and they thus continued to stimulate agriculture, cattle raising, and trade in regions as distant as Bahia, Rio de Janeiro, Pernambuco, and Maranhão.

MISSIONARY ZEAL

Rights of sovereignty over all territories lying to the west of the Tordesillas line were conditional upon Castile's agreeing to undertake the conversion of the native population to the Catholic faith. In order to facilitate the task, the papacy also granted the Castilian crown complete control over the ecclesiastical apparatus required to achieve this end: the right to nominate all bishops and clerics, to build churches and monasteries, and to collect tithes. This was the Patronato Real (royal patronage). The Catholic monarchs and their successors took their obligation seriously. Spanish expansion was motivated in part by the quest for profit, and the Spanish Catholic church in America was to serve in effect as an agent of the state in establishing control over the native population. A missionary spirit and a desire to bring about the conversion of the Indians, reinforced by a sense that Spain had been especially chosen to spread the gospel to the New World, guided the actions of the Spanish crown, at least throughout the first half of the sixteenth century.

The first group of Franciscan friars, twelve in number, arrived in Mexico in 1524, to be followed soon after by the Dominicans, already active in the Caribbean, and the Augustinians. Other regular orders joined later, of which the most influential, especially in the more remote regions of the Spanish empire and in Brazil, were the Jesuits. These were the principal religious orders to whom fell the task of evangelization—the "spiritual conquest." Inspired by religious zeal, and assisted at least in the early stages by the demoralization caused among the Indians by defeat, Franciscans, Dominicans, and Augustinians eagerly sought to overcome the many obstacles in the way of conversion—including large populations spread across vast territories, numerous languages which they did not understand, and the necessity, as they saw it, to destroy all vestiges of native religious beliefs and practices.

Missionaries across the empire employed a variety of methods to achieve their objectives. In the initial stages, especially in the regions that formed part of the great pre-Columbian empires, native temples were pulled down and replaced by great churches and cathedrals, often built by Indian labor on the same sites as the old religious centers. Campaigns were launched to seek out and destroy native idols and other holy objects. Many indigenous customs, such as polygyny, were prohibited. Basic instruction in the rudiments of the Catholic faith was provided, and this was followed, despite some divisions of opinion among the orders, by mass baptisms, a policy favored in particular by the Franciscans. The sons of *caciques* (native chieftains) were selected for special instruction, in the expectation that entire communities would enthusiastically follow them into the Christian church. As the Indian population declined due to disease and the other effects of conquest, friars founded new settlements— the *reducciones,* or *congregaciones*—into which dispersed populations were forcibly moved so as to facilitate the process of conversion and acculturation in European ways. The missionary effort was not, however, entirely destructive. Many regulars took seriously their duty to protect their charges from grasping colonists. Moreover, in Mexico in particular, the more enlightened members

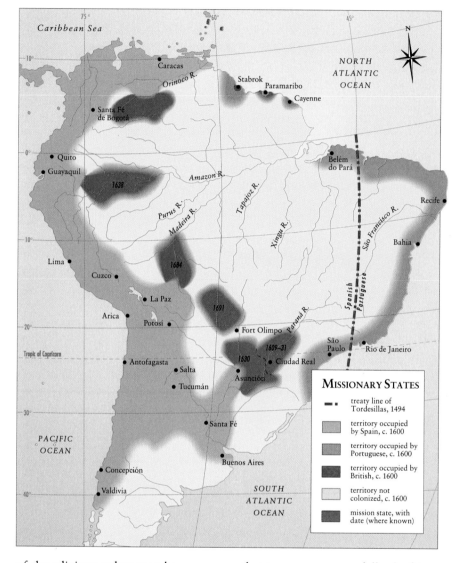

of the religious orders soon became aware that to convert successfully, the friars themselves had to understand Indian culture, language, and religion. Missionaries made great efforts to learn and preach in Indian languages and to study and record Indian customs; in the process, they collected a vast body of data that still serves as an important source for the study of the conquest period. Furthermore, despite the efforts of the religious, the conversion of Indians to Catholicism was never as complete as was initially expected. In many regions, even in those where the missionary effort first began with conviction and enthusiasm, indigenous beliefs were never entirely eradicated. Instead, there emerged a kind of syncretic religion, a fusion of those Christian beliefs that could usefully be adopted with older Indian beliefs, a fusion that is still much in evidence today.

PART III: THE IBERIAN EMPIRES IN AMERICA

The Spanish and Portuguese empires in the Americas expanded and developed in their different ways for more than three centuries. In a first phase, to roughly 1550–1560, immigrants from Spain and Portugal established settlements and sovereignty over the native American peoples they encountered. These colonies then grew and matured into distinctive economies and societies during a long second phase from c. 1580 to c. 1750–1760. A final phase of imperial development then took place in the succeeding half century, when governments in Spain and Portugal sought to exercise closer control over their American possessions, only to see their empires destroyed by movements for independence in 1810–1825.

Into Spain's territories came the institutions of government and religion. Here is the mark of the Inquisition above the doorway to the palace of the Inquisition in Mexico City.

The Spanish-American empire was the first, and became the most formidable of the European empires in the Western Hemisphere. From the Caribbean islands of Hispaniola and Cuba, Spaniards entered the American continents in pursuit of gold, slaves, and new territories to conquer. Colonization of the mainlands started on the northern shores of South America in 1509–1510, but the crucial feats of conquest were in Mexico and Peru, where small groups of Spaniards defeated large Amerindian states and took possession of lands that were to become Spain's richest colonies. In 1519, Hernán Cortés entered Mexico; by 1521, he had overthrown the Aztec state and, on the ruins of its capital Tenochtitlán, he founded Mexico City, later the capital of the viceroyalty of New Spain. In 1532, Francisco Pizarro penetrated into Peru and, after capturing, ransoming, and killing the Inca king Atahualpa, he and his conquistadores in 1533 entered the Inca capital at Cuzco, where they established a base for further conquests in South America. By the mid-sixteenth century, waves of Spanish conquerors and settlers had spread from the core areas of conquest into adjoining regions, where they asserted control over other indigenous peoples. None of the other main areas of conquest proved as rich in returns as Mexico and Peru, but their acquisition enabled Spain gradually to establish imperial sovereignty over the vast territories formed by the great continental mountain chain that ran from the Straits of Magellan through the length of south and central America into Mexico and western North America.

The discovery of immensely rich deposits of silver in Mexico and Peru was particularly important in shaping economic life in Spain's American empire. Mexican and Peruvian silver mines (and to a lesser extent, gold mines in New Granada) provided tremendous wealth for colonists and the crown. Taxes raised from mining and other economic activities supplied the Spanish crown with huge sums of treasure, which made Spain Europe's leading power, and enabled it to build an impressive system of imperial government. The Spanish empire reached a peak of prosperity in the early seventeenth century; the pace of growth in mining and overseas trade then abated until the end of the century. The decline of the imperial economy was not evenly distributed, however. While Spain suffered a deepening economic crisis, Spanish-American economies and societies continued to develop their internal resources, and during the latter part of the seventeenth century they became increasingly independent of the metropolitan economy.

The Portuguese empire in America followed a different trajectory. In the first place, Portugal was slower to colonize its American territory. The main focus for Portuguese expansion lay in Africa and, most importantly, in India. Preoccupied with profiting from trade with those regions, the Portuguese crown neglected Brazil until French interlopers threatened to create colonies there during the 1520s and 1530s. To promote more effective colonization, King João placed a royal governor in Brazil. The first governor-general arrived in 1549, founded the town of Salvador (Brazil's first capital), and took successful action to stimulate settlement and exploitation of Brazilian resources. In 1567, a second royal captaincy was established at Rio de Janeiro, where the Portuguese expelled French intruders intent on colonization and established another base for Portuguese settlement.

After the foundation of Salvador and Rio de Janeiro, settlers began to develop sugar production on a substantial scale, drawing on previous Portuguese experience in Madeira. At first, they used Indian labor, but the death of native peoples from Old World diseases, their inability to cope with hard and continuous agricultural work, and their flight into the interior diminished the labor force available to settlers. In 1559, the crown authorized trade in slaves from Africa to Brazil, thus providing a legal basis for the growth of a massive trade in black slaves and for the formation of the world's first great plantation economy.

Between 1580 and 1640, Spain and Portugal were united under one monarchy, that of the Spanish Habsburgs, and thus Spain's great silver empire in America was brought together with the commercial empires of the slave and spice trades that Portugal had created in Africa and Asia. This great imperial power was remorselessly harassed by French, English, and Dutch enemies, who not only went to war with Spain in Europe but also attacked Spanish colonial trade, raided Spanish-American ports, and sought to establish colonies of their own. Spain could not resist all the pressures, and its rivals successfully challenged Spain's claim to sovereignty throughout the Americas. But while the French, English, and Dutch were able to set up their own colonies in regions of North America and the Caribbean that were not occupied by Spanish colonists, Spain managed to defend the territorial integrity of its American possessions against foreign encroachment. The Portuguese monarchy, which recovered its independence from Spain in 1640, also succeeded in holding Brazil, despite suffering a partial loss of its territory while united with Spain under Habsburg rule. In 1624–1625, the Dutch seized Salvador and, though they were expelled, they returned in 1630 to take control of much of northeast Brazil. This foreign presence lasted until 1654, when Portuguese and Brazilian arms finally dislodged the Dutch from their last strongholds, bringing the whole of Brazil back under Portugal's sovereignty and foreshadowing a period of Portuguese colonial expansion.

From the 1680s, Spain and Portugal competed for territory in South America. Portuguese settlers advanced southward toward the Río de la Plata, where they founded the Colonia do Sacramento and came into military confrontation with Spain, which founded a rival city at Montevideo. Determination to halt each other's expansion on this frontier led to periodic armed clashes until the issue was addressed at the Treaty of Madrid (1750), when Portugal recognized Spanish supremacy on the Río de la Plata in exchange for Spain's commitment to withdraw from the mission regions created by the Jesuits on the Uruguay and upper Paraná Rivers. The treaty did not resolve the issue, however. Portugal and Spain continued to dispute territory in this region until colonial rule ended in the early nineteenth century.

The major threat to the Iberian empires continued to come from outside America, from other European powers that wished to extend their trade and territory. Throughout the eighteenth century, Britain exerted particular pressure on Spain and Portugal as it sought to share in the resources of their empires. The Portuguese monarchy coped with these pressures by a commercial alliance with Britain (the Methuen Treaties of 1703), which allowed Britain to share in its commerce with Brazil. Spain, by contrast, sided with France against Britain and was frequently embroiled in wars that affected its American territories. Governments of both monarchies responded to international competition by seeking to tighten their control over their American colonies, while intensifying exploitation of colonial resources.

By the beginning of the eighteenth century, Brazil and Spanish America were entering upon a new path of demographic and economic growth, and the burgeoning wealth of the colonies was to underpin the revival of their metropolitan powers. In both Portugal and Spain, government ministers became increasingly aware that the future of their monarchies depended on efficient exploitation of their overseas territories and they developed new policies designed to modernize the systems of colonial administration and commerce that had been in force for the previous two centuries. Schemes for the "defensive modernization" of colonial systems began in Spain in the first half of the eighteenth century, and were followed by similar schemes in the Portuguese empire after 1750.

In the Spanish monarchy, colonial reform was associated with the succession of a new dynasty in 1700, when Spain entered a new phase of its political history. With the death of Charles II, last of the Habsburg kings of Spain, the Spanish throne was inherited by Philip of Anjou, grandson of Louis XIV, and power thus passed into the hands of a Bourbon prince who was closely linked to France. The Bourbon succession was not achieved peacefully, as England, the Dutch Republic, and Austria joined in a Grand Coalition to support a Habsburg claimant to the throne against the French-backed Philip. But the War of the

Spanish Succession eventually ended in compromise at the Treaty of Utrecht (1713), and the Bourbon Philip V secured the throne of Spain. Philip had to renounce any future claim to the throne of France, thus frustrating French plans for creating a superstate in which France and Spain would unite under one king. Spain also lost territorial possessions in Europe, and had to make concessions to Britain, including the right to enter Spanish-American ports to trade in slaves. However, in the wake of war, ministers of the Bourbon crown were determined to rebuild Spanish power, and they initiated the first of a series of reforms designed to reinforce the absolute power of the crown, strengthen its administrative and military structures in America, and ensure that American wealth would be exploited for the benefit of the metropolis.

The new thrust of Spanish policy was cautious at first, and major changes awaited the reign of Charles III (1759–1788). Shifts in Portuguese colonial policy also came during the later eighteenth century, beginning during the reign of Dom José I (1750–1777). Their purpose was essentially the same: to ensure that the American territories would make the maximum contribution to the metropolitan economy and government treasury, with colonial commerce promoting reciprocal growth in the economies on both sides of the Atlantic. And, like the Bourbon reforms to the structures of the Spanish empire, the reforms introduced by the Portuguese crown succeeded in imposing a more centralized form of government and in channelling an increasingly large colonial commerce to the metropolis.

Colonial reorganization was associated with an era of growth and prosperity in both Spanish and Portuguese America, and by the end of the eighteenth century the American empires of Spain and Portugal were thriving. But colonial growth did not guarantee their stability. At the close of the eighteenth century, Spain was caught up in a long and exhausting war with Britain, and its empire was eventually to disintegrate when war precipitated the collapse of the Bourbon monarchy in 1808. Portugal was also trapped by the pressures of international war, and its king responded by leaving Portugal in 1807 and, from 1808, making Brazil the seat of the monarchy and center of the empire. For Spain, the fall of the monarchy in 1808 marked the start of a long and ultimately unsuccessful struggle to retain its American empire, ending in 1825 with the loss of its last foothold in continental America. For Portugal, the loss of empire came more peacefully, when in 1822, following the return of King João VI to Portugal, his son Dom Pedro presided over the conversion of Brazil from a colony into an independent monarchy.

The church of Santa Rita, Rio de Janeiro, Brazil, is typical of many colonial building styles imported directly from Portugal.

ROYAL REFORMS

The first efforts at reorganization and reform in Hispanic America were made under Philip V (1701–1746), grandson of the Bourbon Louis XIV of France, with measures directed at rebuilding the Spanish transatlantic trade and asserting closer command over American government. In 1720, the crown took steps to revive Spain's colonial commerce by introducing new regulations designed to ensure regular sailings of the transatlantic fleets, and to prevent foreign contraband. This was matched by political reforms aimed at asserting central control over American administration, notably through the creation of the viceroyalty of New Granada in 1719, the first new viceroyalty to be established since the sixteenth century. The results were disappointing, however. The fleets continued to have difficulty in competing with contraband, while the viceroyalty of New Granada was suppressed in 1723. Under Philip's successor, Ferdinand VI (1746–1759), fresh attempts were made to reform both commerce and government. The viceroyalty of New Granada was definitively reestablished in 1739, and during the Anglo-Spanish War of 1739–1748, the crown replaced the system of fleets that served Spanish South America with individual licensed ships, and legalized the passage of Spanish shipping to Peru and the Pacific coast via Cape Horn. And, from 1750, the crown made more determined efforts to cut back on creole influence in colonial government by reducing sales of offices in the American *audiencias* (tribunals).

The pace of reform accelerated after Spain's humiliating defeat at the hands of the British during the Seven Years War (1756–1763). During the war, Spain lost Havana to the British and, though it was returned under the terms of the Peace of Paris (1763), the fall of this strategic point in Spain's imperial defenses prompted a new reformist offensive during the reign of Charles III (1759–1788). Colonial reorganization began in Cuba, and was then extended to Mexico by José Gálvez. Gálvez's success in Mexico induced the crown to extend reform to other colonies. In 1776, the viceroyalty of the Río de la Plata was established, detaching the silver-rich region of Upper Peru (modern Bolivia) from the viceroyalty of Peru, and redirecting its trade from Lima on the Pacific coast to the Atlantic port of Buenos Aires, which also became the capital of the new viceroyalty. Gálvez, appointed minister for the Indies in 1776, sent officials to Peru, New Granada, and Chile, in order to increase revenues, to strengthen colonial defenses, enlarge Spanish trade, and find the means of making the colonies more productive. Gálvez was, moreover, determined to centralize colonial government by introducing a new official, the *intendant*, who was answerable directly to Spain rather than to the viceroys in America. The system of *intendants* was duly introduced in the Río de la Plata viceroyalty in 1782, in Peru in 1784, and in New Spain in 1786. During the same years, Charles III's government introduced new measures to promote colonial commerce and production. In 1778, the Reglamento de Comercio Libre introduced the principle of freer trade within the empire and aimed to stimulate the export of colonial resources to Spain. During the 1780s and 1790s, the crown also patronized schemes for increasing the output of American mines, through new mining

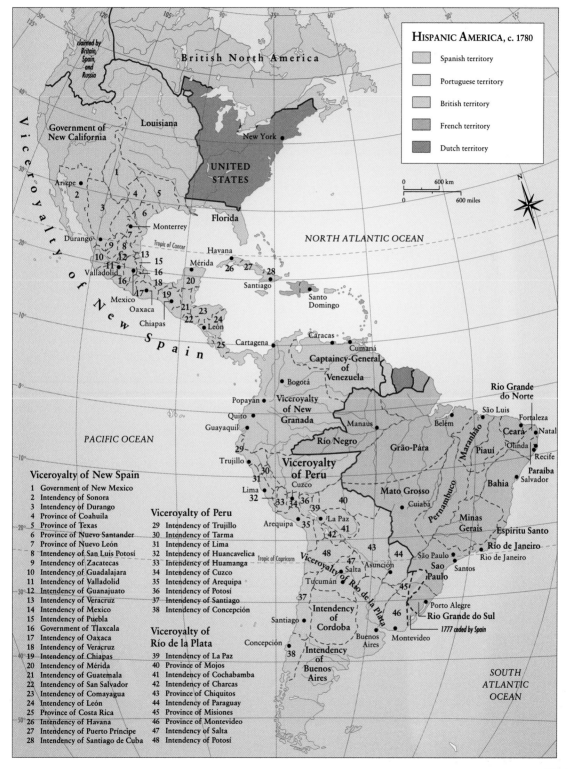

HISPANIC AMERICA, c. 1780

- Spanish territory
- Portuguese territory
- British territory
- French territory
- Dutch territory

British North America

Government of New California

Louisiana

New York

UNITED STATES

Florida

NORTH ATLANTIC OCEAN

0   600 km
0   600 miles

Viceroyalty of New California

claimed by Britain, Spain, and Russia

Arizpe

Durango

Monterrey

Tropic of Cancer

Havana

Mérida

Santiago

Santo Domingo

Mexico
Oaxaca
Chiapas
León

Cartagena

Caracas
Cumaná

Captaincy-General of Venezuela

Bogotá

Popayán

Viceroyalty of New Granada

Quito
Guayaquil

Río Negro

Manaus

Grão-Pará

PACIFIC OCEAN

Trujillo

Cuzco

Viceroyalty of Peru

Lima

Cuzco

Mato Grosso

Cuiabá

Minas Gerais

São Paulo
Sao Paulo
Santos

Arequipa

La Paz

Tropic of Capricorn

Asunción

Salta
Tucumán

Viceroyalty of Río de la Plata

Santiago

Intendency of Cordoba

Buenos Aires

Montevideo

Concepción

Intendency of Buenos Aires

Río Grande do Norte
São Luis
Fortaleza
Ceará
Natal
Olinda
Recife
Paraíba
Salvador

Bahia

Espiritu Santo
Río de Janeiro
Rio de Janeiro

Porto Alegre
Rio Grande do Sul

1777 ceded by Spain

SOUTH ATLANTIC OCEAN

Viceroyalty of New Spain

1. Government of New Mexico
2. Intendency of Sonora
3. Intendency of Durango
4. Province of Coahuila
5. Province of Texas
6. Province of Nuevo Santander
7. Province of Nuevo León
8. Intendency of San Luis Potosí
9. Intendency of Zacatecas
10. Intendency of Guadalajara
11. Intendency of Valladolid
12. Intendency of Guanajuato
13. Intendency of Veracruz
14. Intendency of Mexico
15. Intendency of Puebla
16. Government of Tlaxcala
17. Intendency of Oaxaca
18. Intendency of Veracruz
19. Intendency of Chiapas
20. Intendency of Mérida
21. Intendency of Guatemala
22. Intendency of San Salvador
23. Intendency of Comayagua
24. Intendency of León
25. Province of Costa Rica
26. Intendency of Havana
27. Intendency of Puerto Príncipe
28. Intendency of Santiago de Cuba

Viceroyalty of Peru

29. Intendency of Trujillo
30. Intendency of Tarma
31. Intendency of Lima
32. Intendency of Huancavelica
33. Intendency of Huamanga
34. Intendency of Cuzco
35. Intendency of Arequipa
36. Intendency of Potosí
37. Intendency of Santiago
38. Intendency of Concepción

Viceroyalty of Río de la Plata

39. Intendency of La Paz
40. Province of Mojos
41. Intendency of Cochabamba
42. Intendency of Charcas
43. Province of Chiquitos
44. Province of Paraguay
45. Province of Misiones
46. Province of Montevideo
47. Intendency of Salta
48. Intendency of Potosí

ordinances and schemes for applying modern scientific knowledge to the processes of production.

While these reforms brought growth of colonial commerce and increases in yields of taxation, they also provoked colonial antagonism and triggered major rebellions. These began in 1765, when the city of Quito rebelled against new taxes. More formidable rebellions broke out in Peru and New Granada in 1780–1781, also in opposition to fiscal and administrative reform. The greatest of these is known as the Rebellion of Túpac Amaru, after the name that its leader took to signify his position as the successor to the throne of the Incas. From its epicenter near the city of Cuzco, the ancient capital of the Incas, the rebellion spread to neighboring provinces in Peru and Upper Peru, and even into bordering areas of Chile and the Río de la Plata, as native populations seized the opportunity to protest against the various forms of exploitation to which they were subject. While this great rebellion swept through the southern Andes, involving tens of thousands of people, another major regional revolt broke out in New Granada, where a large rebel force known as the Comuneros demanded the reversal of fiscal and political reforms. Here, rebellion ended peacefully through negotiation; in Peru, the outcome was considerably more violent, and many lives were lost before the crown fully restored its authority.

Although Spain's authority survived these challenges, new threats arose at the end of the century, when creole political adventurers inspired by the American and French revolutions sought to stir uprisings against Spain in the name of freedom and independence. They did not attract any substantial support in the colonies, but changes in the international situation gradually weakened Spain's position in the Americas, and were eventually to give creole revolutionists their chance to break away. Spain sided with France in almost continuous war with Britain in 1796–1808, and bonds with America were substantially weakened during this prolonged conflict. Confronted by British naval superiority, Spain's transatlantic trade broke down, eroding the economic connection between the colonies and parent power. In 1797, Spain lost the island of Trinidad to Britain, British forces invaded Buenos Aires in 1806–1807, and, although these attacks were repelled by local forces, by 1808 Britain was poised to press its attacks in South America in the hope that dissident creoles would take Spanish defeats as an opportunity to rebel.

In the event, it was France rather than Britain that precipitated the collapse of the Spanish empire when, in 1808, Napoleon usurped the throne of his Spanish ally and plunged Spain into internal chaos. The breakdown of authority at the center of the empire led at first to a wave of patriotic support for Spain in America, but this did not last. In 1810, when the defeat of Spain at the hands of the French seemed imminent, citizens of many of the leading cities of Spanish America demanded control of their own governments and established self-governing juntas. Although they did not initially demand independence, the break from Spain had begun, and the way was now open to the eventual struggle for independence and the disintigration of the Spanish empire in the Americas.

In this painting by Goya, Charles III, king of Spain, is out shooting with his dog. When not concerned with hunting, he rebuilt the army and the navy, reformed state finances, and expelled the Jesuits.

EIGHTEENTH-CENTURY PORTUGUESE AMERICA

During the late seventeenth century, Brazil's sugar economy experienced a crisis when competition from Caribbean plantations decreased the price of sugar and increased the price of slaves. However, at the end of the century, a great gold rush began in Minas Gerais, and the boom in gold production continued throughout the first half of the eighteenth century, creating new sources of wealth and opening the interior to an inrush of Portuguese immigrants and black slaves. The boom passed its peak in about 1755, and production then fell back steadily for the rest of the century. Nonetheless, gold mining did much to change Brazil's economy and society. New regions of settlement, based on mining and ranching, were created in south central Brazil; Rio de Janeiro, the port closest to the gold mines, took on a new importance and became Brazil's capital in 1763. The fall in gold output was compensated by renewed growth in overseas demand for sugar, tobacco, cotton, coffee, indigo, and cacao, and Brazil's trade flourished as a result of the growing interest of British merchants, who had come to exercise a powerful influence over Brazil's external trade.

As Brazil became Portugal's leading colony, outstripping in economic importance the other Portuguese colonies in Africa and Asia, so the crown sought to obtain more benefit from it both for the state and the metropolitan country. Under the Marquis of Pombal (chief minister to the crown in 1755–1777), efforts were made to tighten control of Brazil by administrative and tax reforms designed with much the same purpose as those introduced by Bourbon officials in Spanish America. Pombal ensured that responsibility for colonial matters was taken over by a single ministry, that of the Navy and Overseas Territories, and he used the Board of Trade (established in 1755) to try to harness Brazil's trade and resources for the economy of Portugal. The crown tried to reorganize Portugal's commerce by establishing the Company of Grão Pará and Maranhão in 1755, and the Company of Pernambuco and Paraíba in 1759, and Pombal directed his reforming energies toward trying to ensure that the British took less, and Portugal more, of Brazil's trade. He also attacked the power of the Church, expelling the Jesuits from Brazil in 1759–1760, almost a decade before Spain expelled the Jesuits from its American possessions. Defense, too, was high on his agenda. Since the end of the seventeenth century, Portugal had been challenging Spain's rights to sovereignty over the region that bordered Brazil along the Río de la Plata system, and entered into frequent conflict with Spain over this territory during the 1760s and 1770s. Such conflicts involved heavy costs, and it is thus not surprising that Pombal, like his counterpart in Spain, sought to increase royal revenues by increasing the efficiency of the treasury.

By the end of the eighteenth century, Brazil was a highly prosperous and wealthy colony, but Portugal had gained less from reform of its colonial government and commerce than had Spain from its more populous and extensive dominions in America. Portugal suffered from fewer serious challenges to its authority. There were two significant conspiracies directed against Portuguese rule in the eighteenth century, and both were aborted before they could become rebellions. The first occurred in 1789, in the town of Ouro Prêto, when a group

> "This court considers the extermination of the Company of Jesus more useful than the discovery of India."
> *Marquis de Pombal*, chief minister to the crown

of intellectuals and local notables resentful of crown taxation plotted to overthrow royal rule. The conspiracy failed, however; the rebels were betrayed before
they could act, and most were pardoned for their intentions. A second plot took
place in Bahia in 1799, when a few whites, mulattos, and slaves called for political
freedom and social equality. The rebellion was, however, nipped in the bud, and,
after a few executions and punishments, political life returned to normal.

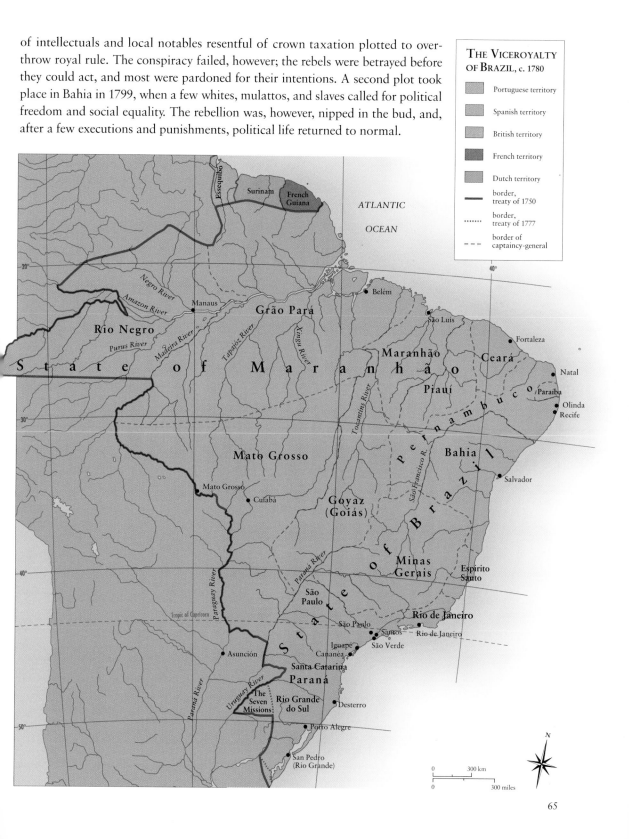

THE VICEROYALTY
OF BRAZIL, c. 1780

Portuguese territory

Spanish territory

British territory

French territory

Dutch territory

border,
treaty of 1750

border,
treaty of 1777

border of
captaincy-general

THE CARIBBEAN: COLONIAL CONTENTION

This illustration from the journal of Captain Beauchesne, c. 1699, shows a hunting scene on the Caribbean Island of Tobago.

The Caribbean became an arena for conflict among Europeans shortly after Spain established the first colonies in the region. From the mid-sixteenth century, foreigners were active in Caribbean waters, interloping in Spanish trade and in time of war attacking Spain's American ports and ships. Then, from the 1620s, the Caribbean began to turn into a microcosm of the competing colonial empires of Spain, France, Holland, and England. While Spanish settlers were established on the larger islands of Cuba, Hispaniola, and Puerto Rico, French and English settlers moved into the smaller islands, which were claimed but not effectively occupied by Spain. First, they established colonies in the Lesser Antilles; later, they encroached directly into Spanish-occupied space. England seized Jamaica in 1655, and French settlers created the colony Saint Domingue in the western half of Spanish Hispaniola, leading to Spain's formal cession of the territory to France in 1697. By the close of the seventeenth century, these islands were all becoming important sources of sugar for European markets, competing with Brazil. To satisfy the growing European taste for sugar and its products, they imported large numbers of African slaves to work the sugar plantations and became export-based slave societies that relied on their metropolitan powers to sustain economic growth and ensure defense against external attack.

Rivalry between European colonial powers led to frequent conflict in the Caribbean. In the late seventeenth century, clashes between rival colonists and navies mingled with the depredations of buccaneers and pirates to create a climate of violence, which was to persist throughout the succeeding century. Now that France and England had important economic and strategic stakes in the Caribbean, their islands became major targets in wartime when each tried to destroy the other's sugar trade. Such warfare became more common and more destructive in the late eighteenth century, as Britain, France, and Spain competed for American territory and trade. The Seven Years' War (1756–1763) was a notable stage in this struggle for empire, involving a contest for territory in both the Caribbean and North America and ending with a treaty (the Peace of Paris) that redrew the map of European empire in the Americas. During the war, Britain inflicted serious damage on French and Spanish islands, taking

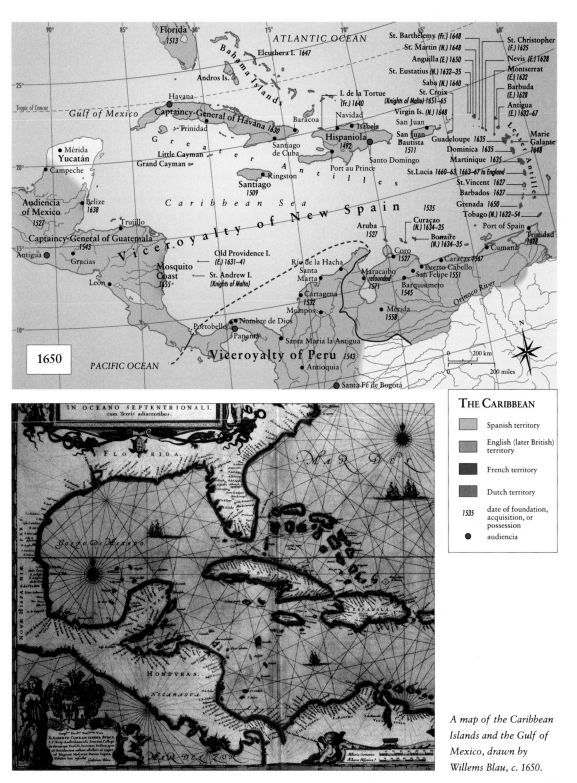

1650

Map labels (upper map): Florida 1513 · ATLANTIC OCEAN · St. Barthélemy (Fr.) 1648 · St. Christopher (F.) 1625 · Bahama Islands · Eleuthera I. 1647 · St. Martin (N.) 1648 · Anguilla (E.) 1650 · Nevis (E.) 1628 · Andros Is. · St. Eustatius (N.) 1632–35 · Montserrat (E.) 1632 · Saba (N.) 1640 · Barbuda (E.) 1628 · Tropic of Cancer · Havana · I. de la Tortue (Fr.) 1640 · St. Croix (Knights of Malta) 1651–65 · Antigua (E.) 1632–67 · Gulf of Mexico · Captaincy-General of Havana 1630 · Baracoa · Navidad · Virgin Is. (N.) 1648 · Trinidad · Greater · Isabela · San Juan · Marie Galante (E.) 1648 · Mérida · Little Cayman · Santiago de Cuba · Hispaniola 1492 · San Juan Bautista 1511 · Guadeloupe 1635 · Yucatán · Grand Cayman · A · Santo Domingo · Dominica 1635 · Campeche · n · Port au Prince · Martinique 1635 · t · Kingston · St. Lucia 1660–63, 1663–67 to England · Santiago 1509 · i · St. Vincent 1627 · Caribbean Sea · l · Barbados 1627 · Audiencia of Mexico 1527 · Belize 1638 · l · Grenada 1650 · 1535 · e · Tobago (N.) 1632–54 · Trujillo · s · Viceroyalty of New Spain · Curaçao (N.) 1634–35 · Port of Spain · Captaincy-General of Guatemala 1543 · Aruba 1527 · Bonaire (N.) 1634–35 · Trinidad 1498 · Antigua · Gracias · Old Providence I. (E.) 1631–41 · Coro 1527 · Caracas 1567 · Cumaná · Mosquito Coast 1655 · St. Andrew I. (Knights of Malta) · Río de la Hacha · Maracaibo refounded 1571 · Puerto Cabello · San Felipe 1551 · León · Santa Marta · Barquisimeto 1545 · Orinoco River · Cartagena 1532 · Mérida 1558 · Mompós · N · Portobello · Nombre de Dios · Panamá · Santa Maria la Antigua · Viceroyalty of Peru 1543 · PACIFIC OCEAN · Antioquia · Santa Fé de Bogotá · 200 km · 200 miles

THE CARIBBEAN

- Spanish territory
- English (later British) territory
- French territory
- Dutch territory
- 1535 — date of foundation, acquisition, or possession
- ● audiencia

A map of the Caribbean Islands and the Gulf of Mexico, drawn by Willems Blau, c. 1650.

An engraving by J. Johnson (far right) shows daily life on a plantation in the parish of Nicola Town, on the Caribbean island of St. Christopher, around the early 1800s.

Guadeloupe, Dominica, St. Lucia, and St. Vincent in the French West Indies, and capturing Havana in Cuba. After the war, however, the distribution of colonial territory in the Caribbean was more or less restored. Britain returned Havana to Spain, and restored all the French islands apart from the Grenadines, Tobago, St. Vincent, and Dominica, preferring to destroy France's empire in North America by annexing Canada rather than retaining important parts of the French West Indies.

The War of American Independence (1776–1783) brought more carnage to the Caribbean, as the powers renewed their struggle for territory. This time, the British islands fell to French forces: Dominica, Grenada, St. Kitts, Montserrat, and St. Nevis were all taken by France, only to be returned to Britain by the Treaty of Paris, whereby Britain acknowledged the independence of its North American colonies. Then, in 1793–1802 and 1803–1815, Britain's wars with Revolutionary and Napoleonic France once more turned the Caribbean into a major theater for warfare, this time with a new twist. In the wake of the French Revolution, the white elites of France's rich sugar-producing colony of St. Domingue turned against the metropolitan power in 1791, and triggered a rebellion that mobilized the free blacks and then stirred major slave rebellions. A prolonged and complex conflict followed, in which slave revolts against the planters also involved successive armed interventions by the French, Spanish, and British, until the Republic of Haiti was established in 1804 as the first independent state to provide citizenship for those who had been slaves. While France lost St. Domingue to slave rebellion, Britain made fresh gains in the Caribbean, taking St. Lucia and Tobago from France, Trinidad from Spain, and rounding out its Caribbean sugar islands by purchasing the Dutch colonies of Demerara, Essequibo, and Berbice on the adjoining South American mainland. When the great Anglo-French wars ended with the Treaty of Vienna (1815), Britain, France, and Spain remained as the major colonial powers in the Caribbean, but the long struggle for dominance in the region was over. The wars of Spanish-American independence deprived Spain of its continental American colonies during the 1820s, and, though it retained Cuba, Puerto Rico, and Santo Domingo in the Caribbean, Spain ceased to be a major power capable of colonial expansion. France and Britain meanwhile turned their attention elsewhere, toward India and the Far East, reflecting the start of a new age of European imperialism in other regions of the world.

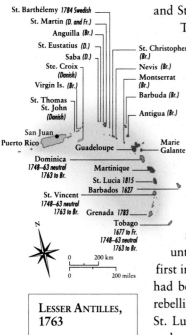

St. Barthélemy *1784 Swedish*
St. Martin *(D. and Fr.)*
Anguilla *(Br.)*
St. Eustatius *(D.)*
Saba *(D.)*
Ste. Croix *(Danish)*
Virgin Is. *(Br.)*
St. Thomas
St. John *(Danish)*
San Juan
Puerto Rico
Dominica *1748–63 neutral 1763 to Br.*
St. Vincent *1748–63 neutral 1763 to Br.*
St. Christopher *(Br.)*
Nevis *(Br.)*
Montserrat *(Br.)*
Barbuda *(Br.)*
Antigua *(Br.)*
Guadeloupe
Marie Galante
Martinique
St. Lucia *1815*
Barbados *1627*
Grenada *1783*
Tobago *1677 to Fr. 1748–63 neutral 1763 to Br.*

N
0   200 km
0   200 miles

LESSER ANTILLES, 1763

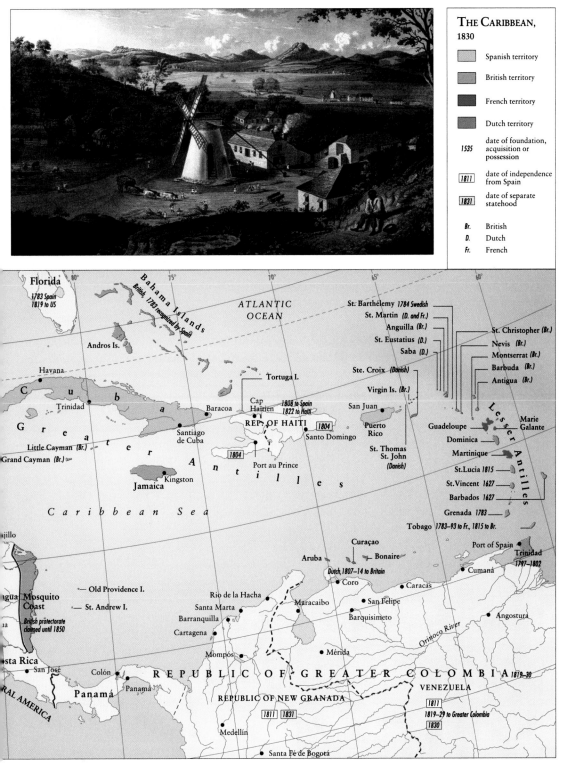

THE CARIBBEAN,
1830

Spanish territory

British territory

French territory

Dutch territory

1535   date of foundation,
acquisition or
possession

1811   date of independence
from Spain

1831   date of separate
statehood

Br.   British

D.   Dutch

Fr.   French

Florida
1783 Spain
1819 to US

Bahama Islands
British, 1783 recognised by Spain

ATLANTIC
OCEAN

St. Barthélemy *1784 Swedish*
St. Martin *(D. and Fr.)*
Anguilla *(Br.)*
St. Eustatius *(D.)*
Saba *(D.)*

St. Christopher *(Br.)*
Nevis *(Br.)*
Montserrat *(Br.)*
Barbuda *(Br.)*
Antigua *(Br.)*

Andros Is.

Havana

C u b a

Trinidad

G r e a t e r

Little Cayman *(Br.)*
Grand Cayman *(Br.)*

Baracoa

Santiago
de Cuba

Tortuga I.

Cap
Haïtien

1808 to Spain
1822 to Haiti

REP. OF HAITI *1804*

1804

Santo Domingo

Port au Prince

Ste. Croix *(Danish)*

Virgin Is. *(Br.)*

San Juan

Puerto
Rico

St. Thomas
St. John
(Danish)

Guadeloupe

Marie
Galante

Dominica

Martinique

St.Lucia *1815*

St.Vincent *1627*

Barbados *1627*

Grenada *1783*

Tobago *1783–93 to Fr., 1815 to Br.*

Lesser Antilles

A n t i l l e s

Jamaica

Kingston

C a r i b b e a n   S e a

jillo

Old Providence I.
St. Andrew I.

agua Mosquito
Coast

*British protectorate
claimed until 1850*

sta Rica

San José

Curaçao

Aruba   Bonaire

Dutch, 1807–14 to Britain

Coro

Rio de la Hacha

Santa Marta
Barranquilla
Cartagena

Mompós

Colón

Panamá   Panamá

RE P U B L I C   O F   N E W   G R A N A D A

1811   *1831*

Medellín

Santa Fé de Bogotá

Maracaibo

San Felipe

Barquisimeto

Mérida

Caracas

Port of Spain

Trinidad
1797–1802

Cumaná

Angostura

Orinoco River

R E P U B L I C   O F   G R E A T E R   C O L O M B I A *1819–30*

VENEZUELA

1811

1819–29 to Greater Colombia

1830

RAL AMERICA
ua

69

PART IV: REVOLT IN IBERIAN AMERICA

The eighteenth century saw a number of challenges to Spanish and Portuguese authority in the Americas. From 1780, revolts in Peru, New Granada, Brazil, and elsewhere sought to redefine the relationship between the colonies and the metropolis. But with the exception of the lengthy Rebellion of Túpac Amaru in Peru, none of these posed a significant threat to imperial control. Few uprisings had any explicitly revolutionary intent. Instead, the downfall of the Iberian empires was triggered by events in Europe. In 1808 Napoleon Bonaparte decided to invade the Iberian Peninsula, ostensibly to defeat Portuguese and British troops defying his blockade of British goods. Within a year it became clear that his intention was nothing short of the complete conquest of the Spanish and Portuguese monarchies. A series of swift military victories yielded much of Spain to French troops. More dramatically, in April 1808 Napoleon's army captured the entire Spanish royal family, who were then imprisoned in France. It was this capture of the Spanish monarchs that sparked off revolution in the Americas.

With the detention of Ferdinand VII and his father, Charles IV, the Spanish empire was deprived of a head. (The Spanish world scorned to recognize Napoleon's brother Joseph as emperor.) In Spain, this void was filled by various so-called Supreme Juntas committed to governing Spain in the absence of the monarchs. These juntas consolidated in late 1808 into a single body, the Junta Central, which summoned an elected *Cortes* (parliament). The Junta Central, and its successor, the Council of Regency, a self-appointed government-in-exile, confidently expected to inherit the legitimacy of the imprisoned Bourbon monarchs. They proved sadly mistaken in this belief. Across Spanish America, the capture of the monarchs and the formation of the Spanish juntas had set off a wave of dissent. Disagreement revolved around the question of who should assume the authority of the deposed monarchs. While few officials favored supporting the intrusive French forces, there was no consensus on how Spanish America ought to respond to the French invasion. Why should America accept the authority of the Junta Central? Beginning in 1809, the deep political division about how to govern the Americas in the absence of the monarch led major cities across Spanish America to overthrow the Spanish colonial bureaucracy. First in Quito, and then in other major cities, governing juntas were established, in competition with those already existing in Spain. These bodies at first proclaimed their loyalty to the imprisoned Ferdinand, but by 1812 most had declared independence from Spain. The unifying role played by Spain was not, however, occupied by any other entity. Instead, Spanish America fragmented into small statelets. Many of these were soon embroiled in enervating struggles with neighboring provinces. Few regions wished to see Spanish authority replaced with control from a nearby rival. The years from 1810 to 1814 thus saw a series of regional revolts and internecine struggles in much of Spanish America.

In many areas, the collapse of Spanish authority unleashed profound hatreds that had been only barely contained during the colonial period. Regions with significant racial divisions were particularly vulnerable. In Mexico, Indian and *casta* (mixed race) followers of the revolutionary priest Father Hidalgo made plain their hatred of the oppressive economic and social order in a series of massacres that convinced many that a race war had begun. Similar events occurred in Venezuela under the leadership of royalist commanders. In the viceroyalty of Peru, fears of an Indian uprising were sufficient to prevent significant revolutionary mobilization by the creole elite. Continued Spanish control was considered far preferable to possible Indian revolt. Likewise in Brazil, a country where whites were heavily outnumbered by black slaves, the creole elite hesitated to disrupt the social order. Fear of black, Indian, or casta rebellion served as a constant check on the radicalness of the revolutionary leaders across Latin America.

Outside of Mexico, the revolutionary leadership during this phase of the war was largely creole. Creoles, individuals of white parentage born in the Americas, had been progressively excluded from colonial authority during the later half of the eighteenth century. The efforts by the Bourbon monarchs to reassert control over their American colonies had led to a hardening of distinctions between the creole elite and *peninsulares,* or whites born in Spain itself. Creoles found it increasingly difficult to gain official posts, and were, as they saw it, victims of a terrible discrimination. A small number, perhaps inspired by the American and French Revolutions, had already articulated radical plans for separation from Spain. Most, however, showed little sign of revolutionary intent until after the French invasion of Spain. Once imperial unity had been shattered, however, disgruntled creoles were among the first to reject Spanish control.

During the years of the Peninsula War (1808–1814), Spain's American colonies were left largely to their own devices. The *Cortes* in Spain was occupied with the war against Napoleon. Its delegates could agree on no effective measures to end the uprisings in America, and in any event had virtually no funds at their disposal. For these reasons, relatively few soldiers were sent from Spain to fight against the revolutionaries. Until the defeat of Napoleon in 1814, royalist and republican armies alike were composed largely of American troops. These conflicts may therefore be considered civil wars. In some areas, such as Mexico, colonial authorities were able to defeat the rebels on their own, with virtually no military assistance from Spain at all. In others, such as Río de la Plata, Spain's failure to intervene militarily destroyed its authority at an early stage in the conflict. Nowhere, with the exception of Mexico, did either side command large armies. At most 6,000 soldiers fought at the decisive battle of Boyacá, which destroyed royalism in Colombia.

After the defeat of Napoleon, Ferdinand VII returned to the Spanish throne. In contrast to the *Cortes*, which was largely liberal in outlook, Ferdinand was deeply conservative. Resolved to erase any vestiges of the French invasion, he immediately ordered that all aspects of Spanish government should return to their pre-1808 state. To do this, Ferdinand would need to solve the "American problem," as Spanish officials called the war in America. At first it appeared that royalists could turn back the clock. In 1815 Ferdinand sent an army to Venezuela, charged with defeating the rebels. This force quickly swept through Venezuela and New Granada, restoring a substantial chunk of South America to Spanish control. Peru had remained staunchly royalist throughout the Peninsula War. Revolt in Mexico had already been crushed by viceroy Calleja. Only the southernmost portion of the hemisphere remained in insurgent hands, and rebels there were embroiled in regional factionalism. It appeared possible that Spain might regain control of its wayward American empire.

Meanwhile, in Brazil, events were following a somewhat different course. In advance of the French invasion of Portugal, the entire Portuguese royal family had fled to Brazil, establishing a temporary court in Rio de Janeiro. The arrival of the Portuguese monarchs in Brazil, a singular event in the history of the Americas, completely altered developments in that colony. Far from separating from the metropolis, the colony replaced the metropolis. In 1815 the Prince Regent João declared Brazil to be a kingdom equal in importance to Portugal itself. Thus in 1815, Spain was securing its American colonies by military conquest, while Portugal decreed that its colonies were no longer colonies at all.

Neither situation proved stable. In the years after Ferdinand's return to the throne, Spain's grip on its colonies weakened. Military assaults led by Simón Bolívar, José de San Martín, and a host of other leaders destroyed Spanish control of South America. Moreover, political developments in Spain dramatically altered the balance of power in the Americas. In 1820, a military revolt originating in Cádiz forced Ferdinand VII to reinstate the constitution created by the liberal *Cortes* in 1812, and to initiate other reforms. The Constitution of 1812 had been in force very briefly in parts of the Americas during the period from 1812 to 1814, and was now reintroduced in Mexico and the other remaining royalist regions. In Mexico, the reappearance of the Constitution of 1812 provoked serious disagreements among royalist officials, only some of whom supported the liberal document. Bickering and infighting among royalist officials ate away any remaining popular support for Spanish rule, and within a year royalist forces withdrew from Mexico, tacitly acknowledging the independence of Spain's first and greatest colony. Elsewhere, the divisions that followed the reintroduction of the Constitution of 1812 fatally undermined remaining Spanish enclaves. Ironically, the document intended by its framers to reunite Spanish America with Spain served in the end as a coup de grâce to imperial control. In Brazil, insistent Portuguese demands that the king return to Lisbon eventually obliged João VI to leave Rio de Janeiro. His son Pedro remained behind. In 1822 Pedro announced Brazil's separation from Portugal, and assumed the title of Pedro I of Brazil. Slight military attempts were made to return Brazil to Portuguese control, but these proved unsuccessful. Brazil's passage to statehood was thus accomplished at the cost of much less bloodshed than in the rest of Latin America. Unlike in other parts of Latin America, where the Spanish crown enjoyed genuine popular support, in Brazil there was little royalist feeling to sustain a lengthy war. Fiscally, Portugal was even less able than Spain to pursue a costly overseas conflict.

By 1825, all of mainland Latin America was free of Iberian control. A hand-ful of islands in the Caribbean remained Spanish, only one of which, Cuba, was to assume any economic importance for its stricken owner. Portugal's foothold on the Americas was definitively eliminated when in 1833 Pedro I abdicated in favor of his son, the Brazilian-born Pedro II. The demise of European control over Latin America, however, should not be read as a sign of some inherent weakness in Iberian colonialism. Spanish control over its American colonies lasted for over three hundred years, much longer than British control over North America. Moreover, the independence of Latin America was primarily the result of events occurring outside the hemisphere. There is little reason to believe that revolution would have broken out in the Americas in 1810 if Napoleon had not invaded Spain.

In place of the Spanish and Portuguese colonies a variety of new states formed. Mexico and Brazil achieved independence as constitutional monar-chies (in Mexico's case swiftly replaced with a republic), but the majority of new states formed as republics. Independence ushered in some significant changes. The new political systems made elections a regular feature of life. The nineteenth century also saw a flowering of journalism, political and otherwise, as well as other forms of literary output. The elimination of Iberian restrictions opened the region's economies to world trade. Most countries enthusiastically embraced the principles of free trade, a policy that brought not entirely positive results. Other aspects of life were scarcely altered by political independence. Landholding systems were barely changed. The plantation, the hacienda (estate), and communal land held by Indians remained the three dominant forms of land tenure. Slavery, the foundation of economic life in regions such as Brazil, was nowhere abolished at independence. In Brazil, involuntary servi-tude continued until 1888. Elsewhere abolition generally occurred during the middle years of the nineteenth century. Social hierarchies remained in many ways unchanged. While independence created a new elite often consisting of military heroes, not all of whom were white, the central importance of race and color in determining social position was not altered. The abolition of the use of racial classifications in official documents, which occurred in many countries after independence, in no way eliminated their power. Nor did inde-pendence bring about a revolution in gender relations. Independence thus did little to alter the social and economic inequalities present in the colonial period. Finally, the countries established at independence were not necessarily coherent nations. The republics of Mexico, Colombia, and Peru did not spring fully formed from the ruins of colonialism. Despite efforts to forge a sense of national identity, not all citizens accepted the new political units. This is not surprising. Some of the new states governed vast areas that had never previously been joined together, or that Spain had made no attempt to inte-grate. Border conflicts were a common feature of nineteenth-century Latin America. Overall, political independence was the beginning, not the end, of a process of change.

"Spain had denied positions of responsibility to American-born creoles. We were never viceroys or governors, save in the rarest of instances; seldom archbishops and bishops; diplomats never; as military men, only subordinates; as nobles, without royal privileges."
Simón Bolívar

REVOLT IN THE CARIBBEAN

At the dawn of the French Revolution, the Caribbean was a colonial zone of coffee- and sugar-producing islands, inhabited by a comparatively small number of whites, free people of mixed race, and hundreds of thousands of black slaves. Since its colonization by Europe in the fifteenth century, the region had produced incredible wealth for the European metropolises. The small size of the individual islands belied their power to generate income. In 1789 Saint Domingue, the eastern half of the island of Hispaniola, alone produced nearly as much sugar as all the British colonies put together, and led the world in coffee production.

A ex-slave, Toussaint L'Ouverture, became leader of the slave revolt. He eventually controlled the whole island of Hispaniola, until tricked by the French into surrender. He was taken a captive to France, where he died in 1803.

These economies relied on a population of black slaves for the production of lucrative export crops. The repressive social apparatus required to maintain plantation society had survived repeated challenges. The French Revolution, however, brought unexpected consequences to the region. Nowhere was this more true than in the rich sugar island of Saint Domingue. There, the *grands blancs*, the great planters and merchants, used the revolutionary movement in France to press for greater autonomy from Europe. The island's free people of color, themselves often slave owners, and the less wealthy whites meanwhile agitated for equal status with the white aristocracy. Slave-owning society was thus divided in August 1791, when a well-organized slave revolt broke out in the north of the island. The slave uprising was unusually successful. Within weeks hundreds of plantations lay in ruins. The revolt was able to survive the capture of its first leader, and by the end of the year a former slave named Toussaint L'Ouverture had emerged as the revolution's most talented leader.

Toussaint's skill extended beyond the military; he proved to be an able politician as well. After fighting French, Spanish, and British forces, he formed an alliance with France when the republican government abolished slavery in French territories in 1793. Toussaint built up his authority over the next eight years, defeating rival leaders and governing an autonomous, though formally French, Saint Domingue. This situation proved unacceptable to Napoleon, who in 1802 sent a large army to defeat Toussaint and restore slavery. The French were successful in the former; Toussaint was captured, and he died in France in 1803. The restoration of slavery proved impossible. Black resistance and yellow fever combined to defeat the French army, and on January 1, 1804, Toussaint's successor, Jean-Jacques Dessalines, declared the formation of the independent state of Haiti. The world's first successful slave revolution had triumphed.

Haiti was alone in pursuing revolution. The other Caribbean islands did not follow its example. Moreover, the movement for political independence that subsequently swept across mainland Latin America also bypassed the Caribbean. Cuba and Puerto Rico remained in Spanish hands. Even Santo Domingo, neighbor of the revolutionary Haitian state, left European control only after Haitian troops invaded in 1821. The reasons for this Caribbean conservatism are not difficult to find. The revolution in Haiti, as well as the uprising of Hidalgo and Morelos in Mexico, terrified Caribbean slave owners. Moreover, islands such as Cuba did not share Haiti's distinctive racial distribution, which forced the white aristocracy into a shaky alliance with the free colored population to maintain the colonial system. The revolution in Haiti was a consequence of that colony's specific history, rather than a general pattern for the rest of the Caribbean. Always vulnerable to maritime attack, closely linked to Europe

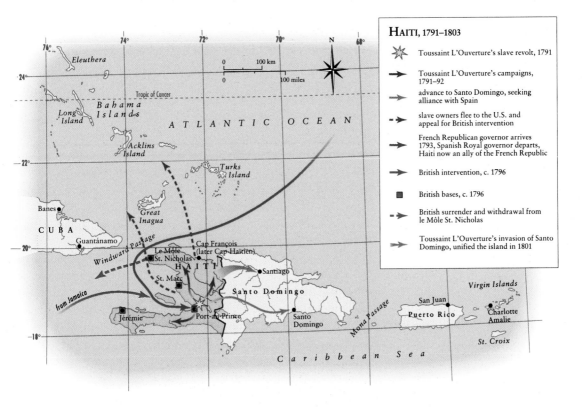

through trade patterns, and nervous about slave unrest, the remaining slaveocracies unhappily watched the political turmoil of the revolutionary years. Four decades earlier, British possessions in the Caribbean had declined to support the rebels in North America for very similar reasons. With the exception of Haiti, the Caribbean colonies entered the nineteenth century largely committed to Europe, to sugar, and to slavery.

INDEPENDENCE MOVEMENTS

The first taste of political independence came in 1806 to the viceroyalty of Río de la Plata, a vast region comprising much of present-day Argentina, Uruguay, Paraguay, Bolivia, and Chile. In that year the populace of Buenos Aires had defeated a British force bent on capturing the city, as part of a larger British campaign against France and Spain. The victory over the invaders was accomplished without any assistance from Spain, or, indeed, from the Spanish colonial bureaucracy in Buenos Aires. This empowering experience of self-defense was to inspire future resistance against outside aggression. Within a year the inhabitants of Buenos Aires defeated a second British force. Spanish authority in the viceroyalty was thus already weakened when, in 1808, news reached the region of Napoleon's capture of the Spanish monarchs and the establishment of the Junta Central. Despite efforts by wealthy Spaniards to seize control of the regional government, by 1809 the creole militia emerged as the most powerful force in the city. Representing a mixture of economic and intellectual interests, the military leaders agreed only on the need to open the economy to foreign trade. In May 1810 the viceroy was deposed; power now resided in the hands of the creole elite, there to remain.

The new authorities in Buenos Aires had ambitions of heading a broad, independent region, but this ambition was not accepted outside of Buenos Aires itself. In the huge hinterland, other forces were at work. The news of the fall of the Spanish monarchy had already reverberated through the viceroyalty, leaving a schism in its wake. In Upper Peru (present-day Bolivia), a region of particular importance because it possessed vast silver mines, reports of Ferdinand's overthrow were met with revolt. In the capital Chuquisaca (later Sucre), La Paz, and elsewhere, juntas of varying degrees of radicalness were established to govern in the absence of the Spanish monarch. As occurred in New Granada, these governing juntas failed to unite against the Spanish, and certainly had little desire to submit to the authority of Buenos Aires. As a result, the incipient revolt in Upper Peru was soon crushed by royalist troops from Peru. In Santiago de Chile, a separate governing junta was established in late 1810. Paraguay, too, rejected the pretensions of Buenos Aires, eventually falling under the idiosyncratic control of José Gaspar Rodríguez de Francia. Meanwhile, a trickle of troops from Spain began to arrive in Montevideo, which had remained in the control of the royalists. Further crippled by internal division, the revolution in Buenos Aires was besieged on all sides.

In a stroke of good fortune, the revolutionary government chose in 1814 to appoint as the head of the army the young José de San Martín, a provincial creole who had fought in Spain. San Martín's ultimate military objective was Lima, capital of the viceroyalty of Peru. In Peru memories of the 1780–1781 Rebellion of Túpac Amaru, when thousands of irregular Indian troops had staged a bloody anti-Spanish insurrection, worked to cement peninsular-creole unity. Fearful of race war, the peninsular and creole elites preferred to bury their differences, maintaining a fierce loyalty of the Spanish crown, and launching largely successful attacks on revolutionary forces to the north, south, and east.

San Martín determined to defeat the Peruvian royalists via Chile, itself now languishing in the grip of the royalists. In 1817 his Army of the Andes set off

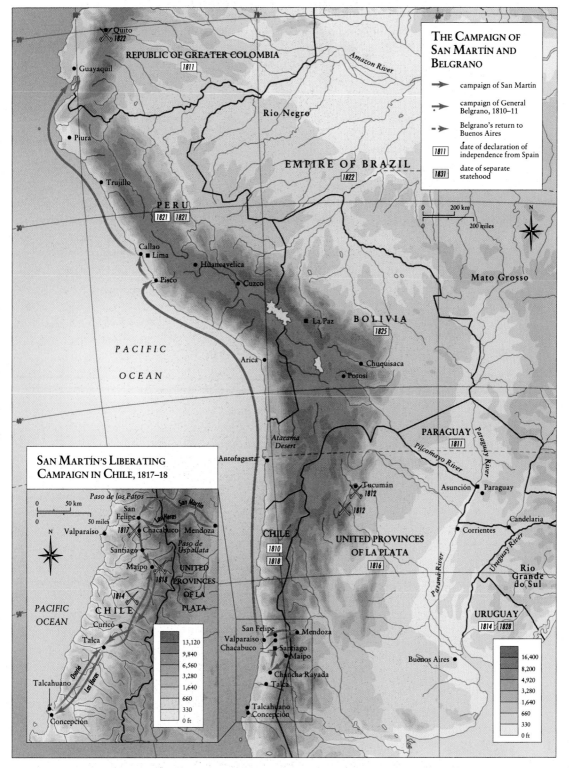

THE CAMPAIGN OF SAN MARTÍN AND BELGRANO

→ campaign of San Martín

→ campaign of General Belgrano, 1810–11

⇢ Belgrano's return to Buenos Aires

1811 date of declaration of independence from Spain

1831 date of separate statehood

REPUBLIC OF GREATER COLOMBIA 1811

Quito 1822

Guayaquil

Amazon River

Rio Negro

Piura

EMPIRE OF BRAZIL 1822

Trujillo

PERU 1821 1821

Callao
Lima

Huancavelica

Pisco

Cuzco

Mato Grosso

PACIFIC

OCEAN

La Paz

BOLIVIA 1825

Arica

Chuquisaca

Potosí

0   200 km
0   200 miles

N

Atacama Desert

Antofagasta

PARAGUAY 1811

Pilcomayo River

Paraguay River

SAN MARTÍN'S LIBERATING CAMPAIGN IN CHILE, 1817–18

0   50 km
0   50 miles

N

Paso de los Patos

San Martín

Valparaíso

Los Heras

San Felipe

Chacabuco

Mendoza

1817

Santiago

Maipo

Paso de Uspallata

1818

UNITED PROVINCES OF LA PLATA

1814

PACIFIC OCEAN

CHILE

Curicó

Talca

Osorio

Los Heras

Talcahuano

Concepción

13,120
9,840
6,560
3,280
1,640
660
330
0 ft

Tucumán 1812

1812

Asunción   Paraguay

Candelaria

Corrientes

Uruguay River

CHILE 1810 1818

UNITED PROVINCES OF LA PLATA 1816

Paraná River

Rio Grande do Sul

San Felipe
Valparaíso
Chacabuco
Mendoza
Santiago
Maipo

Chancha Rayada

Talca

Talcahuano
Concepción

URUGUAY 1814 1828

Buenos Aires

16,400
8,200
4,920
3,280
1,640
660
330
0 ft

77

"The American states need the care of paternal governments to heal the sores and wounds of despotism and war."

Simón Bolívar

for Chile, crossing the Andes and defeating royalist armies at Chacabuco and the important battle of Maipo in April 1818. Naval battles led by the British Lord Cochrane eliminated the final vestiges of Spanish authority in Chile by 1820. San Martín then turned his attention to Peru itself. His forces landed in Pisco, in late 1820, and began to play a waiting game with the viceroy Joaquín de Pezuela in Lima. Trapped in their capital, the royalists chose to abandon Lima in 1821, withdrawing to the Peruvian Andes. They were decisively defeated only in December 1824, at the Battle of Ayacucho, by the forces of Bolívar's ally José Antonio de Sucre. In 1822, following a mystery-cloaked meeting with Bolívar in Guayaquil, San Martín retired to Europe, where he died in 1850.

Simón Bolívar was born in Caracas in 1783, son of an immensely wealthy landowner. Described by all who met him as intelligent, Bolívar was from his earliest years both physically active and strong-minded. As a youth he had traveled across Western Europe, visiting the Paris of Napoleon Bonaparte, for whom he developed a strong, but not uncritical, admiration. While in Rome, he vowed to free his homeland from Spanish control. The fulfilment of this vow was to occupy the remainder of his life.

Bolívar returned from his voyage to Europe in 1807. In his absence, several abortive attempts had been made to incite revolution in Venezuela and neighboring Colombia, but none had attracted any popular support. Bolívar's return to America coincided with the beginning of the revolutionary process. The following year alarming reports began to arrive from Spain. A French army, led by Napoleon's brother Joseph, had invaded Spain, capturing the Spanish royal family and seizing control of the state. These events threw New Granada's and Venezuela's Spanish bureaucracy into disarray. In Caracas, Cartagena, Santa Fé de Bogotá, Quito, and elsewhere, creole revolutionaries deposed the representatives of Spain, establishing juntas dedicated to governing autonomously while Ferdinand VII remained in captivity. What these revolutionaries intended to do should Ferdinand be released was rarely spelled out.

Spanish forces in South America responded as best they could to the wave of revolution afflicting their colonies. With little support from the beleaguered Spanish mainland, South American royalists were obliged to formulate their own policies for dealing with the revolutionaries. In Venezuela, energetic royalist officials soon launched a vigorous and bloody assault on the revolutionaries, recapturing the whole of western Venezuela, the important port of Puerto Cabello, and, in 1812, reentering Caracas. In neighboring New Granada, as Colombia was then known, royalist forces were less successful. There, separate revolutionary movements had broken out in many cities, great and small. Support for the Spanish crown was confined to the northern and southern margins of the viceroyalty. In Santa Fé de Bogotá, Cartagena, Mompós, Socorro, Tunja, Cali, Popayán, and elsewhere, local creoles, discontented with Spanish rule, had established governing juntas.

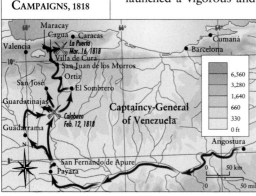

BOLÍVAR'S CAMPAIGNS, 1818

Simón Bolívar, known as "the Liberator," fought the colonial forces of Spain between 1810 and 1824. Such was his reputation that part of Upper Peru was renamed "Bolivia" in his honor.

Within a matter of months, these small revolutionary nuclei had degenerated into squabbles over who was to exercise supreme authority. Power was eventually consolidated into two rival groups based in Cartagena and the old viceregal capital, Santa Fé. Further south, in the Presidency of Quito (present-day Ecuador), Spanish forces were able in 1812 to recapture the regional capital, Quito, which was to remain in royalist hands until 1822.

The leaders of the revolution, as Spanish officials were quick to note, were overwhelmingly drawn from the upper classes. The poorer members of colonial society did not immediately rally to this cry for freedom from Spanish rule, and for some years the movement for independence remained a largely elite undertaking. Chief among these aristocratic revolutionaries stood Simón Bolívar. In the years following Caracas's 1811 declaration of outright independence from Spain, Bolívar rose to a central position in the movement against Spain. Forced in 1815 to flee to the Caribbean, he refined his plans and prepared to take command of the revolutionary movement.

Bolívar returned to Venezuela in 1816 to a changed continent. In 1814, Napoleon's forces had been decisively defeated in Europe. Ferdinand VII, newly restored to the Spanish throne, had assembled a sizable army intended to crush the American insurgents. This force, under the command of General Pablo Morillo, arrived on the Island of Margarita, off the Venezuelan coast, in early 1815. After reestablishing royal control in Venezuela, the army marched into New Granada, recapturing Cartagena after a lengthy siege in December 1815. By the end of 1816, virtually all of Venezuela and New Granada lay in royalist hands.

The royalists however, failed to consolidate their victory. Unpleasant behavior by royalist troops, unreasonable demands for supplies and money, and overall ineptness wore away at the Spanish reconquest. The populations of Venezuela and New Granada turned against the invaders. In 1816, Bolívar's troops penetrated into present-day Guayana, and began to worm their way into royalist Venezuela. Bolívar did not work alone. In the vast plains that lie between Venezuela and Colombia, irregular forces under the command of José Antonio Páez had been leading a debilitating guerrilla war against the royalists. Páez and Bolívar eventually joined forces, formulating a bold strategy to strike at the heart of Spanish control. In 1819, Bolívar led his army westward, over the Andes into New Granada, crossing the bleak Páramo de Pisba in early July. After this tremendous feat, Bolívar's forces defeated Spanish troops at the decisive battle of Boyacá on August 7, 1819. The Spanish viceroy fled to Cartagena, which itself fell to revolutionary forces in 1821. A series of republican victories (Carabobo, Pichincha, Ayacucho) cemented republican control of northern South America.

Although Spanish control of South America was thus eliminated, it was far from clear that an effective alternative had been established. Observing the discord that engulfed Colombia after independence, Bolívar offered the following disillusioned assessment of his life's work: "America is ungovernable. Those who have served the revolution have plowed the sea. The only thing that one can do in America is emigrate." He died in 1830 at the age of forty-seven.

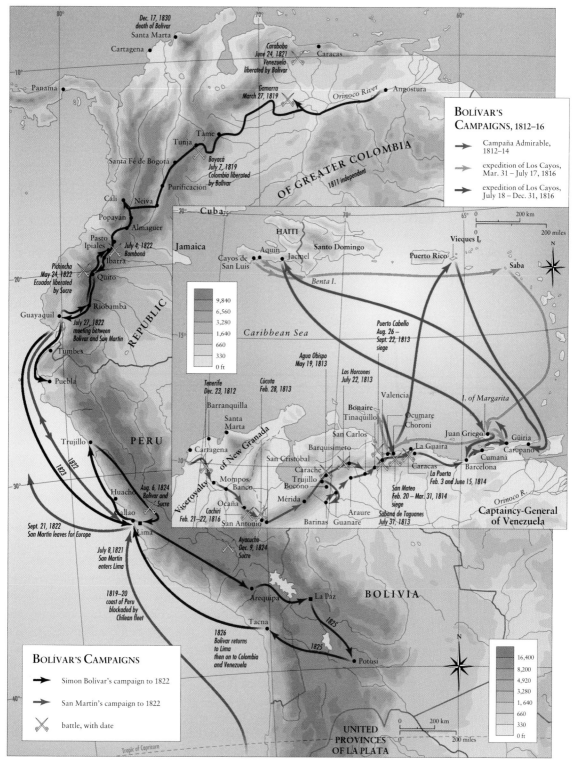

BOLÍVAR'S CAMPAIGNS, 1812–16

→ Campaña Admirable, 1812–14

→ expedition of Los Cayos, Mar. 31 – July 17, 1816

→ expedition of Los Cayos, July 18 – Dec. 31, 1816

Dec. 17, 1830 death of Bolivar
Santa Marta
Cartagena
Panama

Carabobo June 24, 1821 Venezuela liberated by Bolivar
Caracas
Gamarra March 27, 1819
Orinoco River
Angostura

Táme
Tunja
Santa Fé de Bogotá
Boyacá July 7, 1819 Colombia liberated by Bolivar
Purificación

Cali
Neiva
Popayán
Almaguer
Pasto
Ipiales
July 4, 1822 Bomboná
Ibarra
Pichincha May 24, 1822 Ecuador liberated by Sucre
Quito
Riobamba
Guayaquil
July 27, 1822 meeting between Bolivar and San Martin
Tumbes
Puebla
Trujillo

OF GREATER COLOMBIA
1811 independent

REPUBLIC

PERU

Cuba
HAITI
Jamaica
Aquín
Cayos de San Luis
Jacmel
Santo Domingo
Puerto Rico
Vieques I.
Saba
Benta I.

Caribbean Sea

Puerto Cabello Aug. 26 – Sept. 22, 1813 siege

9,840
6,560
3,280
1,640
660
330
0 ft

200 km
200 miles

Agua Obispo May 19, 1813
Los Horcones July 22, 1813
Valencia
I. of Margarita

Tenerife Dec. 23, 1812
Cúcuta Feb. 28, 1813
Bonaire
Tinaquillo
Ocumare
Choroni
Juan Griego
Güiria

Barranquilla
Santa Marta
San Carlos
Barquisimeto
La Guaira
Cumaná
Carúpano
Barcelona

Carraca
San Cristóbal
Carache
Trujillo
Bocono
Caracas
La Puerta Feb. 3 and June 15, 1814

Mompos
Banco
Mérida
San Mateo Feb. 20 – Mar. 31, 1814 siege

Ocaña
Cachiri Feb. 21–22, 1816
Araure
Sabana de Taguanes July 31, 1813
Orinoco R.

Viceroyalty of New Granada
San Antonio
Barinas
Guanare

Captaincy-General of Venezuela

Huacho
Aug. 6, 1824 Bolivar and Sucre
Callao
Lima

1822
1823

Sept. 21, 1822 San Martin leaves for Europe

July 8, 1821 San Martin enters Lima

Ayacucho Dec. 9, 1824 Sucre

1819–20 coast of Peru blockaded by Chilean fleet

Arequipa
La Paz
BOLIVIA
Tacna
1825
1825
Potosí

1826 Bolivar returns to Lima then on to Colombia and Venezuela

BOLÍVAR'S CAMPAIGNS

→ Simon Bolivar's campaign to 1822

→ San Martín's campaign to 1822

⚔ battle, with date

16,400
8,200
4,920
3,280
1,640
660
330
0 ft

200 km
200 miles

UNITED PROVINCES OF LA PLATA

Tropic of Capricorn

MEXICO IN REVOLT

The roots of Mexican independence reach back far into the colonial period. In the colony of New Spain as nowhere else in Spanish America there developed ideas about nationality and Mexican identity on which nineteenth-century revolutionaries could draw. Various messianic movements with murky connections to moves for political autonomy had appeared during the eighteenth century. Many of these had centered on mysterious apparitions of the Virgin. It is thus not surprising that when nineteenth-century creole conspirators developed plans for a revolutionary movement against Spain, they should take as their symbol the Mexican Virgin of Guadalupe. The Virgin was taken by Father Miguel Hidalgo as his emblem when on September 16, 1810, he called for an uprising against peninsular rule.

Hidalgo soon found himself at the head of an extensive revolt. By October 1810 his troops numbered 60,000, and had enjoyed victories at San Miguel el Grande, Celaya, Guanajuato, and Valladolid. The army poised to capture Mexico City itself.

In Mexico the news of the French invasion of Spain had received an ambiguous welcome. In Mexico City, creole calls for the viceroy to assume autonomy clashed with peninsular demands for continued subservience to Spain. Within months, the viceroyalty was in the hands of die-hard royalists, who swiftly blocked any calls for greater independence. The creole and peninsular inhabitants of Mexico City looked with horror on Hidalgo's Indian army, united in their fear of an Indian revolt. Fevered organizing produced a royalist force of some 30,000, headed by Félix María Calleja, a veteran officer with considerable military experience. This force was sufficient to convince Hidalgo to withdraw his troops from their camp on the outskirts of Mexico City. Now on the defensive, Hidalgo and his lieutenant, Ignacio Allende, sustained a defeat at Acapulco in November 1810. The rebels regrouped, only to suffer another defeat outside Guadalajara in January 1811. Within months, Hidalgo was captured and executed. The revolt continued after Hidalgo's death, led by José María Morelos, who endowed the revolution with greater political coherence and military leadership. Morelos's and Calleja's troops battled against each other until November 1815, when Morelos was captured and executed.

Calleja retired as viceroy in late 1816. His successor arrived in Mexico to find the country pacified, if not unified. It appeared that royal control had been restored, but a renewed challenge was to appear in an altogether different quarter. In January 1820, a liberal uprising in Spain threw Spanish government in both Europe and the Americas into disarray. In Mexico, viceroy Juan Ruiz de Apodaca reinstated an abridged version of the liberal Constitution of 1812, simultaneously alienating both conservatives and liberals. Importantly, the deep divisions in peninsular politics were publicly displayed. Spain hardly presented a convincing picture of strength.

Independence finally came to Mexico in the person of Agustín de Iturbide, a former royalist soldier turned revolutionary leader. In 1821 Iturbide articulated his outline for an independent Mexico in his Plan de Iguala. Mexico was to become a constitutional monarchy, closely linked to the Catholic Church. This plan appealed to all major political actors. Spanish forces acknowledged defeat in 1821, and Iturbide proclaimed himself emperor of an independent Mexico.

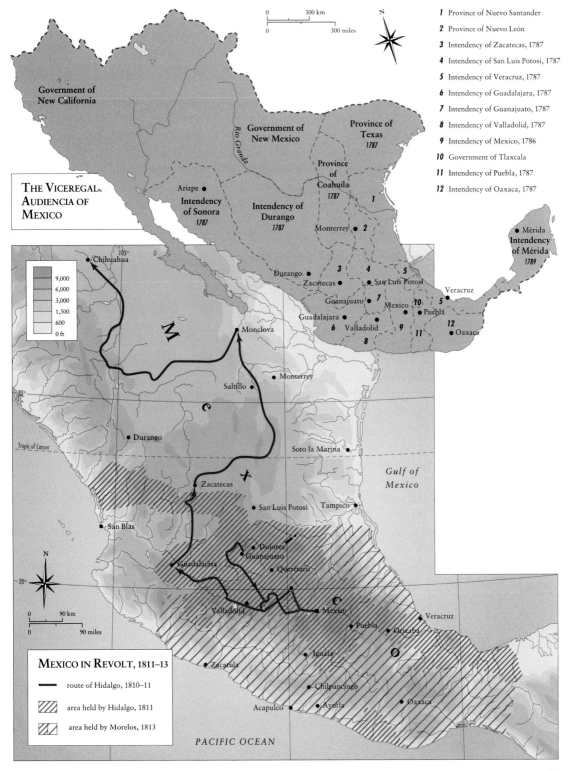

0   300 km

0   300 miles

1 Province of Nuevo Santander

2 Province of Nuevo León

3 Intendency of Zacatecas, 1787

4 Intendency of San Luis Potosí, 1787

5 Intendency of Veracruz, 1787

6 Intendency of Guadalajara, 1787

7 Intendency of Guanajuato, 1787

8 Intendency of Valladolid, 1787

9 Intendency of Mexico, 1786

10 Government of Tlaxcala

11 Intendency of Puebla, 1787

12 Intendency of Oaxaca, 1787

Government of
New California

Government of
New Mexico

Province of
Texas
1787

Rio Grande

Province
of
Coahuila
1787

Arizpe ●

Intendency
of Sonora
1787

Intendency of
Durango
1787

Monterrey ● **2**

1

● Mérida

Intendency
of Mérida
1789

THE VICEREGAL AUDIENCIA OF MEXICO

Durango ●

Zacatecas ●

3   **4**   **5**

● San Luis Potosí

Veracruz ●

Guanajuato ●   **7**

Mexico ● **10**   **5**

Puebla ●

Guadalajara ●

6   Valladolid   **9**

8   **11**

12

● Oaxaca

9,000
6,000
3,000
1,500
600
0 ft

● Chihuahua

105°

M

e

x

Monclova ●

● Monterrey

Saltillo ●

25°

Durango ●

Soto la Marina ●

Tropic of Cancer

Zacatecas ●

San Luis Potosí ●

Tampico ●

*Gulf of
Mexico*

San Blas ●

Dolores
Guanajuato

● Querétaro

Guadalajara ●

N

20°

Valladolid ●   Mexico ■

Veracruz ●

Puebla ●   Orizaba ●

0   90 km

0   90 miles

MEXICO IN REVOLT, 1811–13

──── route of Hidalgo, 1810–11

▨ area held by Hidalgo, 1811

▨ area held by Morelos, 1813

Zacatula ●

Iguala ●

Chilpancingo ●

Acapulco ●   Ayutla ●

● Oaxaca

PACIFIC OCEAN

BRAZIL: TRANSITION TO MONARCHY

Botafogo Bay, Rio de Janeiro, from an engraving made around 1860.

On November 29, 1807, the entire Portuguese court, including the Portuguese royal family, sailed from Lisbon for the New World. The convoy reached Brazil in early 1808, and for the next thirteen years, the Portuguese empire was governed from Rio de Janeiro. The colony had become the de facto metropolis. The reason for this remarkable transfer was Napoleon's invasion of Portugal in 1807. Once it became clear that defeat at the hands of the French was inevitable, the Portuguese monarchs decided to beat a strategic retreat to their most powerful colony.

The impact of this move was profound. The monarchy was obliged to rescind some of the more restrictive commercial legislation, and the British were granted an extremely privileged position with respect to overseas trade. The arrival of the court brought other changes as well. The first printing presses were introduced to Brazil during this period, which also saw the establishment of a state bank, and medical and military academies. Important as the measures were, the court's move to Brazil was critical to the process by which Brazil achieved independence.

During the years that the royal family resided in Brazil, repeated calls were made for their return to Europe. But equally vociferous voices insisted that they remain in Brazil. In the face of these conflicting demands, the court vacillated. In 1815, in an attempt to postpone the promised departure, the Prince Regent João announced the creation of the "United Kingdom of Portugal, Brazil and the Algarves," thereby elevating Brazil to an equal status to Portugal. This act, far from unifying Brazil into a nation, merely highlighted regional resentment against the dominance of Rio de Janeiro. In 1817 a regionalist revolt that began in Pernambuco spread to a number of different provinces. The defeat of these uprisings did not completely restore the credibility of the monarchy, which from 1818 governed with an increasingly siegelike mentality. Unwilling to contemplate reform, the monarchy was unable to respond to either the aftermath of war in Portugal or regional discontent in Brazil. Crisis occurred in 1820. In August of that year Portuguese troops in Oporto mutinied, much as Spanish troops had done in Cádiz eight months earlier. Their demands included the return of the king from Brazil, as well as the summoning of an elected *Cortes* or parliament. This event initiated uprisings in several Brazilian cities, culminating in April 1821 with João VI's return to Portugal, leaving his son Dom Pedro as temporary regent in Brazil.

The next year saw an intensification of the three-way struggle between Dom Pedro and the advocates of Rio de Janeiro's supremacy on the one hand, Brazil's other provinces, and the *Cortes* in Portugal. In province after province, local notables established governing juntas that implicitly challenged the authority of either Dom Pedro, the *Cortes*, or both. Dom Pedro retained a tenuous grip on power until August 1821, when orders arrived from Lisbon for his immediate

"Since they want a king of their own, it had better be you."
King João of Portugal,
to his son Dom Pedro

return. This command was taken as signaling the Portuguese *Cortes*'s intention of returning Brazil to its colonial status. As such, it met with nearly unanimous hostility in Brazil itself. Although provinces such as São Paulo or Bahia did not wish to be sidelined by Rio, neither did they want renewed subservience to Lisbon. On January 9, 1822, bowing to pressure, Dom Pedro announced his intention of remaining in Brazil. This decision, broadly welcomed in Rio de Janeiro, commanded much more equivocal support elsewhere in Brazil, where local elites still resented the dominance of Rio. A number of provinces continued to acknowledge the authority of the *Cortes*. However the *Cortes*, in a series of inept moves, managed to alienate what support it retained in Brazil. On September 7, 1822, Dom Pedro announced the independence of Brazil. Within five weeks he had been acclaimed Brazil's first emperor. Attempts to defend the authority of the *Cortes* by military force were roundly defeated, largely through the assistance of Sir Thomas Cochrane, commanding a rapidly assembled navy. By the end of 1823, Brazil had separated from Portugal with a minimum of bloodshed.

TRANSITION TO MONARCHY, 1807–22

- Portuguese possessions
- → Portuguese royal family flee Napoleonic invasion, November 1807

PART V: POSTCOLONIAL MALADIES

The first fifty years of independence, roughly from 1820 to 1870, were unsettled if not turbulent times for most of the newly independent nations of Latin America as they struggled to forge the necessary institutions and a sense of national identity that would enable them to overcome a host of problems—political, social, economic, and even, on occasion, external. Creating strong central governments able to withstand destructive factionalism as well as regional threats to their national authority was no mean task. In general, nations were weak and vulnerable to encroachments by neighboring states and, on rarer occasions, by foreign powers. Compounding the difficulties in building viable nations was the meager success most countries had in developing successful and productive economies.

To the outside world, Latin America was a resource-rich region that seemed to offer attractive opportunities for trade and for investment in mining schemes. Foreign merchants led by British traders entered the scene in numbers in search of new opportunities arising from the demise of Iberian control in nearly all parts of the Americas, save for Cuba and Puerto Rico. The prospect of genuine free trade with all countries was appealing to foreign traders as well as to some domestic groups, but it posed dangers to local manufacturers organized on artisan lines who had thrived during the colonial era.

But the real potential for trade and national development was far less promising as there were daunting social and economic obstacles, not to mention an uncertain political picture. On the economic plane, a number of new republics in Spanish America began their lives as independent countries with economies that had been devastated during the independence struggle, and this included the former colonies of most economic importance to Spain. As a result of the wars of independence, physical capital had been destroyed and financial capital had fled. The mining economies of New Spain (now Mexico) and Upper Peru (now Bolivia) were in ruins and this dealt a blow to all the ancillary industries that had served them in adjoining territories. Like the time before independence, the mass of the population was illiterate and was either living in an impoverished state or at a subsistence level, especially those countries of Spanish America which had large Indian communities. The new independent nations had small middle classes with the bulk of the population living outside the economic mainstream, thus the consumer market for finished goods was tiny.

During the 1820s, in both Spanish America and in Portuguese America (Brazil), Indians and blacks constituted more than half of the population. Mixed bloods, that is, mestizos and mulattos, comprised over a quarter of the Spanish-American population and slightly less than one-fifth of Brazil's population. The white population in Brazil was nearly a quarter of all inhabitants, whereas it represented something under one-fifth in Spanish America. Most people in Latin America lived in rural areas, while the cities, although growing, were not generally of any great size.

Important as it was to improve the shaky state of postcolonial economies, the paramount task in the immediate decades after independence was to develop effective political institutions able to gain the allegiance of the populace and the obedience of interior regions. In many countries of Spanish America, central areas, which had either political or economic power, experienced difficulties in forcing their will over outlying regions. Added to this, a particular feature of those Spanish-American territories in the forefront of the military struggle against Spain was the emergence of military chieftains or leaders, known as *caudillos*. It was in the decades after the wars of independence that the typical caudillo (authoritarian ruler) first emerged.

At the heart of the political insta-bility cropping up in Spanish America from the 1820s onward was the fact that there was no consensus on vital political issues and that a debate, often violent, raged on such matters as to whether states should have central-ized or federal systems, whether con-servative values instead of liberal or reformist values should prevail, and whether the church should have a dominant or less dominant position in society.

The first three decades of indepen-dence until mid-century were by far the most unstable period. Various Spanish-American countries saw fre-quent changes of government and even bouts of civil war. By comparison, Portuguese America (Brazil) enjoyed greater stability under monarchical rule, even though the autocratic prac-tices of the first emperor, Pedro I, enflamed some separatist feelings in diverse parts of the country. Under his successor, Pedro II, the nation remained stable and unified even though the ongoing debate about the future of slavery was a divisive political issue in Brazil until the institution's abolition in 1888.

Antonio José de Sucre, soldier and patriot, leader in the wars of liberation, seen here at the battle of Ayacucho in 1824.

In Spanish America, political instability was extreme in a number of coun-tries. Mexico during the period from 1821 to 1850 had fifty governments and was subject to frequent military coups, with the caudillo General Antonio López de Santa Anna in and out of government. Due to its internal weakness, Mexico was unable to maintain its postcolonial territorial integrity and, by mid-century, it had lost half of its territory as a result of the secession of Texas and the war with the United States in the 1846 to 1848 period. Argentina was another country wracked with civil conflict as interior provinces resisted the efforts of Buenos Aires, ruled by the dictator Juan Manuel de Rosas, to estab-lish its hegemony over the confederation known as the United Provinces of La

Plata. Colombia's government faced intermittent civil war from 1839 to 1842 over assorted issues relating to regionalism, clericalism, and personal questions about the president. Peru experienced internecine political struggles even at times to the point of anarchy until Ramón Castilla seized power in 1845 and ruled the nation with a firm but benign hand until 1862. Bolivia, lacking a landed aristocracy or some form of power elite to give it stability, suffered endemic political volatility and was constantly at the mercy of military leaders inside or just outside its borders. The Dominican Republic in the Caribbean probably

had the most protracted and lengthy struggle to maintain its independence and to control its destiny of any of the colonies that broke with Spain in the first part of the nineteenth century. Neighboring Haiti ruled the country from 1822 to 1844 and later Spain, at the request of the government of General Pedro Santana, reassumed control of the nation in 1861, but relinquished its hold in 1865, when its position was becoming untenable.

The weakness and debilitating political infighting in Spanish-American countries promoted external difficulties for these nations. Poorly demarcated frontiers, an inheritance from the colonial experience, and ongoing disputes about trade and resources were other powerful combustibles. In addition, Spain found it difficult to rec-

Despite disputes between the newly independent South American nations, vast tracts of land remained to be exploited by the existing population and by emigrants from Europe who began to occupy areas like Monte Verde in Brazil.

oncile itself to the loss of the bulk of its colonies in the Americas, even though Britain and the United States had been quick to recognize the new nations, and the latter had seen fit in 1823 to issue the Monroe Doctrine warning to European nations, most notably the Holy Alliance countries, not to assist Spain in any attempt to reconquer the lost possessions. Spain's actual threat to the new republics of the Americas was probably more apparent than real.

External disputes were, however, frequent in the first fifty years of independence, and there were both minor and major wars that involved Latin American states with their neighboring countries and even with powers outside the region. Among the conflicts were the Brazilian-Argentine confrontation over Uruguay in 1826 to 1828, the Chilean action against the Peruvian-Bolivian confederation in 1837, the French blockade of the port of Buenos Aires in 1838, the Anglo-French blockade of the Río de la Plata from 1845 to 1848 directed at the Rosas government, the war between Mexico and the United States from 1846 to 1848, the French invasion of Mexico in 1862 to install Maximilian von Habsburg as emperor of that country, and the War of the Triple Alliance from 1865 to 1870 between Paraguay on one side and

Argentina, Brazil, and Uruguay on the other. Yet another war, and a major conflict at that, was the War of the Pacific during 1879 to 1883, pitting Chile against Peru and Bolivia.

While the Latin American region had to face no little political turbulence in the first fifty years after independence, the worst period, the years from the 1820s to the 1850s, was over, and for some countries an era of acute internal political chaos had ended. In Argentina, the powerful city and province of Buenos Aires in the 1850s and 1860s had finally tamed the regional caudillos and effected a national organization on its own terms. After the early 1860s, a stable Argentina could focus more single-mindedly upon national economic development. In the Latin American region, a greater sense of nationhood was also beginning to gain real currency and this could be seen in the 1860s in important countries. Mexico was a case in point as Benito Juárez led a national resistance movement that defeated the government of Emperor Maximilian in 1867. The decade of the 1860s also marked the dénouement of French and Spanish attempts to install monarchical governments in the Americas either controlled or subservient to them. The independence of Latin American countries was being seen increasingly as irreversible. At the same time, Spain's hold over its few remaining colonies was in some jeopardy as the important Cuban colony was in a state of open insurrection from 1868 to 1878.

To a large extent, the overriding national task in the first fifty years of independence had been to create a sense of nationhood and to engineer a national consolidation providing an elementary political unity. In these directions there was clear progress. Large countries like Argentina, Brazil, Colombia, Mexico, and Venezuela could be relieved that they had held in check regional or separatist tendencies posing a threat to their territorial integrity.

In other spheres of national life, the era from 1820 to 1870 produced no very great social or economic changes in most countries. Economies were either stagnant or had low rates of economic growth that gave them little scope for creating sizable employment or for raising the amount of prosperity in society. Even a country like Chile, which could be seen as something of a qualified success in political and economic terms during the period, still had high levels of unemployment and underemployment in its great economic heartland, the agricultural region of the Central Valley. As in the colonial period, the export of primary products (raw materials and foodstuffs) was by default the mainstay of economic endeavor, but this was no panacea, as few countries possessed the staple products most in demand by the industrializing countries of Western Europe and North America. At the same time, manufacturing, above all artisan activity, was more in the doldrums than ever before, due to the widespread adoption of free trade after the collapse of Iberian rule.

Contrary to the prevailing pattern in much of Latin America, a certain amount of social and economic change did occur within certain regions of a few countries. From the 1830s onward, Brazil, in response to rising world demand for coffee, was rapidly increasing its coffee plantations in its southeast in an area north of Rio de Janeiro running westward to São Paulo. This boom was producing a new planter elite and was sparking off a demand for labor that was hard to meet in the period up to 1870 in view of the restrictions placed on the overseas slave trade in 1850, the practical difficulties of shifting slave labor from the northeast to the southeast, and the reluctance of potential emigrants in Europe to offer their labor to a slaveholding country. But even so, dramatic changes were following in the wake of the rise of the dynamic staple product coffee. In Argentina, the rapid conversion of Buenos Aires province from the 1820s into a livestock region rearing sheep and cattle stimulated a sharp rise in the rural and urban population of that area, even though Argentina had yet to make its true market as a major foodstuff-exporting nation by 1870.

In tandem with Latin America's unremarkable economic growth in the 1820 to 1870 period, population growth was relatively modest and averaged around one percent per annum in the first three decades after independence. What was significant, of course, was that the demographic growth rate, certainly that in the years from 1820 to 1850, was lower than the rate in the later stages of the colonial era. A factor holding down population growth was the fact that the region's large Indian population, highly concentrated in Mexico, parts of Central America, and in the Andean nations, lived in austere conditions on the basis of subsistence agriculture incapable of supporting larger populations. Efforts to bring Indian communities into the mainstream of economic life, including attempts to end communal landholdings, were never fully successful in changing the marginal role that Indians had in the society and the economy.

But there were exceptions to the general population picture, especially in those countries where fairly dynamic economic changes were taking place in particular regions. Land settlement in part of the Argentine Pampas, most notably in Buenos Aires province, helped to triple the population of the nation and also the city of Buenos Aires in the years from about 1825 to 1869. Brazil, with its expanding southeastern coffee economy, experienced strong demographic growth, which was especially high before 1850, when legislation banning the importation of African slaves began to be more fully implemented, thus closing off an important source of new labor for coffee farms. In some countries, certainly Argentina and Brazil, urbanization accelerated in capital cities and commercial centers; nonetheless, most people in Latin America continued to live in rural areas, and only a small minority lived in the cities. About 10 percent of all Argentines inhabited Buenos Aires in 1869, and about 3 percent of Brazilians resided in Rio de Janeiro in 1872.

From independence up to 1870, Latin America was clearly in a new era with a changed political landscape. The main beneficiaries of the new political order were the creole minority, who generally exercised political power or who contested it in the mutually destructive struggles that ensued over the period. Of course, there was not absolute creole monopoly of power, as mestizo leaders also emerged and, rarer still, even a national leader of Indian extraction could arise, as with Benito Juárez in Mexico.

But, in a real sense, there was no clean break with the region's colonial past. The social composition of society bore considerable resemblance to the Iberian era, even though the apex of society had changed as Iberians were no longer the elite, replaced by creoles, with a sprinkling of upward-moving mestizos. There had been no truly significant enlargement of the middle class. Like before, a majority of the population in both Spanish and Portuguese America was composed of Indians and blacks, most of whom lived at the subsistence level. Although slavery had been abolished in nearly all countries by the middle of the nineteenth century, Brazil and Cuba being the exceptions, the economic lot of the free slaves had not really been transformed.

The reality was that Latin American countries in the 1860s were badly in need of economic development and lacked the capital and an adequate infrastructure—only token railroad building had occurred—required for an economic leap forward. Compounding the problems was the fact that skilled labor was in short supply. Argentina, for one, was unable to adapt the Pampas for farming as it lacked both experienced cereal grain growers as well as a transport infrastructure. Brazil, with slavery seen as a controversial institution, was badly in need of a new source of manpower for the expanding southeastern coffee industry.

In social terms, the rather stratified and hierarchical society of the colonial period, with its great gulf between the few that were well-off and privileged and the many who were poor, had not changed dramatically. The concentration of wealth characteristic of the colonial era persisted. One of the great hallmarks of the colonial period, the hacienda (great estate), not only remained, but had been strengthened by the land policies of many countries. If there had been any fears by landowning creoles in colonial Spanish America that independence might unleash forces threatening their large landed domains, this had been put to rest. In some countries—Argentina was a prime example—land concentration greatly accelerated in the years and decades after independence. Fifty years of independence had shown Latin America to be volatile in political terms but conservative in social and economic matters.

Vast areas of Argentina, like the Pampas, remained in the control of a few families, who would become richer as the market for beef exports to affluent industrialized countries developed.

THE COLONIAL LEGACY

At the dawn of independence, the new nations of the Americas faced a future full of opportunities and challenges. Independence presented Brazil with a great change, but there was also continuity as the new state moved easily and peacefully from being an important possession of the Portuguese crown to an independent monarchy ruled by Pedro I, who, although the heir to the Portuguese throne, defied the authorities in Portugal and declared Brazilian independence in 1822. In Spanish America, however, the transition from colonies of Spain to independent republics was more prolonged and bloodier, and, in areas where major fighting occurred, the devastation was considerable.

Whereas the smooth transition from colony to independent empire boded well for Brazil's political stability, most Spanish-American countries faced a far different scenario. Their colonial inheritance would lead in the opposite direction toward political instability and intercountry territorial conflict. That the colonial experience of Spanish America would engender such problems is clear. The chief beneficiaries of the independence wars, the creoles, were largely unprepared for the governmental positions that they would assume. During the colonial period, Spain had assiduously tried to keep creoles out of high offices usually monopolized by peninsular Spaniards. But Spain also bequeathed a Hispanic tradition of strong executive government which was diametrically opposed to the United States system which stressed checks and balances in the three great branches of the state. While the Hispanic tradition would appeal to conservative forces in the new republics, it would collide and jar with those forces of a liberal or reformist persuasion. Given the differing traditions, the implantation of constitutional government on republican lines was destined to require a lengthy and conflict-ridden period of adaptation.

But the legacy of Spanish colonialism not only betokened some internal instability within states; it also contributed to some volatility in the relations between the newly independent countries. This was virtually guaranteed by the balkanization of Spain's vast empire in the Americas. The great liberator Simón Bolívar in the 1820s feared that the breakup of important Spanish administrative jurisdictions would open the way for intraregional conflict and external weakness, and his premonitions were amply borne out by experience. The fact that the old colonial boundaries were not always demarcated with precision meant that numerous frontier areas would be disputed by the new republics. Also, Spain's periodic reorganization of some administrative units created some confusion as to which viceroyalty or *audiencia* (tribunal) had the ironclad claim to a particular territory.

Right from the start, the four major colonial administrative units—the viceroyalties of New Spain, New Granada, the Río de la Plata, and the audiencia of Lima—were strongly affected by the outcomes of the independence struggles. The countries of Central America split away from Mexico in 1823 and formed the Central American Confederation, which fractured into five independent states in 1838. By 1830, the republic of Greater Colombia had split into three independent nations: Colombia, Ecuador, and Venezuela. The viceroyalty of the Río de la Plata was pulled apart by the independence movements as leaders like

José Gervasio Artigas on the eastern shore of the Río de la Plata (Uruguay) and Dr. José Gaspar Rodríguez de Francia in Paraguay wanted either autonomy from Buenos Aires (Artigas) or full independence (Francia). Both of these leaders would plant the seed of nationhood in their lands. The breakup of Spain's old administrative units ensured that numerous boundary and territorial disputes would bedevil the relations of neighboring states of Spanish America in the nineteenth and twentieth centuries. This would certainly add an element of precariousness in the external relations of neighboring states of Spanish America, and it would be a contributing factor or even a direct cause in some of the region's major wars of the last two centuries.

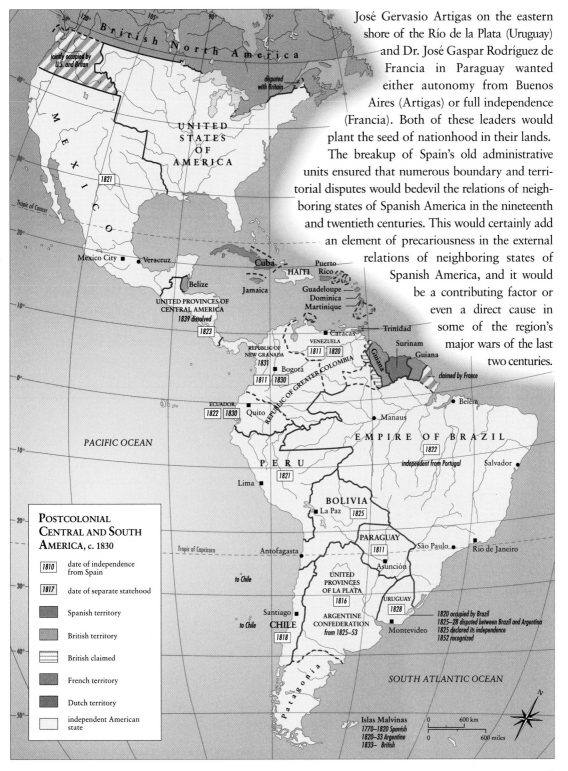

POSTCOLONIAL CENTRAL AND SOUTH AMERICA, c. 1830

| 1810 | date of independence from Spain |
| 1817 | date of separate statehood |

Spanish territory

British territory

British claimed

French territory

Dutch territory

independent American state

THE RISE OF THE CAUDILLO

The wars of independence and the onset of nationhood for Latin American countries gave birth to a political phenomenon that would be most prevalent in the period from the 1820s to the 1850s but, in a more random way, would survive in other forms in the second half of the nineteenth century and even in the present one. The phenomenon was the rise of the *caudillo*—in other words, the military chieftain or strongman.

What can be called the institution of caudillism was very much Hispanic in origin and was basically confined to Spanish America. Initially, caudillos were generally leaders on horseback with a military following who operated at local, provincial, or even national levels. Many of the first caudillos were fighters or veterans of the wars of independence. These charismatic leaders dispensed patronage and spoils, expected complete loyalty from their followers, and reserved all governmental functions for themselves, acting as executives, legislatures, and judiciaries rolled into one. Many regional caudillos had little time for bureaucracies; a few were even illiterate.

That caudillism was Hispanic to its core seems clear, inasmuch as Portuguese America (Brazil) never developed a replica of this political institution. Brazil, which gained its independence by peaceful means, had in many ways different military traditions from those of its Spanish-American counterparts. It is true, however, that from the mid-nineteenth century onward into the twentieth century, Brazil developed its *coronelismo* or *coronel* system, which produced power brokers, usually rural or small-town political bosses, who possessed either political or economic power in their communities. Unlike the quintessential Spanish-American caudillos of the 1820–1850 era, who were often in conflict with central governments, the Brazilian coronel was usually a component of the national status quo and was, in many ways, an agent of social control. Frequently, individuals who carried the real or honorary title of coronel were planters or ranchers or, in the present century, professional men or industrialists who were granted their titles from National Guard units in northeastern Brazil. While caudillos would emerge in both small and large nations in Spanish-America, the practice thrived best in countries where populations and important economic activities were most dispersed and this usually applied to the bigger states. Smaller nations, especially those where populated centers and economic pursuits were more concentrated, were less fertile grounds for the proliferation of caudillos, although a national leader might come to the fore exhibiting some of the mannerisms and traits of the caudillo. Probably the most celebrated caudillos of the first half of the nineteenth century were Argentina's regional caudillo Juan Manuel de Rosas, Mexico's military caudillo Antonio López de Santa Anna, and Venezuela's national leader José Páez, the independence hero and commander of the horsemen of the plains. These great historical figures, however, left a mixed legacy. Páez was restrained in his exercise of power from 1830 to 1846 and can be credited with holding his country together. Rosas and his fellow caudillos maintained a rudimentary form of unity for the Argentine confederation, and thus utter chaos and fragmentation were avoided. Santa Anna, on the other hand, handled Mexican affairs in a reckless and irresponsible way.

Of all the Spanish-American republics, no country after independence was more affected by caudillism than Argentina. Probably the first great caudillo was the independence war hero Martín Güemes, the governor of Salta. Numerous provincial caudillos were on the scene, such as Rosas of Buenos Aires; Estanislao López of Santa Fe; Juan Facundo Quiroga of La Rioja, who dominated provinces from Catamarca to Mendoza; Ricardo López Jordán of Entre Ríos; and Angel Vicente Peñaloza of La Rioja, among others. In a sense, Argentina's regional caudillos as federalists were united in their hostility to the forces advocating a highly centralized state, the Unitarians, but they still fought each other on occasion, and some resisted the attempts of Rosas to impose the will of Buenos Aires over other provinces of the Argentine confederation. In the end, the great leader of Entre Ríos, Justo José de Urquiza, defeated Rosas in 1852, and the celebrated Argentine dictator was forced to live in England as an exile.

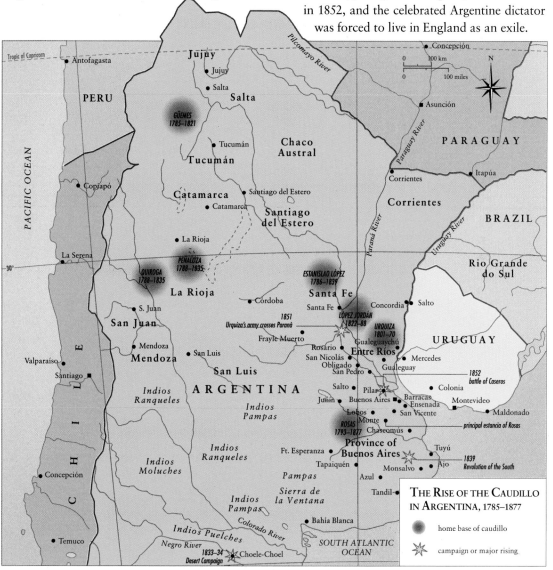

THE RISE OF THE CAUDILLO IN ARGENTINA, 1785–1877

home base of caudillo

campaign or major rising

OUTPOSTS OF STABILITY

In a Latin American region where political unrest was almost the norm for many countries during the 1820s and through the 1860s, only a few countries escaped real turbulence, even though they were not always exempt from fairly limited political disorders. In particular, Brazil, Chile, and Paraguay stood out as regional pillars of stability. Their success in avoiding the political pitfalls visible elsewhere was due more to special circumstances than to any common denominator present in all three cases.

Superficially, Portuguese America (Brazil) was not subject to the political upheavals and violence that were so characteristic of the Spanish-American world. The argument has been put forth that the Portuguese by nature have been less confrontational and more willing to seek the compromises necessary to avoid political catastrophes than their Hispanic-American counterparts. The merit of such an argument remains to be proved, but it is clear that there was a smooth transition from colony of the Portuguese monarchy to an independent imperial state. Brazil's emperors in the nineteenth century are widely credited with holding together a large territory that could conceivably have split into a northeastern policy and a center-south one. While the nation's emperors were by nature autocrats, they eschewed an absolutist approach and accepted a system of constitutional monarchy. Under their imperial system, there was the semblance of a democratic order as certain posts of government were allocated through electoral means. Due to the limited form of democracy in a rather stratified and hierarchical society, Brazil was not tightly subjected to a highly centralized governmental setup. In a large country with widely dispersed economic centers—the sugar and cotton economy of the northeast and the emerging coffee economy of the southeast—a truly centralized and autocratic governmental form would have exacerbated regional frictions. As it was, Brazil was largely free of acute political difficulties, although it did in fact suffer some civil conflicts in the 1840s.

The comparative political stability of Chile and Paraguay, which had adopted the republican form of government, was of course due to factors unique to themselves. Chile's ability to avoid the disorders common to many Spanish-American countries owed something to geography and the nation's social system as well as to the remarkable political leadership of a determined conservative elite. In a long and geographically diverse land composed of an arid almost unpopulated northern area, an agriculturally rich central area, and a southern area of forests and lakes, it was the fertile central region that was, in the decades after independence, the dominant force in national politics and national economic life. The country had a relatively simple social structure composed of a landowning elite on one hand and a large mass of illiterate rural laborers, many of whom provided labor for the great estates that were the backbone of the economy, on the other. Essentially, a conservative alliance governed the land with a strong presidency and a highly centralized state administration. With stable political conditions, Chile developed a reasonably sound economy based primarily on agriculture and secondarily on mining. The fact that Chile had a compact economic heartland and a skillful and reasonably united elite kept the country from descending into the unrest and anarchy of so many of the Spanish-American republics.

Paraguay was the other Spanish-American nation that enjoyed a rare political stability from independence up to the disastrous War of the Triple Alliance. From 1865 to 1870, three strong leaders, essentially dictators, strove to create and maintain a self-reliant nation beholden to no other neighboring state and in the process helped to forge a national identity. The first leader, Dr. José Gaspar Rodríguez de Francia, catered to his xenophobia by severing trade links with other adjoining countries. His successor, Carlos Antonio López, eased up on the country's isolation and encouraged some trade with the outside world to strengthen the economy. His son and successor, Francisco Solano López, put a military emphasis to his rule, and Paraguay assumed the guise of a South American Prussia, but he ultimately plunged his country into a ruinous war with neighboring states that not only crushed the nation but undermined the stability enjoyed for almost six decades.

While it is hard to identify a common factor that would explain why Brazil, Chile, and Paraguay enjoyed relative political stability in the decades after independence, it would seem clear that internal economic and social conditions in the three countries militated against the rampant factionalism, regionalism, and caudillism so pronounced in other Latin American states.

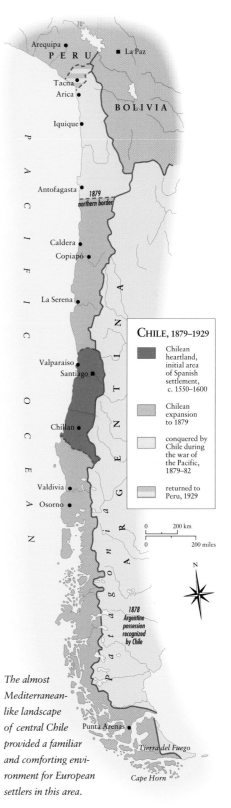

CHILE, 1879–1929

- Chilean heartland, initial area of Spanish settlement, c. 1550–1600
- Chilean expansion to 1879
- conquered by Chile during the war of the Pacific, 1879–82
- returned to Peru, 1929

1879 northern border

1878 Argentine possession recognized by Chile

The almost Mediterranean-like landscape of central Chile provided a familiar and comforting environment for European settlers in this area.

MEXICAN–AMERICAN WAR

For Mexico, the war that was fought with the United States from 1846 to 1848 was the defining moment for its efforts to maintain the territorial integrity of a vast landholding that the country had laid claim to when it declared independence from Spain. In 1821, the New Spain domain of the mother country extended from the Isthmus of Panama to the border of the Oregon territories, and it encompassed half of the population and half of the wealth of Spanish America. Of course, the population of that enormous tract was very much concentrated in what became Mexico proper; as Spain had made only token settlements, in the vast lands of California, Texas, and the Colorado River Valley.

At independence, Mexico faced a herculean task of consolidating and maintaining the great landmass claimed. Almost immediately the Central American states broke away in 1823 and formed the Central American Confederation. This loss was accepted with some resignation, but Mexico's real concern was to preserve the North American territories. It faced, however, two major difficulties in the first decades of national existence. First, the national task of the country was to create a strong central government able to impose internal order and to administer its large expanse effectively, but this was not to be achieved. Second, Mexico faced an extremely grave external threat posed by the relentless westward push of American citizens who were beginning to spill into territory claimed by the Mexican government.

The combination of Mexico's internal weakness and the migration of American nationals into the Texas territory soon produced a crisis. In 1836, U.S. settlers in Texas rebelled against the central Mexican government and, after defeating the army of General Santa Anna, declared independence. The status of the newly independent republic of Texas immediately created tension and friction in the relationship between Mexico and the United States, as Mexico refused to recognize the Texan government, while in the United States the debate raged about whether the slaveholding territory of Texas should be annexed.

The army led by Santa Anna, president of Mexico, was defeated after bloody hand to hand fighting with United States troops at the battle of Cerro Gordo on April 18, 1847.

The eventual decision by the American government to annex Texas in 1845 put the two nations on a war collision course. The entry of U.S. troops into the disputed area between the Nueces River and the Rio Grande was the catalyst for war as Mexican forces counterattacked and the conflict unfolded. In May 1846 Washington declared war, and the conflict known today in Mexico as the War of the North American Invasion began.

While neither nation had been fully prepared for war, Mexico, with its poorly organized and poorly supplied armed forces, was at the greater disadvantage. Over time, U.S. forces launched their attacks from widely dispersed theaters of operation. In August 1846 U.S. navy units in the Pacific seized key ports in California, which effectively brought that region under their control. General Zachary Taylor's army in September 1846 launched its campaign directed at Monterrey and later, in February 1847, defeated General Santa Anna's army at Buena Vista. Already, Colonel Stephen Kearny's forces seized Santa Fe in August 1846 and then struck out to join the U.S. naval forces at San Diego, an action that ended Mexican resistance in California.

In 1847 the war was reaching a decisive stage. The army of General Winfield Scott started a major thrust in March 1847 when it captured the city of Veracruz and then, on the march to Mexico City, defeated Santa Anna's forces. The latter victory cleared the way for Scott's army to enter Mexico City in September 1847, and the Mexican government was forced to flee to Querétaro. The war had now been lost by Mexico, and in February 1848 the Mexican authorities signed a peace treaty with the United States whereby the Americans agreed to pay $15 million in recognition of the ownership of enormous new territories from Texas to California, approximately half of Mexico's national territory.

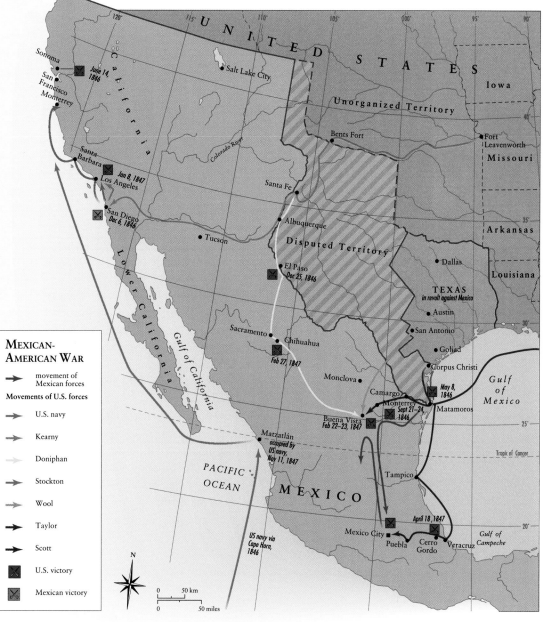

MEXICAN-
AMERICAN WAR

→ movement of
Mexican forces

Movements of U.S. forces

→ U.S. navy

→ Kearny

→ Doniphan

→ Stockton

→ Wool

→ Taylor

→ Scott

☒ U.S. victory

☒ Mexican victory

THE WAR OF THE TRIPLE ALLIANCE

The bloodiest war fought by Latin American nations in the nineteenth century was the conflict known as the War of the Triple Alliance, which pitted Paraguay in a very unequal struggle against the combined forces of Argentina, Brazil, and Uruguay. This war had very significant geopolitical ramifications, and its effect on Paraguay for decades was devastating.

Just prior to the conflict, Paraguay was a politically stable nation with a small but quite diversified economy. It was very much a regional military power with an effective and well-regarded army. In some respects, Paraguay conveyed the picture of a Prussia in South America, and there was a clear sense of nationhood. The fact that Paraguay was able to build a national identity in the decades after independence owed much to the internal disunity in Argentina, which frustrated any designs by Buenos Aires governments to establish claim to their hegemony over Paraguay. Paraguayan national development was also helped by the fact that the country was not confronted militarily by Brazil, which was more of a potential rather than a real military power before the outbreak of hostilities.

Paraguay's autocratic leader, Francisco Solano López, who idolized Napoleon, fancied himself and his nation as the arbiter of the balance of power of his region. To both Argentina and Brazil the regional designs of the Paraguayan dictator-president were a concern. Both nations feared that López might appeal to and encourage separatist sentiments in areas bordering Paraguay, in Entre Ríos and Corrientes in the case of Argentina and in southern states in Brazil showing some dissatisfaction with imperial rule.

But the actual catalyst for the war stemmed from Brazilian intervention in Uruguayan politics, which resulted in the replacement of the Blanco party government of Uruguay with the Colorado party government of General Venancio Flores. López had counted upon Argentina to join him in opposing the Brazilian move, but, when the Buenos Aires government made an about-face and supported Brazil, the Paraguayan leader made the rash and ill-advised decision to march his troops across Argentina territory toward Uruguay, and thereby ignited a disastrous five-and-a-half-year war. In one fell swoop, Paraguay's able fighting machine was locked in combat with the forces of Argentina, Brazil, and Uruguay, under the control of General Flores.

Broadly speaking, there were two main phases to the long war. In the initial nine months, Paraguay's army of 38,000 men was on the offensive. Afterward, however, the prospects for López's army turned more bleak with the death of the best of his soldiers and the increasing shortages of weapons, medicine, and food. With the mobilization of manpower in Brazil, the most formidable member of the Triple Alliance, Paraguay was soon fighting on the defensive in its own territory in a war of attrition that could only favor the side with superior resources and manpower. In addition to that, Paraguay was at a technological disadvantage with military equipment, inasmuch as Triple Alliance soldiers were equipped with Enfield and repeater rifles, while López's forces basically used flintlock muskets.

On the defensive, during the second phase, the Paraguayan army on its own territory held out valiantly for three years at the fortress of Humaitá near the confluence of the Paraguay and Paraná Rivers. This strategic position stymied for a considerable period of time the naval and ground advance of the Triple Alliance forces along the Paraguay River. But, once the siege was ended, Paraguayan forces were on the retreat, and the capital, Asunción, fell in January 1869. Undeterred by his defeat, Marshal López raised a new army, and the war went on until the battle of Cerro Corá of March 1, 1870, when Brazilian troops killed the Paraguayan leader. With the death of López, the war was over.

The war and its aftermath were nothing short of catastrophic for Paraguay, whose losses were staggering. But wartime casualties were high for all sides, with Brazil's losses alone amounting to about 100,000 dead and 65,000 wounded. The Paraguayan population at the end of the war had been cut in half as a result of combat deaths, disease, and malnutrition; furthermore, females now constituted three-quarters of the entire population. Paraguay was occupied for seven years by Brazilian forces, and 25 percent of the nation's land was annexed by Brazil and Argentina. What had been a strong and unified republic under autocratic rule had become a weak and faction-ridden nation susceptible to political instability.

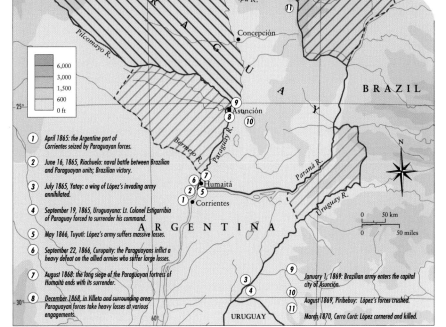

THE WAR OF THE TRIPLE ALLIANCE

✗ battle

Paraguay territorial change following the war

⬚ ceded to Brazil, 1870

⬚ ceded to Argentina, 1874

⬚ disputed with Bolivia

① April 1865: the Argentine port of Corrientes seized by Paraguayan forces.

② June 16, 1865, Riachuelo: naval battle between Brazilian and Paraguayan units; Brazilian victory.

③ July 1865, Yatay: a wing of López's invading army annihilated.

④ September 19, 1865, Uruguayana: Lt. Colonel Estigarribia of Paraguay forced to surrender his command.

⑤ May 1866, Tuyutí: López's army suffers massive losses.

⑥ September 22, 1866, Curupaity: the Paraguayans inflict a heavy defeat on the allied armies who suffer large losses.

⑦ August 1868: the long siege of the Paraguayan fortress of Humaitá ends with its surrender.

⑧ December 1868, in Villeta and surrounding area, Paraguayan forces take heavy losses at various engagements.

⑨ January 1, 1869: Brazilian army enters the capital city of Asunción.

⑩ August 1869, Piribebuy: López's forces crushed.

⑪ March 1870, Cerro Corá: López cornered and killed.

WAR OF THE PACIFIC

Of the wars in South America in the nineteenth century, few had such transcendental importance for the nations involved as did the War of the Pacific, fought by Chile against Peru and Bolivia in the years from 1879 to 1884. The war had both a geopolitical and economic significance as Chile defeated its Andean rivals and gained the nitrate-rich provinces of Tarapacá (Peru) and Antofagasta (Bolivia), while Bolivia lost its access to the Pacific Ocean. That war not only established Chile's geopolitical preeminence in its part of the Andean region, but provided the country with the valuable mining resource of nitrate and, in the process, shifted its economic destiny in the direction of a mining economy, where the nation would hold a virtual world monopoly upon nitrates used for agriculture and for munitions.

The Andean countries of Chile, Bolivia, and Peru, from the early years after their emergence as independent states, harbored conflicting designs and interests that would be the cause of future conflict. Chile went to war in the years from 1836 to 1839 to prevent the formation of a Peru-Bolivian Confederation under the leadership of the revolutionary war general Andrés Santa Cruz. Chile's action had its commercial reasons, namely the abrogation of the Chilean-Peruvian trade treaty of 1835, but it also felt the confederation threatened the regional balance of power. While Chile was successful in its aim to dissolve the Peru-Bolivian Confederation, it did little to resolve the underlying problem of the ownership of the land in the Atacama region jointly claimed by Bolivia and Chile.

What appeared to be worthless terrain in the 1830s began to take on a far more attractive look from the 1840s onward, as world attention began to be focused first upon deposits of guano (the dried excrement of seabirds), and later on nitrates found in coastal regions of Peru and Bolivia. Rising interest in nitrates, which like guano were used as a fertilizer, ensured that the desolate Atacama spaces were now seen as potentially valuable property. With the discovery in 1840 by a Frenchman that guano was a first-class fertilizer, and with Chilean suspicions that large quantities of this resource might lie in the Atacama desert, Chile announced in 1842 that its northernmost boundary lay at the twenty-third parallel. Bolivia immediately disputed the claim and demanded that the southernmost limits of its territory be recognized as near the twenty-sixth parallel. The seeds for the eventual Pacific coast war were thus sown in the early 1840s.

In the decades after the 1840s, Peru's intense exploitation of guano deposits, which provided the country with its main source of export revenue, began to be played out by the end of the 1870s, and thus attention shifted to the mining of nitrates found in abundance in the Atacama desert. Peru leased out mining extraction licenses to concerns often of foreign nationality in its provinces of Tacna, Arica, and Tarapacá. Bolivia also did the same and, to defuse the threat of armed conflict, it concluded a treaty with Chile in 1866 whereby the two signatories set their boundaries at the twenty-third parallel and agreed to exploit jointly the mining resources between the twenty-third and twenty-fifth parallels.

The actual catalyst for the war occurred in the 1870s, when Peru and then Bolivia imposed measures that affected foreign concessionaires, including Chilean interests. Believing the Bolivian actions contravened treaty obligations,

A view of Valparaíso Bay, c. 1880, an important focal point for Chilean shipping and port of supply for forces involved in the War of the Pacific.

Chile sent an ultimatum to Bolivia, which was unheeded. Chile then sent its forces to occupy Antofagasta, and the ensuing hostilities between the two countries brought Peru into the war to support its Bolivian ally. Despite being outnumbered, Chilean armed forces destroyed the Peruvian army and in the first two years of war occupied all of the Bolivian territory in the Atacama desert, Peru's provinces of Tacna, Arica, and Tarapacá, and also the cities of Callao and Lima in Peru. The all-conquering Chilean nation was thus able to dictate peace terms in the Treaty of Ancón of October 23, 1883. Under that treaty, and a later treaty with Bolivia in March 1884, Chile gained the Antofagasta region and Tarapacá from Peru, with Chilean administrative control for ten years of the Tacna and Arica provinces pending a plebiscite, which in point of fact was never held.

This conflict was one of the major wars in Latin America and its consequences were far-reaching. It also confirmed Chile as the dominant power in the Andean region.

Ancón
Lima
1881
Callao
Chorillos
⑤
Chileans land at Pisco and advance to Lima, taken early 1881
Pisco
Ica

PERU

L. Titicaca

Arequipa
Sorata
La Paz

Moquegua

⑤
Jan. – June 1880
Chilean blockade

Tacna
18°
Tacna
1929 Chile – Peruvian border
④
Arica
March 1880
Chilean forces land near Arica

Arica

1883 Chile –
Peruvian border

Oruro

Lake
Poopó

Sucre

Pisagua

②
Nov. 1, 1879
Chilean forces land

Iquique

Potosí

BOLIVIA

Uyuni

Tarapacá

original Peru – Bolivian border

Quillagua

Villa Montes

Tocopilla

PACIFIC OCEAN

N

Mejillones
23°

1842 claimed by Chile

Antofagasta

1866 treaty

Jujuy

①
Feb. 14, 1879
Chilean forces land and occupy surrounding districts
24°

Salta

original Chile – Bolivian border
Paposo

Taltal

ARGENTINA

0   100 km
0   100 miles

Chañaral

Caldera

CHILE

Catamarca

THE WAR OF THE PACIFIC,
1879–84

→   Chilean attack

✕   battle

- - -   Chilean border, 1842–1929

▨   Chilean occupied, 1883–93

Copiapó

Atacama

La Rioja

16,000
12,000
10,000
6,000
3,000
1,500
600
0 ft

75°
70°
65°

PART VI: FOUNDATIONS OF MODERN LATIN AMERICA

In the years from 1870 to 1945, Latin America experienced major changes, especially in the economic sphere where the foundations for more modern economies were laid. Political and social changes for most countries were far less dramatic and did not alter fundamentally existing conditions, except perhaps in the case of a small number of countries that received unusually heavy inflows of European immigrants. What could be called an economic transformation was inextricably linked to such external factors as the influx of foreign investment and technology, the growing overseas demand for Latin American foodstuffs and raw materials, and the large-scale movement of people from Europe to parts of the region.

But the period from 1870 to 1945 was not an unbroken era of heady economic expansion. Actually, the high point in Latin America's economic transformation occurred from about 1870 to the outbreak of World War I, when extremely high levels of investment and economic growth were registered. After the economic dislocations of the First World War, Latin America had to be content with more moderate growth and expansion in the 1920s, before the region was sorely tested by a harsher economic climate during the Depression of the 1930s and World War II. Thus, in the long time span from 1870 to 1945, there were two periods with their own distinctive characteristics. The first was from 1870 to 1930, when the region became and remained closely integrated into the world economy as an exporter of foodstuffs and raw materials. The second period, from 1930 to 1945, was a transition stage when questions were being asked as to whether, in the light of changes in the international economy, Latin America could rely primarily on the export of primary products to provide for its social and economic needs.

By 1870, Latin American politicians and intellectuals contrasted the greater progress and stability of Northern Hemisphere nations with the perceived limitations of their own societies. Most put their hopes on unfettered economic liberalism as the way forward. Some fell under the sway of the European philosophy of Positivism, which stressed the application of the methodology and spirit of science in order to bring about order and progress to nations. Britain and Continental Europe, with their ideas and economic accomplishments, appeared to be the model or partner for the economic and social uplift of the region. And while Latin American elites yearned for an economic transformation, political leaders and intellectuals in some countries hoped that economic advancement could be combined with a social transformation. Important figures in Argentina like Domingo Sarmiento and Juan B. Alberdi sought to modify the prevailing Hispanic culture and civilization by incorporating appropriate features of European and North American culture in Argentina. Like other members of the Argentine elite, they saw immigration from Europe as a necessary agent of change. In Mexico, Porfirio Díaz and his close supporters embarked upon a program of economic liberalism and reform aimed at transforming not only the economy but the Indian cultural milieu that they neither understood nor valued.

International economic conditions from 1870 to 1913 provide the explanation for the economic transformation of Latin America. That period produced one of the greatest explosions in world trade, which was stimulated by the free movement of capital and immigrants across borders, combining the existence of open markets with a minimum of trade barriers. For Latin America, it was a golden age when capital and immigrants entered the region in record amounts. Foreign investment was fundamental to the development of a transport infrastructure, railroads in particular, and to the creation or support of export activities producing staple products for sale in Europe and North America. In the four and a half decades before 1914, three distinctive types of export-oriented economies arose in Latin America, namely the agricultural economy based on temperate zone products, the tropical zone agriculture economy, and the mining economy.

Argentina and Uruguay were prime examples of temperate zone agricultural economies engaged in livestock raising and cereal grain production. A far larger number of countries fitted the description of tropical zone agricultural economies, and this included states in Central America and the Caribbean islands that specialized in such products as coffee, cane sugar, and bananas. Brazil produced both tropical and temperate zone products but was best known as the world's foremost producer of coffee. A number of countries like Chile, Peru, and Bolivia could be depicted as mining-type economies.

While most Latin American countries were now established fixtures in world commodity trading, only a minority had really strong export economies, whereas the states of Central America and the small nations of South America like Ecuador, Bolivia, and Paraguay had relatively unproductive economies. In contrast, however, a number of nations had become major players in the world trade of their particular commodity products. Argentina was now a major wheat- and corn-exporting country and the greatest meat exporter. Brazil was the dominant coffee producer in the world. Cuba became in the 1910s the largest world exporter of cane sugar, and Chile emerged as the most significant, if not monopoly, producer of nitrates destined for agricultural and munitions purposes.

However, Latin America's sudden economic transformation in the years before 1914 was not a balanced development. Rather it was lopsided. The production of primary products for export was highly developed. Domestic manufacturing, while stimulated to some degree by the growth of national income and population numbers, was not sufficiently protected from overseas competitors and remained the unfavored Cinderella of the economy. From a purely national perspective, development within a given country was often greatest in those geographical zones where export production was concentrated and least or not at all in other less favored regions. Argentina was a notable case in point where development was very much confined to one great region, the Pampas, whereas outlying areas to the north or the south were not major beneficiaries of national economic expansion. Most Latin American countries remained agricultural economies, with a modern sector producing products for the international market and a sizable traditional sector working on a subsistence basis or producing at no great profit for the internal market.

Paralleling the economic expansion was a sharp increase in the Latin American population, which between 1850 and 1900 doubled from about thirty to sixty-one million people. The rate of demographic increase, averaging at about 1.25 percent per annum in the second half of the nineteenth century, was on a rising trend as it averaged 1.7 percent per annum from 1900 to 1930 and gave Latin America an estimated population of 104 million by 1930. While the population surge was general to most countries, the fastest rate of growth took place in the Southern Cone of South America, that is, the countries of Argentina, Chile, Paraguay, Uruguay, and in southern Brazil. In particular, the population growth rates of Argentina and Uruguay far outstripped those of other nations and reflected the special attraction of those lands to European immigrants. Along with general population growth, cities and towns were also increasing in size, even though Latin America continued to be a region where most people lived in the countryside and were engaged in rural occupations. The modernization of agriculture geared to export had provided new employment opportunities for rising national populations. While most countries had extremely large rural-based populations, Argentina and Uruguay went somewhat counter to the prevailing trend, with the very rapid urbanization that was occurring in their territories. The capital cities of Buenos Aires and Montevideo in particular proved a magnet for large numbers of immigrants, and Argentina and Uruguay by 1914, and in fact beyond, were destined to have substantial numbers of people living in urban areas.

Strong population and economic growth tended to overshadow the more moderate social changes taking place in most countries. Overall, the basic make-up and structure of what were usually two class societies, an upper class and the mass of the populace, had not markedly changed that much, inasmuch as national middle classes, although expanded after 1870, were still not large by North American or Western European standards. In countries with large Indian populations, the economic transformation process had failed to integrate most Indians into the mainstream of the national economy. The same was true with blacks in Brazil, given the fact that much of the labor required in the expansion of the nation's coffee industry was provided by European immigrants. Insofar as income distribution was concerned, wealth concentration, far from lessening, had been accentuated. Landholdings used for export agriculture were now much more valuable and, in the case of Argentina, the large landowners of the Pampean region were now rich beyond their dreams and recognized the world over for their wealth and affluent lifestyle.

While Latin America as a whole at the turn of the twentieth century had not undergone any real social transformation, Argentina and Uruguay were exceptions to the rule. Thanks to great economic advance and the massive influx of European immigrants, these two countries in culture and ethnic stock were much more Europeanized and now boasted the largest middle classes of the entire region. Even so, the great social changes in Argentina tended to occur in the Pampas rather than in the length and breadth of this large nation.

Along with Latin America's fairly muted social changes, political moderniza-tion was inclined to lag behind economic developments in the years from 1870 to 1930. Still on the agenda of many countries was the need to achieve political sta-bility and to fashion strong political institutions. Constitutional rule and broader political participation remained live issues in many states. Traditional elites, certainly large landowners, sought to retain their influence on or control of gov-ernment at a time when new social forces were beginning to challenge the status quo. In the first decades of the twentieth century, only a handful of countries had functioning multiparty political systems. Chile and Uruguay were probably the most conspicuous examples of this. In Argentina, the wealthy cattle owners of the Pampas, who had dominated national political life for many decades, finally lost their power monopoly thanks to the electoral reform law of 1912 and the rise of the middle-class party, the Radical Civic Union, which was elected to power in 1916 and remained in elective office until 1930. Brazil, however, had its own distinctive political system brought into being when the monarchy fell in 1889. That country lacked national political parties; instead, political bosses in the most important Brazilian states determined who would occupy the presi-dential office. In Mexico, in the aftermath of its great and far-reaching revolu-tion, a one-party system assumed shape at the end of the 1920s. For most Latin American nations, above all the smaller countries in the Caribbean Basin and in South America, political power usually remained in the hands of national oli-garchies or military leaders. Ironically, in certain nations in the Caribbean area that had seen intervention by the United States for the ostensible purpose of pro-viding political or financial stability, the armed forces or the constabularies trained by the Americans sometimes became the springboard for the emergence of dictators like Rafael Trujillo in the Dominican Republic and Anastasio Somoza in Nicaragua.

In international terms, Latin America's alignment to the world trade econo-my in the period from 1870 to 1930 fostered a much closer interaction between the region and outside nations. Investment, trade, and ethnic links with Europe, for example, were now strengthened immeasurably, with the relationship strongest between European countries and nations in the Southern Cone of South America, such as Argentina, Brazil, Chile, and Uruguay. Britain was by far the most significant overseas investor and trader with Latin America and had a massive investment stake in Argentina far greater than that in other individual countries of the region. The economic interaction between Britain and Argentina was so important to both parties that the twentieth-century historian Henry Ferns alluded to pre-1930 Argentina as being an "informal member of the British Empire." While European nations had forged strong economic ties with countries in South America, the United States from about the 1890s onward was showing increased political and economic interest in Latin America, with initial attention focused on Mexico, Central America, and island nations like Cuba.

The outside world was now taking more notice of a Latin American region with the capability of exporting low-cost foodstuffs and raw materials and, as a result, an enhanced capacity to import manufactured goods on a large scale. This was certainly true of important commodity product exporters like Brazil, Chile, Cuba, and above all Argentina, which from the turn of the century was becoming one of the attractive overseas markets for consumer and industrial products, not to mention raw materials like coal. However, many of the smaller countries, although with better export capabilities, had economic and political structures that were far from ideal. Nowhere was this more the case than among the Caribbean islands and Central American countries, which specialized in one or two tropical products for export capabilities, but were vulnerable to political instability. These states formed the model for the derisive and perhaps unfair term of "banana republic," which conjured up the picture of sleepy tropical nations run either chaotically or under strongman rule. In point of fact, the Caribbean Basin from 1870 to 1930 became fertile ground for intervention, often of a military kind, by outside powers. In the years from about 1871 through 1897, on countless occasions, a succession of European nations used force or the threat of gunboats to back up the commercial claims of their citizens against a number of countries, notably Haiti, the Dominican Republic, Nicaragua, Venezuela, and Colombia. Later, the United States took on the mantle of hemispheric policeman and actively intervened in the political and financial affairs of numerous Caribbean Basin countries.

With the beginning of the world depression of the 1930s, Latin America entered a new era that ended almost six decades of economic activity, usually with strong growth resulting from the production of foodstuffs and raw materials for export. Latin American countries would now face a more difficult economic environment in the short and long terms as a result of changes taking place in the international economy. In particular, Britain and other European countries, which in the aggregate were the largest buyers of the region's primary products, were no longer willing or able to maintain their level of purchases and were scaling back their imports. This was certainly the case with temperate zone agricultural products, especially meat. Thus, in the years from 1930 to 1945, which embraced the Depression and World War II period, Latin American nations were under pressure to diversify their economies, if possible, to limit the hardship and dislocation caused by depression and war.

Smaller countries with tiny manufacturing bases had little option but to defend their export industries and ride out the Depression as best they could. Nations with a fair degree of home industry and scope for more extensive industrialization had two alternatives, namely either to give priority in their recovery programs to promoting domestic manufacturing or to work primarily to defend their embattled agricultural producers with only secondary encouragement to home manufacturers. By and large, most opted to defend their traditional export industries by concluding trade agreements with the main overseas buyers of their products. Argentina was a case in point; the conservative coalition government of President Agustín Justo concluded the Roca-Runciman Treaty with Britain to assure market access for the politically influential refrigerated beef trade in exchange for tariff and foreign exchange concessions to the United Kingdom.

While the anti-Depression response of most countries was to defend hard-pressed primary producers, a common feature of many national recovery programs was the abandonment of laissez-faire economic attitudes in favor of greater state intervention in the economy and even, in some cases, to resort to outright economic nationalism. Examples of the latter were Bolivia's expropriation of the oil fields owned by Standard Oil of New Jersey in 1936 and Mexico's nationalization of its foreign-owned petroleum industry in 1938.

Mirroring the economic crisis of the 1930s were more unsettled political conditions. In 1930, a succession of civilian governments in Central America and South America were removed by the military or by movements backed by armed forces. Most significantly, General José Uriburu in Argentina staged a coup in 1930 that ended fourteen years of constitutional rule by Radical party governments, and in Brazil the revolution of 1930 brought to power the master-politician Getúlio Vargas. Even countries with more established democratic credentials were not immune to political turbulence. President Gabriel Terra in Uruguay organized an in-power coup d'état in 1933 in order to modify the nation's political institutions, and he ruled as a moderate dictator until the elections of 1938.

Political and economic uncertainties continued in the World War II period. Latin America, however, was very much in a period of transition as new remedies were being called for to cope with unresolved social and economic needs. There were, of course, signs of the winds of change. Larger countries like Argentina, Brazil, and Mexico in the early 1940s were beginning to deviate from the pattern of economic development followed since 1870 when they began to consider ways and means of accelerating industrialization through import substitution. What had been unthinkable before—favoring the interests of the manufacturing industry over and above those of agriculture—was now being realistically considered. At the same time, some signs of political change were in the air. The military revolution of 1943 in Argentina was a milestone, as the officers in power began to chart new political and economic directions. The military regime supported the initiative of Colonel Juan Perón, a leading figure behind the revolt, to win trade union support for their government. That charismatic officer established close relation with trade unionists giving a mighty impetus to trade unionization in Argentina and, in the process, unleashed forces that in time would make workers major participants in the nation's political arena, an unprecedented development in Argentine history. In Guatemala in 1944, the disaffection of university students and sections within the military forced the dictator Jorge Ubico from office, paving the way for the election in 1945 of Dr. Juan José Arévalo, who came into the presidency on a program of social reform that was an anathema to landowners as well as to conservative elements in business and the military.

Clearly by 1945, Latin America was set to enter into a new phase in its historical experience that would bring new political, social, and economic challenges.

IMMIGRATION, 1870–1930

The period from 1870 to 1930 saw a large influx of immigrants, mainly from Europe, coming to the Latin American region. Apart from the United States, which received the greatest volume of immigrants, Latin America was one of the largest recipients of European immigrants. Mass immigration in the region really began in the 1870s and reached its peak in the decades before the outbreak of World War I, although it continued at a high level until about 1930.

For Latin America, the heaviest stream of immigrants came from countries in southern Europe, especially Spain, Portugal, and Italy, but an appreciable current of people also set forth from Eastern European nations. The principal reason for the outflow of Europeans was economic, particularly in the last three decades of the nineteenth century, when rural labor was being dislodged from traditional pursuits as a result of the need of European agriculture to rationalize to meet worldwide competition. But, political reasons were not absent; pogroms in Poland and Russia motivated some Jews to emigrate, some of whom would come to Argentina in large numbers.

The immigration pattern in Latin America was uneven; only a small number of countries received a really massive European immigration. Five countries were major recipients, notably Argentina, Brazil, Cuba, Uruguay and, to a lesser degree, Chile. There was a common denominator in the flow of people to the first four countries. They were the nations offering the greatest economic opportunities because they had an acute shortage of manpower for economies being structured around the export of agricultural products in great world demand. Argentina and Uruguay, which had traditionally operated pastoral activities, needed immigrants with farming experience.

Italian emigrants leaving Milan for Genoa or Marseille to sail to the New World, as shown in this illustration from April 1900.

In terms of numbers, Argentina in the years from 1870 to 1930 received approximately four million European immigrants and Brazil about half that number. About 600,000 European immigrants settled in Uruguay, but, given that country's small size and small population before 1870, the impact upon the nation's social composition was the greatest of any country in Latin America. In Cuba, the 600,000 or so immigrants who settled on the island were mostly Spaniards arriving, ironically, after Spain's rule was ended by the Spanish-American War of 1898. Chile, which was developing as a mining economy, received an estimated 200,000 European immigrants in the period in question.

To other Latin American countries, the flow of immigrants was much more modest. Some Chinese and Japanese immigrants came to Andean nations, Peru above all. Central American nations received something of a trickle, although Costa Rica throughout the nineteenth century received Galician and Basque settlers from Spain and became the most Europeanized nation in Central America.

Among Latin American elites, and certainly in those countries where labor shortages impeded the development of export agriculture, it was almost an article of faith in the late nineteenth century that European immigrants were indispensable for the economic and social modernization of their societies. While numerous governments set out to encourage immigration into their countries, the fact remains that only a handful of nations were truly attractive to Europeans.

IMMIGRATION, 1875–1930

from Europe

from Japan

from the Caribbean

from Mexico and Central America

population estimates, in millions of inhabitants, by country, 1900

UNITED STATES OF AMERICA

Washington

MEXICO

Mexico City

Havana

Tropic of Cancer

CUBA

Jamaica

HAITI

DOMINICAN REP.

Lesser Antilles

Spanish

GUATEMALA

HONDURAS

EL SALVADOR

NICARAGUA

COSTA RICA

PANAMA

Caracas

VENEZUELA

Trinidad and Tobago

British Guiana

French Guiana

Surinam

Bogotá

COLOMBIA

Quito

ECUADOR

Belém

Manaus

BRAZIL

PERU

Lima

BOLIVIA

La Paz

Germans, Austrians, Hungarians

Rio de Janeiro

São Paulo

Tropic of Capricorn

PARAGUAY

Asunción

Italians and Spanish

Portuguese

Santiago

CHILE

ARGENTINA

URUGUAY

Buenos Aires

Montevideo

SOUTH ATLANTIC OCEAN

Japanese

Mexico during the long dictatorship of Porfirio Díaz (1876–1911) appealed to immigrants, but, potential emigrants in Europe, unattracted to labor conditions and wage levels, never came in great numbers.

In the few countries receiving mass immigration, there were striking economic and social effects. Foreign immigrants, especially Italians who became tenant farmers, were instrumental in making the Pampas region one of the world's great farming regions. Immigrants pursued urban as well as rural activities and became an important component of an expanding middle class in those countries receiving a mass immigration. Argentina and Uruguay by 1930 stood out as the Latin American nations with the largest middle classes in percentage terms.

FOREIGN INVESTMENT, 1870–1930

In the decades before 1870, a major impediment to greater economic development in Latin America was the chronic shortage of financial capital. The lackluster economic performance of most countries stunted the creation of domestic capital in many Latin American nations.

The capital panorama, however, changed dramatically from about 1870 onward. The scope in Latin America for developing new agricultural and mining enterprises as well as a vast infrastructure clearly excited the interest of European investors in the 1870s and beyond, as it would American investors from the 1890s onward. As a result, foreign investment flowed into Latin America in massive amounts, especially in the period from 1870 to 1913.

Two types of foreign capital investment were important in helping to propel an economic leap forward. One was the investment made by foreign companies in land, buildings, and equipment in order to produce goods or services. The other was portfolio investment whereby capitalists would extend loans or buy bonds and securities from Latin American entities, almost invariably governments.

The newfound inflow of foreign investment into Latin America was part of a worldwide phenomenon, which was one of the great ages in the international movement of capital. Europe, in the decades up to 1914, was the overwhelming source of capital to be invested across national boundaries. Of the estimated $44 billion of foreign investment worldwide in 1914, six Western European countries had $38.4 billion alone. The top world investors, Britain, France, and Germany, had the preponderance, $32.8 billion, while the United Kingdom possessed more than 40 percent of total world foreign investment. Britain was the leading foreign investor in Latin America and had a total investment of almost £1 billion in 1913. But 1914 was the high-water mark of European investment in Latin America. World War I not only stopped the fresh flow of capital from Europe, but it forced some of the combatant nations such as Britain and France to sell off portions of their overseas investments, and Germany, at the end of the day, lost almost its entire stock. The calamitous war left a legacy of a European economy sapped of its pre-1914 vitality and no longer capable of exporting prodigious amounts of capital to regions like Latin America. Before 1890, the United States had comparatively few foreign investments; however, from the 1890s on there was a rapid buildup of American investment, with an initial focus in the Caribbean and such key countries within it as Mexico and Cuba. Still, South America was not totally neglected, as the U.S. had sizable mining investments in Chile and Peru by 1914.

In the 1920s, the United States became the principal supplier of capital to Latin America and took over Britain's role as the chief source of portfolio investment, as Wall Street bankers dispensed loans on a large scale. While the buildup of U.S. investment was notable, Britain in 1930 still retained its place as the largest foreign investor in Latin America. Overall, foreign investment played an enormous role in what has been called the economic transformation of Latin America in the years from 1870 to 1930. This activity, however, would be subjected to new and severe stresses and strains in the harsher and more austere economic climate during the Great Depression and World War II.

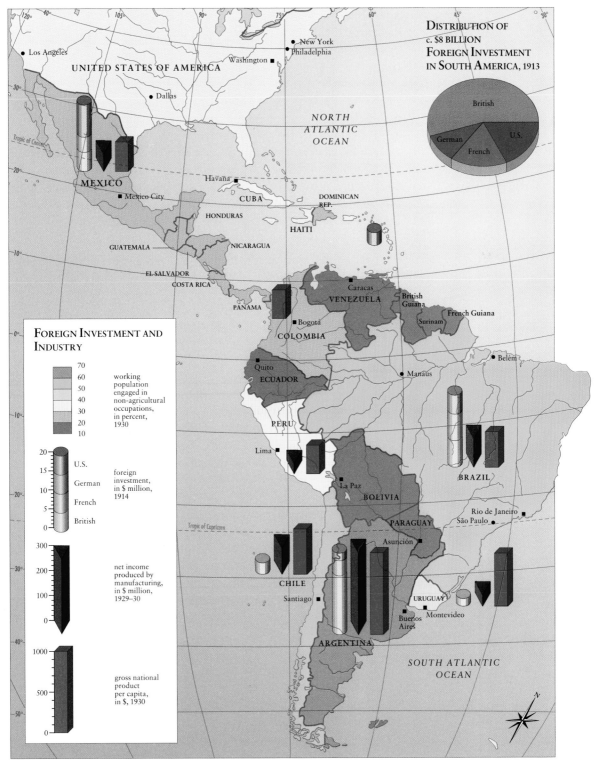

DISTRIBUTION OF
c. $8 BILLION
FOREIGN INVESTMENT
IN SOUTH AMERICA, 1913

British
German
French
U.S.

FOREIGN INVESTMENT AND
INDUSTRY

70
60
50
40
30
20
10

working
population
engaged in
non-agricultural
occupations,
in percent,
1930

20
15
10
5
0

U.S.
German
French
British

foreign
investment,
in $ million,
1914

300
200
100
0

net income
produced by
manufacturing,
in $ million,
1929–30

1000
500
0

gross national
product
per capita,
in $, 1930

THE MEXICAN REVOLUTION

In a region that had had a largely conservative political and social order since independence, the Mexican Revolution of the 1910s struck Latin America like an earthtremor. Not only was it the most violent of the revolutionary upheavals, with combatant and civilian casualties from all causes estimated at anywhere from one to two million people, but it was Latin America's first social revolution and one than changed the political, social, and economic landscape of Mexico.

Prerevolutionary Mexico had been divided by acute political and social tensions. The thirty-five-year rule of Porfirio Díaz and his technocratic advisors, who set out to modernize the economy and society of Mexico with a program of economic liberalization, alienated broad sections of national life. Indian communities and the peasantry had been aggrieved with the regime's agrarian policies, which led to greater land concentration in fewer hands. Workers for their part were resentful of low wages and poor working conditions. Liberal opinion in urban areas and northern rural regions, which wanted a restoration of democracy, was outraged in 1910 when the aging dictator Díaz reneged on his promise not to seek reelection. In addition, Mexicans in general took umbrage at the blatant favoritism accorded to foreign investors and to immigrants.

Once the insurrection began, the broad grouping of antigovernment forces prompted Díaz to renounce power in 1911, and later fight the attempts of reactionary elements to regain and stay in power. Conspicuous among the revolutionaries were political liberals like Francisco Madero, who sparked off the revolution in 1910, peasants, workers, and northern ranchers and their allies. Rebel forces in the north were led by the colorful leader Pancho Villa, with his small private army, and also by the wealthy rancher Venustiano Carranza, who had strong rural support. In the south the legendary leader Emiliano Zapata led a peasant army determined to redress the land injustices of the Díaz period.

By 1914, the revolutionaries had largely overcome the conservative resistance, but splits had developed between Carranza's army on one hand and the forces of Zapata and Villa on the other hand. While the proponents of radical agrarian reform could mobilize more manpower, the position of Carranza's forces was stronger, thanks to the able generalship of Alvaro Obregón and their control of the customs-house receipts of rich Veracruz State (Province). The constitutional assembly convened in 1916 in Querétaro by Carranza and his partisans produced in time the famous Constitution of 1917, which although modeled on the liberal Constitution of 1857, went much further than had been expected with its provisions on labor rights, its restrictions on the Church, its commitment to land reform, and, significantly, its declaration that all land, including subsoil deposits, has a social purpose and is essentially part of the State's domain.

The Constitution of 1917 gave Mexico a revolutionary credo and established national goals. Moderate liberals like Carranza had been forced by the revolutionary climate to accept elements of the radical agenda. But the power struggle within the diverse revolutionary movement continued unabated even though the

Carranza grouping had gained ascendancy in 1916 with its control of the cities and the railroad lines. But the continuing struggle among the erstwhile revolutionary allies took a heavy toll on the great leaders of the Revolution with the assassination of Zapata in 1919 and Carranza in 1920. The death of Zapata was a major blow for the movement that he led, calling for radical agrarian reform.

In the 1920s, although Mexico was not totally free of turmoil, the destiny of the nation was in the hands of revolutionaries who reflected the liberal strand of thought. But the hunger for land by the peasantry remained, as the only really extensive redistribution of rural properties occurred during the lifetime of Zapata in areas controlled by his forces in southern Mexico. (President Lázaro Cárdenas, during his term of office in the 1930s, would address the land problem by distributing to the peasantry seventeen million hectares of land in the form of communal holdings, the so-called Ejido system.) With concern for the need to give the revolutionary movement an institutional structure, outgoing president Plutarco Calles and his close associates created in 1928 a national revolutionary party, which in 1940 was renamed the Institutional Revolutionary Party. Thus was born a period of one-party government, which has lasted until recent times.

MEXICAN REVOLUTION, 1910–17

main area of revolution

Major rebel leaders' area of control

Pancho Villa, 1914

Carranza, 1913

Madero, 1911

Zapata, 1914

U.S. intervention, with date

WORLD WAR I AND THE LEAGUE OF NATIONS

In 1914, Latin America was at the margin of an international power system centered on Europe. In the Western Hemisphere itself, periodic attempts by the United States from 1889 onward to foster Pan-Americanism met a restrained response from Latin American states that were strongly critical of Washington's interference in the sovereign rights of Caribbean Basin countries. Latin American governments did not think in terms of any collective approach to regional matters and put their emphasis upon the relations between states on a strictly bilateral basis.

The outbreak of hostilities in Europe in 1914 was as unexpected as it was a shock for a Latin American region now inextricably linked to an international economy whose dynamic core was close to Britain and Western Europe. Those Latin American nations with the strongest economic ties with Europe suffered most, especially in the first two years of the war; conversely, nations now in the U.S. economic orbit experienced less hardship. The capital flow from Europe, a vital element in Latin America's economic transformation, virtually ceased for the duration of the war. Trade with Europe was thrown off course as European manufacturers were forced to suspend their shipments of finished goods, while Latin American commodity exporters faced shipping space shortages, limiting the volume of their exports.

The region's economic circumstances were not, however, uniformly bleak as two groups benefited from the international calamity. Home manufacturers who processed locally available raw materials faced lessened foreign competition and could increase their turnover while the war lasted. At the same time, American industrialists and financiers began an offensive to step into the shoes of their European counterparts. Nations like Chile, who had traditionally relied upon capital and trade from Britain and Germany, welcomed dealings with the Americans in order to lessen their dependence upon Europe.

In the realm of international relations, Latin American states made no common response to the war and its combatants. Before the United States' entry into the war, Latin American governments remained neutral, although public opinion was usually more partial to the Allied cause rather than that of the Central Powers. In 1917 the United States became involved in hostilities, and eight countries, namely Brazil, Cuba, Costa Rica, Guatemala, Haiti, Honduras, Nicaragua, and Panama, subsequently declared war on the Central Powers. A further five countries— Bolivia, the Dominican Republic, Ecuador, Peru, and Uruguay—broke diplomatic relations with Germany and its allies, but a hard core of seven nations, namely Argentina, Chile, Colombia, Mexico, Paraguay, El Salvador, and Venezuela, remained steadfastly neutral. The unwillingness of the Argentine and Mexican governments to take a position on the conflict owed more to hostility toward the United States than to any pro-German sympathies.

At the end of the war, U.S. president Woodrow Wilson introduced his idea to create a League of Nations, which would provide international collective security to prevent future wars. Many Latin American countries saw the new League of Nations as an international institution that could be used as a counterweight to American power in the Western Hemisphere. Nonetheless, the

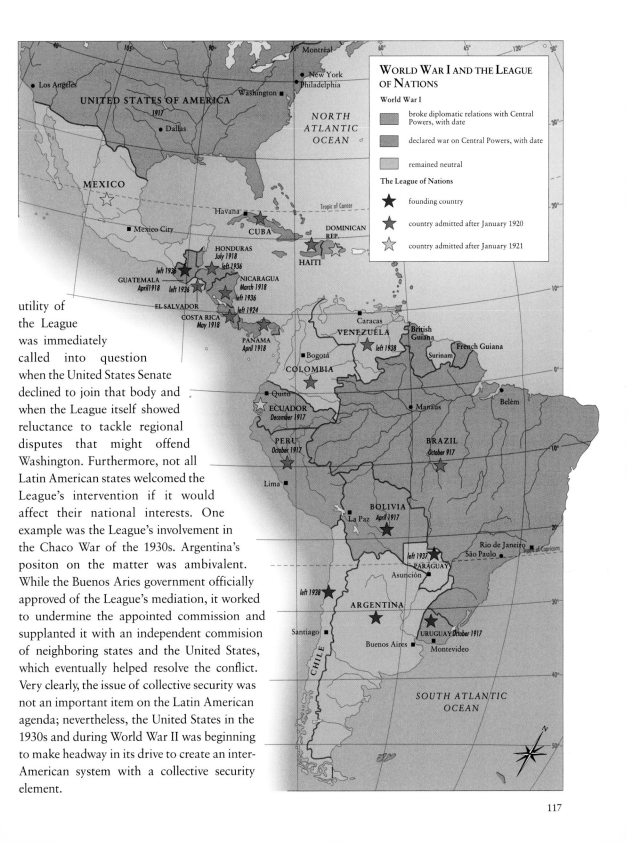

utility of
the League
was immediately
called into question
when the United States Senate
declined to join that body and
when the League itself showed
reluctance to tackle regional
disputes that might offend
Washington. Furthermore, not all
Latin American states welcomed the
League's intervention if it would
affect their national interests. One
example was the League's involvement in
the Chaco War of the 1930s. Argentina's
positon on the matter was ambivalent.
While the Buenos Aries government officially
approved of the League's mediation, it worked
to undermine the appointed commission and
supplanted it with an independent commision
of neighboring states and the United States,
which eventually helped resolve the conflict.
Very clearly, the issue of collective security was
not an important item on the Latin American
agenda; nevertheless, the United States in the
1930s and during World War II was beginning
to make headway in its drive to create an inter-
American system with a collective security
element.

RAILROADS, 1870–1945

Although Latin America's first rail line was built in Cuba in 1837, and although Argentina, Brazil, Chile, Peru, and Colombia had short railroad lines operating in the 1850s, the real age of railroad building occurred roughly from 1870 to 1930, with suspension of most construction projects during World War I. It was during this time that the basic outline of the rail systems in effect today took shape. Great feats of engineering were made to overcome some awesome natural barriers within countries, particularly in the Andean countries as well as in certain areas of Mexico and Brazil.

What drove the rail construction boom, along with the missionary zeal of foreign and domestic railroad apostles, was the availability of international finance. A profusion of railroad projects was being funded in London and other capital centers. It seemed to make little difference whether the railroad schemes were proposed by foreign interests or domestic groups—private interests, provincial governments, or national governments—international capital was usually forthcoming. Railroad construction was designed and sanctioned with little reference to any overall national transport plan. The heavy reliance on foreign finance was unavoidable, but it did encumber both foreign-owned and domestically-owned railroad companies with heavy foreign debts to service. During the Depression of the 1930s and World War II, privately owned railroads would find greater difficulties in the servicing of their foreign obligations.

While virtually all Latin American countries acquired some sort of railroad network, however small, the biggest rail systems were created in a relatively small number of nations that were important world exporters of agricultural or mining products. As a result, Argentina by 1930 had a rail network of about 25,000 miles, Brazil one of almost 20,500 miles, Mexico by 1911 one of perhaps 13,000 miles, Cuba one of 9,200 miles, and Chile one of 5,700 miles. Most other countries had rail trackage ranging from over 100 miles to something less than 2,000 miles. Large nations like Colombia and Venezuela had rail lines totaling about 1,900 and 600 miles respectively. In the case of the former, Colombia did not have a terrain ideal for an extensive rail network. Basically, smaller countries, certainly those in Central America, had rail lines built usually for the specific purpose of moving products like bananas and coffee from plantations

LATIN AMERICAN
RAILROADS

major railroads

to embarcation ports. Uruguay, however, was something of an exception among small countries as it possessed an extensive railroad system with 1,865 miles of track by 1914.

Only in the cases of Argentina, Chile, and Uruguay could it be said that their railroads had something of the character of a national rail network. Even so, the massive Argentine rail system was unbalanced, with a disproportionate amount of track in the Pampean zone, which had become one of the great grain- and beef-producing regions of the world. Brazil's railroad system was heavily concentrated in the southeastern part of the country, and the great coffee-producing area of São Paulo State had the greatest share of the track as well as the most important railroad companies. Most of the Brazilian rail companies operated in only one or two states (provinces), and there was no rail linkup between the northeastern and southeastern regions, which had to depend on coastal shipping as their communication link. In Mexico, in spite of the stipulations of the Porfirio Díaz government which awarded railroad concessions, the American rail companies who built the railroads only provided a north-south linkup of Mexico to its northern neighbor, but never established the east-west lines that would have better unified the country and its internal market.

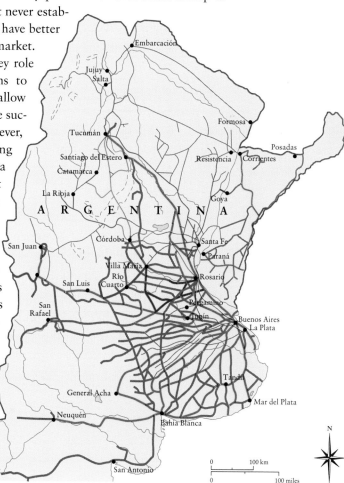

Undoubtedly, railroads played a key role in enabling Latin American nations to lower internal transport costs to allow their commodity products to compete successfully in the world market. However, they were never designed to bring together the disparate regions within a country into one large internal market and they remained largely dependent upon foreign finance. Both British- and American-owned rail companies were prominent in the region by 1930, although this was the high-water mark of the foreign presence, as the trend from the 1930s onward was toward the nationalization of privately-owned railroad lines.

ARGENTINE RAILROADS

Railroads, c. 1895	Railroads, c. 1948
—— British ownership	—— broad gauge 5'6"
—— state ownership	—— standard gauge 4'8 1/2"
—— other ownership	—— narrow gauge 3'3"

UNITED STATES INFLUENCE

Beginning in the 1820s, Latin America was witness to the gradual but inexorable rise of the United States to regional preeminence in the nineteenth and twentieth centuries. Early on, there were signs that the United States, driven by strategic, political, and economic aims, aspired to a position of dominance in the Western Hemisphere. The fledgling North American republic was a fervent advocate of independence and republicanism. The Monroe Doctrine of 1823 warned European nations that the United States would not tolerate any new attempts to recolonize the independent lands of the Americas. While security concerns were uppermost, the United States had political and commercial objectives too, but the nation, preoccupied by the slavery issue and westward expansion, lacked the opportunity, expertise, and means to achieve them. British commercial expertise and the unrivaled power of the Royal Navy were more potent facts of life in the region during the first half of the nineteenth century and even beyond.

But, from the 1860s, the United States was rapidly gaining credibility as a rising regional power. The mobilization of American troops on the Mexican border in 1865 persuaded the French to withdraw their military support from the unfortunate Emperor Maximilian in Mexico. In the 1890s, European nations began to grudgingly acknowledge the United States' sphere of influence in the Caribbean Basin, but not in Latin America as a whole. In 1895, Washington successfully pressed Great Britain to submit the border dispute between British Guiana and Venezuela to arbitration. Later, the Spanish-American War of 1898 enabled Washington to be the midwife for Cuban independence and to make Puerto Rico a protectorate. And, in 1903, the United States helped to engineer Panama's independence from Colombia, opening the way for the building of the Panama Canal.

The first three decades of the twentieth century saw an even greater surge of U.S. influence and activity in Latin America. President Theodore Roosevelt set the tone with his famous Corollary to the Monroe Doctrine, affirming his country's right to act as an international policeman in the Americas to remedy any political and economic misdeeds, and thus to preempt any action by European powers. The years from 1904 to 1933 were an era of active intervention by the United States in the internal affairs of a number of Caribbean Basin nations. The intervention took many forms, such as the creation of political protectorates, the assumption of financial control over national custom houses, the use of economic pressure, and the recourse to outright military intervention in such countries as the Dominican Republic, Cuba, Panama, Nicaragua, Mexico, and Haiti.

In the wake of its security and political concerns, the United States was developing powerful economic interests in the region. In the initial decades of the twentieth century, the United States became the dominant trader and investor in the Caribbean Basin, with heavy stakes in the Cuban and Mexican economies. After 1914, and particularly in the 1920s, the United States became an important economic factor in Latin America as a whole and made serious inroads into the commercial and financial positions of European nations like Britain in important Southern Cone markets in Argentina, Brazil, Chile, and Uruguay.

The American drive for regional hegemony produced a strong backlash in

> "I would dedicate this nation to the policy of the good neighbor—the neighbor who respects himself, and because he does so, respects the rights of others . . ."
> *Franklin Delano Roosevelt*, 1933

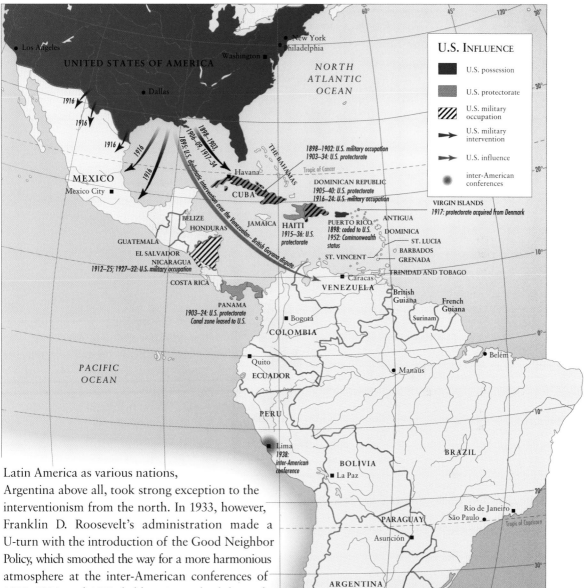

U.S. INFLUENCE

- U.S. possession
- U.S. protectorate
- U.S. military occupation
- U.S. military intervention
- U.S. influence
- inter-American conferences

UNITED STATES OF AMERICA

Los Angeles

Washington

New York
Philadelphia

NORTH
ATLANTIC
OCEAN

Dallas

1916

1916

1916

1916

1895: U.S. diplomatic intervention over the Venezuelan– British Guyana dispute

1898–1903

1905–09; 1917–34

MEXICO

Mexico City

1898–1902: U.S. military occupation
1903–34: U.S. protectorate

Havana

THE BAHAMAS

Tropic of Cancer

CUBA

DOMINICAN REPUBLIC
1905–40: U.S. protectorate
1916–24: U.S. military occupation

VIRGIN ISLANDS
1917: protectorate acquired from Denmark

BELIZE
HONDURAS

JAMAICA

HAITI
1915–36: U.S.
protectorate

PUERTO RICO
1898: ceded to U.S.
1952: Commonwealth
status

ANTIGUA
DOMINICA
ST. LUCIA
BARBADOS
GRENADA

GUATEMALA

EL SALVADOR
NICARAGUA
1912–25; 1927–32: U.S. military occupation

ST. VINCENT

TRINIDAD AND TOBAGO

COSTA RICA

Caracas

VENEZUELA

British
Guiana

French
Guiana

PANAMA
1903–24: U.S. protectorate
Canal zone leased to U.S.

Bogotá

COLOMBIA

Surinam

PACIFIC
OCEAN

Quito

ECUADOR

Belém

Manaus

PERU

Lima
1938:
inter-American
conference

BOLIVIA

La Paz

BRAZIL

Latin America as various nations, Argentina above all, took strong exception to the interventionism from the north. In 1933, however, Franklin D. Roosevelt's administration made a U-turn with the introduction of the Good Neighbor Policy, which smoothed the way for a more harmonious atmosphere at the inter-American conferences of 1933, 1936, and 1938, held against a backdrop of worrying developments in Europe and the Far East. Washington's price for closer regional cooperation was the disavowal of the policy of intervention. Closer, more formalized inter-American links paid dividends for Washington, as most nations of the region followed its lead in proclaiming neutrality in the first years of World War II and later supported the United States once it had entered the war.

PARAGUAY

Rio de Janeiro
São Paulo

Tropic of Capricorn

Asunción

ARGENTINA

Santiago

CHILE

URUGUAY

Buenos Aires
1936:
inter-American conference
1935–38:
Chaco peace conference

Montevideo
1933:
inter-American conference

SOUTH ATLANTIC
OCEAN

THE GRAN CHACO WAR, 1932–1935

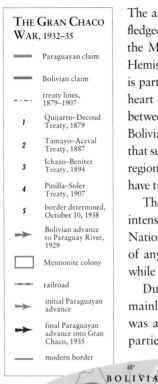

THE GRAN CHACO WAR, 1932–35

━━━━ Paraguayan claim

━━━━ Bolivian claim

━ ・ ━ ・ treaty lines, 1879–1907

1 Quijarro–Decoud Treaty, 1879

2 Tamayo–Aceval Treaty, 1887

3 Ichazo–Benítez Treaty, 1894

4 Pinilla–Soler Treaty, 1907

5 border determined, October 10, 1938

➤ Bolivian advance to Paraguay River, 1929

☐ Mennonite colony

━━━ railroad

➤ initial Paraguayan advance

➤ final Paraguayan advance into Gran Chaco, 1935

━━━━ modern border

The armed conflict in the 1930s between Bolivia and Paraguay was the only full-fledged war fought out by states of the Americas in the twentieth century. Apart from the Mexican Revolution, it was the bloodiest military encounter in the Western Hemisphere this century. The war was contested in the Chaco Boreal, which in turn is part of the Gran Chaco region that stretches into parts of three countries in the heart of the South American continent. The territory in dispute, a wedge of land between the Pilcomayo and Paraguay Rivers running up to the Andean foothills of Bolivia and the Brazilian border, is a largely arid region, but with flood plain areas that suffer inundation after any summertime tropical rainstorms. While much of the region is barren scrubland, the central and southern reaches of the Chaco Boreal have tracts of forests interspersed between flat savannah terrain.

The threat of war in the Chaco and the actual hostilities themselves provoked intense diplomatic activity in capitals of the Americas as well as at the League of Nations in Geneva, not only to stop a bloodbath but to avoid the possible widening of any hostilities, given that Chile and Peru were sympathetic to Bolivia's cause while Argentina was suspected of favoring Paraguay.

During the war and long after, a popular view held that the war was fought mainly over petroleum; nonetheless, this grossly oversimplifies a struggle that was also a legacy of the colonial and nineteenth-century experience of both parties. At independence, both Bolivia and Paraguay went through the formal motions of claiming what seemed to be an economically unimportant territory, which had never had precise administrative boundaries drawn during Spanish colonial days. Throughout much of the nineteenth century, neither nation had done much to settle the area, but Bolivia's defeat in the War of the Pacific and its loss of coastal land on the Pacific Ocean changed everything. In Bolivian eyes the Chaco territory acquired strategic importance as an access point from the Paraguay River to the estuary of the Río de la Plata and the Atlantic Ocean. Paraguay, for its part, saw the extension of its boundaries as almost a psychological necessity in the light of its crushing defeat in the War of the Triple Alliance.

After the War of the Pacific, both countries posted detachments in the Chaco, and Bolivia in 1885 started building a port on the upper Paraguay River, near Bahía Negra. The building of forts by both nations led to sporadic military friction, which only intensified in succeeding decades a flurry of diplomatic activity and the conclusion of numerous treaties in the hope of defusing the dispute.

Events in the 1920s, however, escalated an already critical situation. The discovery of oil in Bolivia by Standard Oil of New Jersey and the development of the Camiri oilfields near the Chaco only seemed to make it more vital for Bolivia to have sovereign access to the Paraguay River. At roughly the same time, in 1924 Paraguay sharply raised the level of confrontation by authorizing 5,000 Mennonite settlers from Russia to found their Filadelfia colony in the middle of the disputed area.

By the 1920s, both sides were being drawn into a military confrontation. While neither country actively plotted war, and while the mass of the respective populaces were unaware of the issues at stake, there was some sentiment within Bolivia's ruling oligarchy for settling the Chaco dispute by force against an apparently weaker adversary, as a way of revindicating Bolivia's status in its region and as a way to obtain a lifeline to the sea. In that decade, Bolivia borrowed heavily from Wall Street bankers and earmarked some of the loan proceeds for armaments.

In 1928, when Paraguayan forces overran the Bolivian-held Fort Boquerón, the stage was set for sporadic skirmishes that lasted until 1932. Intensified international mediation bore little fruit, and full-scale war broke out in June 1932. On the face of it, Bolivia seemed to enjoy all the advantages in the form of greater manpower, superior financial resources, and a great supply of war material, but Paraguay had military trump cards of its own, namely an outstanding military leader in Colonel (later General) José Félix Estigarribia and an army better adapted to fight in steamy lowland conditions and one patriotically motivated to repel an enemy in territory close to the country's economic heartland on the eastern side of the Paraguay River. From 1932 to 1935, Estigarribia's army, using brilliant encircling tactics, pushed the Bolivian forces out of the disputed area and up against Bolivia's Andean foothills. Once in this position, and now defending what was seen as home territory, Bolivia's largely Indian soldiers fought with tenacity and fortitude.

By the middle of 1935 a stalemate had been reached, and the two nations were exhausted by their human and material losses. Under the auspices of international mediation, a truce was signed that required the demobilization of the respective armies to 5,000 men each. With its territorial gains, Paraguay wanted a peace that would ratify its possession of most of the Chaco. Bolivia, resigned to the thwarting of its strategic aims, wanted the rollback of the Paraguayan advance from the proximity of the Camiri oilfields as well as a suitable port on the upper Paraguay River. After three torturous years of negotiations at the Chaco Peace Conference set up in Buenos Aires under the auspices of Argentina, Brazil, Chile, Peru, Uruguay, and the United States, a treaty was drawn up and signed in July 1938. Under the agreement, Paraguay gained in effect the disputed territory, while Bolivia won a corridor to a port on the upper Paraguay River.

The costly war had important but divergent results. For Paraguay, the victor, its territory was more than doubled. For Bolivia, however, the shock of the military defeat had a profound impact in sowing discord and disillusionment, which in time would help incite the 1952 Bolivian revolution.

WORLD WAR II

The Latin American experience during the Second World War differed in some important respects from that of the earlier world conflict in that the region adopted a more unified response to the hostilities, and economic dislocations, on balance, were not quite as traumatic. In an international sense, the Latin American states, with the notable exception of Argentina, forged common positions and maintained a surprising solidarity with the United States. Upon the outbreak of war in Europe, the United States and the twenty Latin American republics declared their neutrality and established a zone of neutrality that was declared off limits to belligerents. Once the United States entered the war in 1941, all the remaining nations, save Argentina, came out initially or gradually in support of the Allied cause. Nine nations, all of the Central American states plus Cuba, Haiti and the Dominican Republic, declared war immediately on the Axis powers of Germany, Italy, and Japan. In early 1942, all of the remaining states, except Argentina and Chile, severed diplomatic relations with Axis countries. Brazil and Mexico in the same year declared war and, in time, sent some combat units to Europe and the Far East, respectively, where they acquitted themselves well. Chile in 1943 joined fellow nations in breaking diplomatic links with the Axis powers. Only Argentina stood out against collective action, although once the tide had turned in the fortunes of the United Nations, it succumbed to Washington's heavy pressure and ruptured relations with the Axis countries in 1944 and later declared war in March 1945.

Latin America furnished valuable support to the United Nations in general and to the United States in particular. In spite of pockets of support for Germany and Italy in various countries within society and even within the military, the pro-Allied policy of Latin American governments never became a particularly live issue in political circles or the intelligentsia throughout the wartime period. Invaluable assistance was rendered to the United States in the form of military bases, communication facilities, the disruption of Axis intelligence-gathering networks, and the access to vital raw materials for the war effort. In the geographical areas of greatest strategic concern to the Americans—the Caribbean Basin and Brazil— Washington could count upon friendly and cooperative governments. Brazil, especially, was indispensable as a jumping-off point to move airplanes and material to different combat theaters, and it played a crucial role in antisubmarine warfare in the South Atlantic. Overall, Latin American cooperation enabled the United States to disrupt the commercial and intelligence activities of Axis nationals. Brazil, Colombia, Ecuador, and Peru in 1940 and 1941 acquiesced to allow Washington to shut down or to take over German and Italian airlines piloted by military reserve officers, and throughout the war, many countries cooperated with the American campaign to blacklist firms and persons trading with Axis nations.

The substantial wartime assistance of Latin America was predicated on the idea that Washington would take into account the region's social and economic problems during the conflict and beyond. In point of fact, the United States did try to reciprocate. Economic aid was dispensed, with the greatest assistance going to the countries of highest strategic importance, like Brazil. Also, the United States made sure that Latin America was not totally cut off from the flow of

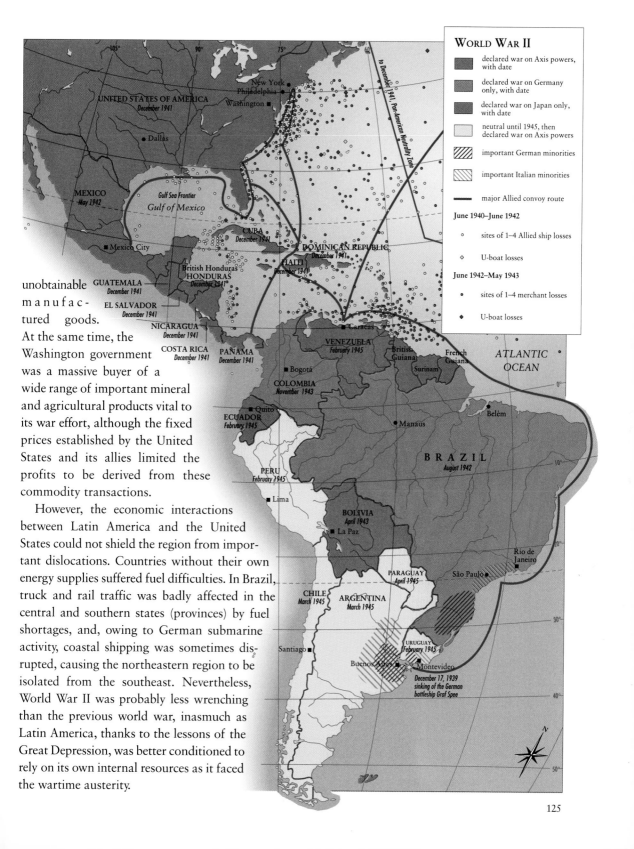

unobtainable manufactured goods. At the same time, the Washington government was a massive buyer of a wide range of important mineral and agricultural products vital to its war effort, although the fixed prices established by the United States and its allies limited the profits to be derived from these commodity transactions.

However, the economic interactions between Latin America and the United States could not shield the region from important dislocations. Countries without their own energy supplies suffered fuel difficulties. In Brazil, truck and rail traffic was badly affected in the central and southern states (provinces) by fuel shortages, and, owing to German submarine activity, coastal shipping was sometimes disrupted, causing the northeastern region to be isolated from the southeast. Nevertheless, World War II was probably less wrenching than the previous world war, inasmuch as Latin America, thanks to the lessons of the Great Depression, was better conditioned to rely on its own internal resources as it faced the wartime austerity.

WORLD WAR II

declared war on Axis powers, with date

declared war on Germany only, with date

declared war on Japan only, with date

neutral until 1945, then declared war on Axis powers

important German minorities

important Italian minorities

major Allied convoy route

June 1940–June 1942

○ sites of 1–4 Allied ship losses

◇ U-boat losses

June 1942–May 1943

• sites of 1–4 merchant losses

◆ U-boat losses

PART VII: CONTEMPORARY LATIN AMERICA

In 1945, Latin America was poised to open a new chapter in the region's historical experience and to enter its real age of industrialization. It was not to be an easy epoch, as the region was to experience extreme political turbulence and even revolutionary upheaval. On the horizon was the transformation of most countries with large rural-based populations into societies where cities and towns would hold the majority of the inhabitants.

Latin America was not to follow the industrial blueprint charted in North America and Western Europe; instead, the region was about to forge its own distinctive path with all of the pitfalls that it would entail. There was a feeling of urgency that the region could not afford a gradual transformation but had to telescope an industrial process that had taken many decades in Europe and North America into a few generations in Latin America. As a result, large countries like Argentina, Brazil, and Mexico, along with some other industrially advanced nations, opted for crash industrialization by severely restricting imports of manufactured products. Latin America was about to pioneer an industrializing strategy that would be known as Import-Substitution Industrialization (ISI). But conditions for rapid industrialization were less than optimal, even in those countries best able to implement the new strategy. For one thing, rural Latin America was not uniformly prosperous, owing to the concentration of land in few hands and the existence of sizable numbers of landless peasants in most countries, save Argentina and Uruguay. Along with that, the low level of wages for urban workers meant that the internal market for domestic manufactured products was not large. Ideally, Latin American countries needed a political leadership capable of fashioning policies that enjoyed widespread support within a democratic context.

By contrast to the experience of North America and Western Europe, Latin America embarked upon its industrial journey at the same time that it was engulfed in a population explosion. Due mainly to medical successes in reducing infant mortality, the Latin American demographic growth rate in the 1960s had shot up to a record rate of 2.9 percent per annum, contrasted with the 1.7 percent annual rate from 1900 to 1930. The range in demographic rates varied from a low of 1.9 percent per annum in Cuba to 3.8 percent per annum in Costa Rica. Significantly, large and populous countries like Brazil and Mexico had population growth rates higher than the Latin American average. Mexico illustrated well the quickening rate of demographic growth inasmuch as it had taken fifty years for the nation to double its population from 1900 to 1950, while it only took twenty-two years for the population to double again and reach a figure of 53.4 million by 1972.

An accompaniment to population increase was the rapid and widening urbanization of Latin America. To the rural unemployed and underemployed, the cities were seen as the fount of opportunity in factories or in service sector jobs, especially in government bureaucracies or state enterprises. The fact that neither industry nor government could create jobs fast enough did not deter the flood of people from interior locations to capital cities and other industrial centers. The result was a proliferation of urban slums as well as the growth of employment in the so-called informal economy operating at the margin of the legal, mainstream economy and engaged in small-scale activities in the areas of textiles, construction, and transport, among other things. The rapid growth of cities has created some of the largest urban conglomerations of the world, such as Mexico City, Buenos Aires, and São Paulo. In both large and small countries, capital cities and the main industrial centers grew to sizable proportions.

Against a background of change in different countries, a large responsibility was on the political order to find remedies for the social and economic problems facing their societies. The region was still struggling to develop the political institutions adequate to the challenge. As ever, the struggle centered on whether democratic or dictatorial rule would prevail. Prospects for democracy after World War II were mixed. The brightest hopes and the best democratic traditions were found in nations on the continent of South America, but this varied dramatically from nation to nation. In other geographical areas, Mexico appeared to be in a stage of guided democracy in which the Institutional Revolution Party saw its mission as providing one-party government in order to foster national development and to ensure economic progress. While there was no guarantee that it would lead to genuine democracy, the military was now firmly under the control of civilian authorities. But in Caribbean island countries and in Central America, with the one exception of Costa Rica, there was no tradition of democracy with free elections, and the military threat to civilian government was ever-present.

In the early post-1945 period, various nations in the South American continent appeared to be making the best progress with representative government. Chile and Uruguay continued to be the pillars of democracy in Latin America. In Brazil, the bland dictatorship of Getúlio Vargas ended in 1945, and the country reverted back to the democratic path and looked set for constitutional rule. In Argentina, almost three years of outright military government ended with the presidential election of 1946, which put Juan Perón into office with the strong backing of organized labor, the military, and the church. The meteoric rise of Perón and the emergence of the movement bearing his name, Peronism, signaled the full incorporation of the trade union movement into the Argentine political process, but it also heralded a divisive polarization of national politics that would bode ill for future political stability. In other parts of South America, however, traditions of democracy and constitutional government were less well established.

With politicians and governments increasingly aware of the need to promote national development, Latin America hoped to enlist outside support for this endeavor. In particular, there were hopes and expectations that the United States would become a partner in the drive to modernize the economic structure of the region. The United States in 1945 occupied by default an unparalleled position in Latin America as the major buyer of regional products and, until the economic recovery of Europe in the 1950s, it was the only source of outside capital and technology badly needed by the region to help with its economic diversification. Latin American hopes for massive financial aid from the United States were rapidly dashed when it was clear in the late 1940s that Cold War imperatives dictated that other regions, Europe in particular, were of higher priority for U.S. economic aid.

"From today onward we shall industrialize the country so that our work may be done by Argentine workers and so that they may earn what foreign workers earned before. This is what industrialization means to us." *President Juan Perón, 1948*

Washington showed scant interest in channeling public funds to Latin America and made clear its view that private capital—foreign and domestic—was the best catalyst for the development of the region. This stance only highlighted the reality that U.S. multinational companies once more were not only investing heavily in petroleum and other traditional interests, but also increasingly in the manufacturing activity around which were being built high walls of protection. While the United States was ignoring the development needs of Latin America, it had succeeded in its aim to bring into being an inter-American system for regional security and an institutional apparatus, the Organization of American States. However, relations between the United States and Latin America in the late 1940s and in the 1950s were becoming more prickly, and anti-Americanism, somewhat muted during World War II, now assumed more visible proportions.

During the 1940s and 1950s, the larger countries along with a handful of other relatively advanced nations pursued with vigor measures to promote home industry. Their policy measures had an economic nationalistic tone to them, and some of these countries imposed restrictions on direct foreign investment (such as Mexico and Perón's Argentina), even though there was a steady buildup in the region of foreign investment, particularly American. To foster economic growth, leading practitioners of highly protectionistic import substitution policies, such as Argentina, Brazil, Chile, and Uruguay, turned their backs on economic and monetary orthodoxy and engaged in a form of deficit financing that produced chronic inflation and the specter of economic instability. These and other countries were in an unremitting struggle to contain the scale of unemployment with good rates of economic growth. In the political sphere, a blow for Latin American democracy was struck in 1958, when Venezuela ended its periodic bouts of dictatorial government with the ousting of the dictator Marcos Pérez Jiménez, which heralded the commencement of a new era of democracy and constitutional rule. But there were contrary signs as well when the armed forces of Argentina overturned the constitutional government of Juan Perón in 1955 and when Dr. François "Papa Doc" Duvalier was elected president in Haiti in 1957 to start what turned out to be an era of dictatorship for the impoverished Caribbean nation.

The decade of the 1960s exposed the underlying political and economic vulnerabilities of the Latin American region. The new strategy of crash industrialization adopted by leading nations large and small had broadened and deepened the industrial structure of these countries and provided a stimulus for the growth of their economies, but it was proving to be no cure-all for resolving the social maladies of their societies. The clamor for reform measures to improve social conditions appeared to be rising, one example of which was the formation in the early 1960s of militant peasant leagues in northeastern Brazil. The 1960s in fact produced real political unrest and showed some evidence of a desire for radical revolutionary change in Latin America. The overthrow of the Batista dictatorship in Cuba in 1959 by a revolutionary movement led by Fidel Castro was a milestone in Latin America's political history and a clear inspiration to movements in other parts of the region that were advocating violent social change. Cuba's adoption of state socialism on Marxist-Leninist lines, its growing ties with the USSR, and its support in the 1960s for guerrilla organizations with Marxist leanings brought about an implacable hostility of the United States. The latter, fearing a revolutionary domino effect in the Americas, strengthened its support and military aid for both democratic governments and anti-Communist dictatorial regimes. The Alliance for Progress, initiated in 1961 by the Kennedy administration, was an undisguised attempt by the United States to engage in joint social and economic assistance projects with Latin American countries tailored with an eye to attracting the support of groups favoring peaceful reforms of an evolutionary, not revolutionary, nature. The United States also discarded its inhibitions about non-intervention when in 1965 the Johnson administration sent American marines directly into the Dominican Republic to end a civil war that Washington feared might result in the emergence of a Castro-style government. Overall, the 1960s could not have been more tumultuous. Widespread guerrilla activity and the threat of social upheaval produced a strong military response as armed forces toppled civilian governments in Brazil, Argentina, and Peru. Untypically, the military government of General Velasco in Peru initiated an extensive program of social and economic reform to preempt any clamor for even more radical alternatives.

The turbulent political scene in Latin America seemed to enter a new stage in the 1970s. The fear in Washington that new Cubas would arise throughout the region had subsided somewhat as the Castro government, now accepting the more cautious counsel of Moscow, no longer advocated publicly or supported directly "national liberation" movements in Latin America. But the threat of radical change was present in Southern Cone countries; in 1973 the military in Chile violently overturned the elected government of the Marxist-inclined President Salvador Allende, while the armed forces in Uruguay and Argentina in 1976 deposed their civilian governments and went all-out to crush major guerrilla movements committed to social revolution. The Argentine military's "Dirty War" against guerrillas and sympathizers was extremely costly in human terms.

Parallel to the political concerns in the 1970s were those of an economic nature. Higher world oil prices, a fall in world economic growth rates, and the stagnation of world trade rocked most Latin American nations, particularly those that were not important oil producers. Inflation was now a more universal problem, and Argentina and Chile at times experienced bouts of hyperinflation. But a potential economic debacle for the region was avoided as international bankers stepped into the breach and began to make, perhaps foolishly, large-scale loans to a number of countries in Latin America and the developing world. Thanks to heavy foreign loans, most nations were able to avoid serious foreign exchange difficulties and maintain respectable economic growth rates; furthermore, governments were able to continue at a high level expenditure on central administration operations and on state enterprises, many of which were loss-making.

Nonetheless, the economic lifeline offered by the foreign bankers from 1973 onward was only a temporary respite. Mexico in 1982 detonated the world foreign debt crisis of the 1980s by announcing that the sharp fall in world oil prices had obliged it to suspend the debt servicing on its massive foreign debt. That bombshell ushered in a crisis that enveloped other heavily indebted countries of Latin America and the Third World, and it cut off further international loans. Latin America was now plunged into its worst recession since the 1930s. It also exposed the shaky foundations of national development strategies that relied heavily on a major role for the state in the economy and a type of industrial protectionism that shielded home industrialists from foreign competition, but stifled efficiency and the ability to compete in the world market. The virtual collapse of state finances and the grim economic outlook forced national soul-searching as to the way forward, whether to batten down the hatches and declare a debt moratorium on terms favorable to debtor nations or to jettison the prevailing economic approach in favor of more open, liberalized economies geared toward exportation. The general blueprint for the latter alternative was clearly that of the dynamic economies of East Asia and also the strong export economy of Pinochet's Chile. With the sharp economic downturn, a number of military governments in South America found themselves under economic and political pressure to restore civilian rule, and Argentina in 1983, Uruguay in 1984, and Brazil in 1985 saw the reestablishment of democratic government. Even Pinochet's Chile was not free from the democratic ferment, and in 1989 the military gave way to democratic elections after first making a constitutional change that created a special institutional role for the armed forces.

While militarism was on the wane in South America, and democracy was making a comeback, political and international conditions were at a dangerous point in Central America, which had become the flashpoint of Latin America in the 1980s. At the heart of the problem was the upheaval in Nicaragua, where the long dynastic rule of the Somoza family was finally ended in 1979 after a bloody civil war that put in power the Sandinista Front of National Liberation, which had warm ties with Cuba and was antagonistic to the United States. The Reagan administration, fearful that the fires of social revolution might spread in Central America, stepped up its economic and military aid to the area and created the Caribbean Basin Initiative, granting trade concessions to nations of the geographical region. United States support for anti-Sandinista rebels, the Contras, escalated a conflict that looked likely to inflame Cold War rivalry in the Caribbean. The collapse of the Soviet Union, however, curtailed the material support given to Cuba and the Sandinistas and led to the defusing of the conflict in the area. In addition, the Sandinistas lost the election of 1990, bringing to power Violeta Chamorro, heading an anti-Sandinista coalition.

From the late 1980s, various countries began to chart new economic directions moving away from state intervention, protectionism, and import substitution. Argentina and Peru among others were conspicuous in the 1990s in opening up their economies through liberalization and privatization measures which helped to bring inflation under control. Brazil in the 1990s scaled down to a good degree its excessive protection for domestic industry, and in 1994 introduced stabilization measures to bring inflation down to low levels by contemporary standards. In the late 1990s the Brazilian economic powerhouse in Latin America, with an expertise in the export of manufactured goods, including technological products like airplanes and military equipment, worked towards restructuring its economy to make it a more dynamic presence in the world trade arena.

Like the economic picture, the political scene of Latin America in the 1990s contrasted sharply with that of previous decades. The great ideological debate raging in the region for decades over the merits of Marxism versus capitalism was now muted, if not over, as the pendulum shifted toward greater acceptance of the market-oriented economy and toward democratic government. The military came under a tighter civilian reign than earlier, and by 1998 no serving officer occupied a presidential chair, although President Fujimori of Peru enjoyed an especially close relationship with the military, and the war against drugs raised the military profile in countries like Colombia and Mexico. Nations that were operating one-party governments, like Cuba and Mexico, were put on the defensive. Castro's Cuba continued to reaffirm the monopoly rule of the Cuban Communist party, but in Mexico, in 1997, President Ernesto Zedillo and his administration allowed freer elections, after which opposition parties gained more governorships, control of the congress, and the mayoralty of Mexico City.

In the sphere of international relations, the United States retained its position as the dominant external power interacting with Latin America. While its economic dominance was no longer what it was in the 1940s and 1950s, the United States remained the most important trader and investor in the region in the late 1990s, even though Japan and European countries like Britain and Germany became major investors. The American economic position with Mexico was strengthened by the formation of the North American Free Trade Association (NAFTA) in 1994 between the two countries and Canada. Significantly, the United States is the principal market for Latin American exports of non-traditional products like manufactured goods. Washington's expressions of interest in the creation of a Western Hemisphere free trade area was received with interest in Latin America, even though the powerful Brazilian nation expressed reservations about any scheme established on U.S. terms. As Americans debated about the desirability of concluding new free trade agreements with individual Latin American countries, Brazil appeared to be making some headway with its aim of a South American trading bloc, with the Common Market of the South, the Mercosur, the core of such an entity.

The newfound economic and political stability that a number of Latin American countries attained by the end of the decade made the region more attractive for foreign and domestic investment, but it still has its precarious side. Overall, future prospects seem brighter for the industrially advanced large and small countries than for the small agrarian-oriented nations still highly dependent upon tropical agricultural production. All countries, however, face the problem of how to translate economic stability and growth into an instrument that will provide gains and uplift for the larger population and not just a well-off minority. Thus, in the interest of political stability, Latin American nations cannot falter in their push for greater and more equitable national development.

DICTATORSHIP VS. DEMOCRACY

During the post-1945 period there has been an unremitting struggle between the partisans of democracy and the forces of authoritarianism and dictatorship. Militarism has posed a serious threat to civilian authority. The struggle has encompassed those nations that before 1945 had either partially or fully developed democratic traditions, as well as countries with a very limited democratic heritage or the virtual absence of the culture of democracy. In a larger sense, the issue of dictatorship or democracy was not just an internal battle for the spoils of office and group preferment, but it also included increasing struggles from the 1960s onward with guerrilla movements, some of a Marxist persuasion, advocating far-reaching revolutionary change in Latin America.

At the end of World War II, the triumph of the United Nations, which had held aloft the standard of democracy, raised hopes that there would be a democratic fallout in Latin America. Initially, there were hopeful signs that the pendulum would be swinging more toward the democratic camp. Brazil and Argentina in the 1940s reverted to constitutional rule. In the 1950s, Colombia and Venezuela ousted military men occupying the presidential chairs, and both countries have operated constitutional democracies ever since. But the picture was mixed. General Alfredo Stroessner assumed power in Paraguay in 1954 to start what would be a thirty-five-year dictatorship. In Guatemala in 1954, the elected president, Jacobo Arbenz Guzmán, who had introduced a program of agrarian reform, was toppled by Guatemalan exiles led by Colonel Carlos Castillo Armas, who were supported by the United States. The armed forces in Argentina in 1955 brought down the elected government of Juan Perón. In Haiti in 1957, the infamous Duvalier regime started out democratically but soon degenerated into a thuggish dictatorship.

Whatever hopes there were for greater democratization in Latin America were dashed in the 1960s by a vast upsurge in guerrilla activity, which in turn produced a climate of uncertainty that encouraged a trend toward rampant militarism in the region, with much of it taking place on the continent of South America. Unlike the militarism of the past, which produced personalistic regimes like that of Trujillo in the Dominican Republic, Somoza in Nicaragua, Batista in Cuba, and Stroessner in Paraguay, the increasing emphasis was upon an institutionalized military response whereby juntas or military officers placed in power were given their authority from the armed forces as a corporate body. In Brazil and Peru, the military institutes of those countries taught an ideology known as the national-security doctrine, which called upon the military to assume a role of leadership in society to defeat forces threatening the internal stability of the nation. The doctrine contemplated a prolonged military stay in government to root out presumed causes of political instability.

In the 1960s and 1970s, the trend in Latin America was toward either personalized military rule or institutionalized military government, with the latter type very much in evidence in the South American countries of Brazil, Peru, Argentina, Chile, and Uruguay. In the case of the two latter countries, these paragons of democracy had succumbed to the regional vice of dictatorship. In many Central American countries, the role of the military seemed to differ somewhat from that

POST-1945 MILITARY INVOLVEMENT IN POLITICS

✦ military coups and/or takeover, with date

▨ country where lengthy military regime occurred

1953–57 dates of lengthy military regime

1953–89 Stroessner dates of a strongman dictatorship

UNITED STATES OF AMERICA

Washington ■

PACIFIC OCEAN

MEXICO

Mexico City ■ • Veracruz
Puebla

Havana
CUBA
✦ *1952–59 Batista*
1952 *1959 Castro*

HAITI Tropic of Cancer
✦ *1957–86 "Papa Doc" then "Baby Doc" Duvalier*
1991

Puerto Rico

DOMINICAN REPUBLIC
✦ *1930–61 Trujillo*
1963

1991–94

NORTH ATLANTIC OCEAN

GUATEMALA
✦ *1954, 1963, 1982, 1993*

HONDURAS
✦ *1957, 1963, 1972, 1978*
1932–48 Carias

NICARAGUA
1936–79 Somoza dynasty

BELIZE
HONDURAS JAMAICA
GUATEMALA Tegucigalpa
Guatemala City
NICARAGUA
■ Managua
EL SALVADOR
San José
✦ *1932–82 (military dominant element in the power elite)*
1948 1979
COSTA RICA Panama City

PANAMA
✦ *1968–81 Torrijos period*
1968

GRENADA
Port of Spain ■ TRINIDAD AND TOBAGO

VENEZUELA GUYANA
Caracas Georgetown ■ Paramaribo ■
1948–58 SURINAM Fr. Cayenne
1948 G.

COLOMBIA
■ Bogotá
✦ *1953–57*
1953

Quito ■
✦ *1963–66 1972–79*
1963 ECUADOR

PERU
✦ *1962, 1968*
1968–80

Lima ■

BRAZIL
✦ 1964
1964–85

■ Brasília

BOLIVIA
✦ *1951, 1964, 1969, 1971, 1978, 1979, 1981*
La Paz ■
1964–82 (mostly under control of military officers)

1953–89 Stroessner

Rio de Janeiro ■

Tropic of Capricorn

CHILE
✦ 1973
1973–90 Pinochet

Santiago ■

✦ *1954, 1989*
PARA.
Asunción ■

ARGENTINA
✦ *1955, 1962, 1966, 1976*
Buenos Aires
1955–58 1976–83

URUGUAY
Montevideo ■ ✦ 1976
1976–84

Falkland Is. to UK

N

of their counterparts in South American states, inasmuch as it seemed to see its function as supporting an increasingly embattled oligarchy either in or outside power.

During the 1980s, military governments that had either crushed or contained guerrilla movements in most countries found increasing difficulties in handling national economic affairs in the face of the foreign debt-induced financial crises of the decade. Added to this, the badly discredited Argentine armed forces, in the wake of their defeat in the South Atlantic War with Britain, were obliged to cede their control of national affairs to an elected civilian government. Throughout the 1980s, one by one, military governments in South America were forced to allow national elections and accept civilian control of their nation's destiny. The Pinochet government in Chile consented to a resumption of civilian rule only after a change was made in the constitution that acknowledged the special role of the military.

IDEOLOGICAL CONFLICT AND REVOLUTION

While Latin America in its first century and a quarter of collective national experience had proved to be surprisingly unrevolutionary, the region after 1945 was politically volatile and seething with unaddressed social problems, such as the widespread landlessness of peasants, a very unequal pattern of income distribution, the low level of wages combined with unsatisfactory working conditions, the poor provision of basic services including health care, and poor education systems, among other things. Conditions were explosive, and one early sign of serious social discontent in the region was the Bolivian Revolution of 1952. What started out as an urban-based antigovernment insurrection swiftly developed into a wider uprising of miners and peasants, who, at the end of the day, brought about an extensive land reform that changed irrevocably the social fabric of the country. Although some of the urban revolutionaries were Marxists, the United States surprisingly gave its belated support to the revolution and provided foreign aid to the new regime.

Although the Bolivian Revolution constituted Latin America's second great social upheaval after that of Mexico in 1910, it was the third great social uprising, the Cuban Revolution of 1959, that was to be the most celebrated in the contemporary period. The overthrow of the Batista regime by Fidel Castro, Ernesto "Che" Guevara, and others produced, against a backdrop of intense American hostility, a radical social transformation that was to create the region's first example of a socialist state built on Marxist-Leninist lines. The Castro government expropriated American and other foreign properties, established state control over the means of production, and introduced widespread social reforms designed to benefit low-income groups in the nation. The United States in 1961, through Cuban émigré proxies, tried unsuccessfully to overthrow the new revolutionary government in the ill-fated Bay of Pigs military venture and later initiated an economic blockade on Cuba that has stood to this day. For its part, Castro's Cuba hastily established close relations with Washington's Cold War rival, the USSR, in the expectation that this would provide support for the nation's security along with the economic assistance vitally needed by an economy utterly dependent on the near-monocrop of sugar.

The growing ties of Cuba to an external power antagonistic to the United States not only made something of a dead letter of the Monroe Doctrine, but also ensured that Latin America would be part of the Cold War scenario. This was made chillingly clear when the Cuban missile crisis of 1962, which was precipitated when the Soviet Union placed intermediate-range nuclear missiles in Cuba, brought the world to the brink of an atomic war. Whatever ambivalence Washington might have had about movements calling for widespread social reform were cast aside in the 1960s, as the United States aligned itself more firmly with democratic or dictatorial governments opposed to radical or Marxist prescriptions for the social ills of Latin America.

The combination of deep-seated social problems, the spread of Marxist thinking in some circles of Latin American society, and the rise of Castro's Cuba as a beacon for revolutionary change made Latin America an even more

Juan Domingo Perón and his wife, Eva Duarte Perón, waving to an enthusiastic crowd from the balcony of the Executive Mansion or Casa Rosada on Plaza de Mayo, Buenos Aires, on May Day 1951.

unstable region, and there was a notable upsurge in revolutionary activity in the 1960s. Countless guerrilla movements of Marxist leanings became prominent, and revolutionary Cuba in that decade lent its active and material support to favored groupings. Guerrilla leaders of some note sprang up in nations like Peru, Colombia, Bolivia, Brazil, and Guatemala, but none of them were destined to achieve the success of their Cuban counterparts, as military counter-insurgency tactics proved vigorous and effective. This was also the fate of the legendary guerrilla leader Che Guevara, who, in an attempt to ignite a conti-nentwide revolution, was captured by units of the Bolivian army in 1967 and was summarily executed on the spot.

In the following decade of the 1970s, important countries in South America faced extreme social turbulence or even violent internal conflict. The Popular Unity program of President Salvador Allende in Chile, which was committed to implementing reforms on Marxist lines, triggered off in 1973 a violent military reaction, as the armed forces led by General Augusto Pinochet brought the gov-ernment down. In Uruguay, the military in 1974 assumed de facto political control and extinguished the insurgency threat of the Tupamaros, who had been since the 1960s the most effective urban guerrilla force in Latin America. Argentina, which seemed on the threshold of a bloody civil war in the first half of the 1970s, experienced a coup in 1976 by the armed forces, which deposed President Isabel Perón and then launched the famous Dirty War, which crushed the guer-rilla forces of the Montoneros and the People's Revolutionary Army.

By 1980 guerrilla activity in South America had been severely checked in most countries. There was one notable exception, however, as Peru in the 1980s and

"All that I am, all that I have, and all that I feel belong to Perón."
Eva Perón

The confident and charismatic revolutionary leader Fidel Castro led a small revolutionary group of some 300 guerrillas and defeated the corrupt Batista regime, taking over Cuba's government in January 1959.

early 1990s faced one of the most violent movements in the form of the Maoist-inspired Sendero Luminoso (Shining Path). Until the capture of its leader in 1992, Shining Path was a serious destabilizing force in Peru. But the real focus of revolutionary activity in Latin America in the 1980s was not in South America but in Central America. The assumption of power in Nicaragua in 1979 by the Sandinista Front of National Liberation, with its close ties to Cuba and its antagonism toward the United States, set the stage for serious confrontation in the 1980s. The United States was concerned about Sandinista support for the Farabundo Martí Front of National Liberation in El Salvador, but there was an even greater and more dangerous issue that had Cold War ramifications, namely the increasing of economic and material aid that Cuba and the Soviet Union were furnishing the Sandinista government. Events in Europe, however, notably *glasnost* and the eventual demise of the USSR, guaranteed that the ideological challenge to American hegemony in the Caribbean would fail.

By the late 1990s, revolutionary activity in Latin America was a far cry from what it had been in previous decades. Prospects for violent social change dimmed. Revolutionary organizations of some note continued to operate in Peru and Colombia, but with less of the same ideological fervor of previous times. While armed revolution no longer seemed to pose a threat to the stability of most nations, a country like Mexico could still be jolted in 1994 and thereafter by a peasant uprising in the economically weak Chiapas State, bringing to national prominence the Zapata Army of National Liberation. Colombia is facing an even more serious upsurge of guerrilla activity as insurgents operate freely in large areas of the hinterland.

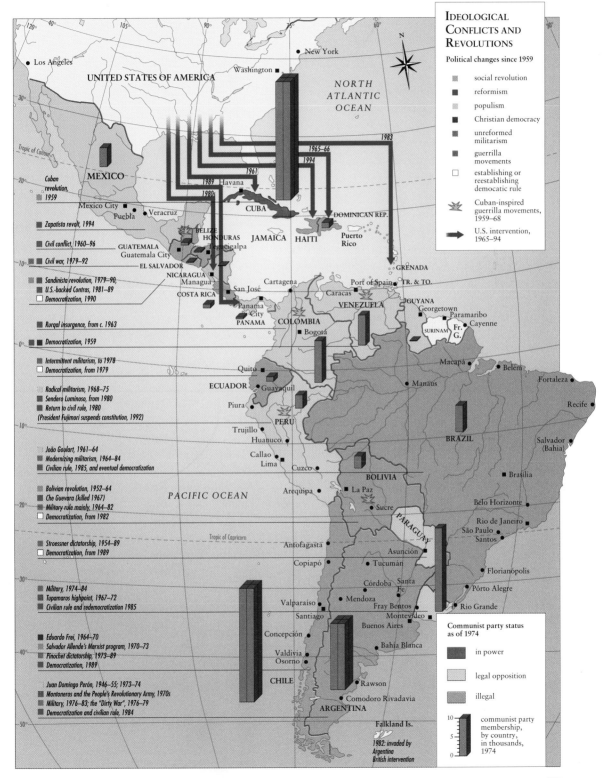

IDEOLOGICAL CONFLICTS AND REVOLUTIONS

Political changes since 1959

- social revolution
- reformism
- populism
- Christian democracy
- unreformed militarism
- guerrilla movements
- establishing or reestablishing democatic rule
- Cuban-inspired guerrilla movements, 1959–68
- U.S. intervention, 1965–94

Cuban revolution, 1959

Zapatista revolt, 1994

Civil conflict, 1960–96

Civil war, 1979–92

Sandinista revolution, 1979–90; U.S.-backed Contras, 1981–89 Democratization, 1990

Rural insurgence, from c. 1963

Democratization, 1959

Intermittent militarism, to 1978 Democratization, from 1979

Radical militarism, 1968–75 Sendero Luminoso, from 1980 Return to civil rule, 1980 (President Fujimori suspends constitution, 1992)

João Goulart, 1961–64 Modernizing militarism, 1964–84 Civilian rule, 1985, and eventual democratization

Bolivian revolution, 1952–64 Che Guevara (killed 1967) Military rule mainly, 1964–82 Democratization, from 1982

Stroessner dictatorship, 1954–89 Democratization, from 1989

Military, 1974–84 Tupamaros highpoint, 1967–72 Civilian rule and redemocratization 1985

Eduardo Frei, 1964–70 Salvador Allende's Marxist program, 1970–73 Pinochet dictatorship, 1973–89 Democratization, 1989

Juan Domingo Perón, 1946–55; 1973–74 Montoneros and the People's Revolutionary Army, 1970s Military, 1976–83; the "Dirty War", 1976–79 Democratization and civilian rule, 1984

Communist party status as of 1974

- in power
- legal opposition
- illegal

communist party membership, by country, in thousands, 1974

1982: invaded by Argentina British intervention

GROWTH AND INFLATION

In the post-1945 years, Latin American countries anticipated the need of high rates of economic growth to meet popular expectations and to provide sufficient employment for societies in the midst of population explosion. The memory of the stagnation of the depression and war years only reinforced the commitment to substantial growth rates to be valued for their capability of increasing wealth as well as savings to be invested back into the economy.

In the 1950s and 1960s, the good economic growth rates in most countries were due mainly to higher manufacturing output geared to the demand of internal markets. The main sources of job creation were in the areas of manufacturing and in service sector activities, particularly in the governmental sphere. While economic growth for most countries was well above the region's demographic rate of about 3 percent per annum, Latin America was far from enjoying boom conditions, as urban unemployment and rural underemployment stayed at high levels in many countries. In addition, the Latin American region from the 1950s onward enjoyed the unenviable reputation of being the inflation capital of the world. Ironically, it was only a minority of countries that were now chronically afflicted with inflation rates well above those of the developed countries. The so-called banana republics, small, economically weak countries highly dependent upon tropical agriculture, had relative monetary stability and low inflation rates. But it was the more economically important nations of the Southern Cone, namely Argentina, Brazil, Chile, and Uruguay, that had chronic inflation, and it was precisely these countries that were in the forefront of the crash industrialization drive taking place in Latin America. Another rapidly industrializing country, Mexico, was able to avoid serious inflation problems, thanks to the increasing alignment of its economy with the United States.

Within the Southern Cone as well as in other parts of Latin America, an academic debate raged over the question of inflation and growth. What could be called the "monetarist school of thought" took an orthodox viewpoint that the easy money policies of governments were responsible for chronic inflation. A contrary body of opinion, the so-called "structuralist school of thought," blamed inflation on the structure of the Latin American economy and accepted endemic inflation as the necessary price to pay to ensure acceptable rates of economic growth.

The growth prospects and the monetary stability of most Latin American countries faced ever greater challenges in the 1970s. A universal fear in the region was that further scope for import substitution was diminishing and likely to impair the growth opportunities of manufacturing industry. But the prime worry was the state of the world economy and the stagnation of world trade. The Latin American countries, however, won a temporary economic boost in the form of access to foreign bank loans. Because of this, Latin American governments in particular were able to use foreign borrowings to maintain high levels of public expenditure and thus keep their economies growing. During this decade, high rates of inflation became a more widespread problem in the region and Argentina and Chile at different times faced something close to hyperinflation.

The real moment of truth for the growth and monetary stability of Latin

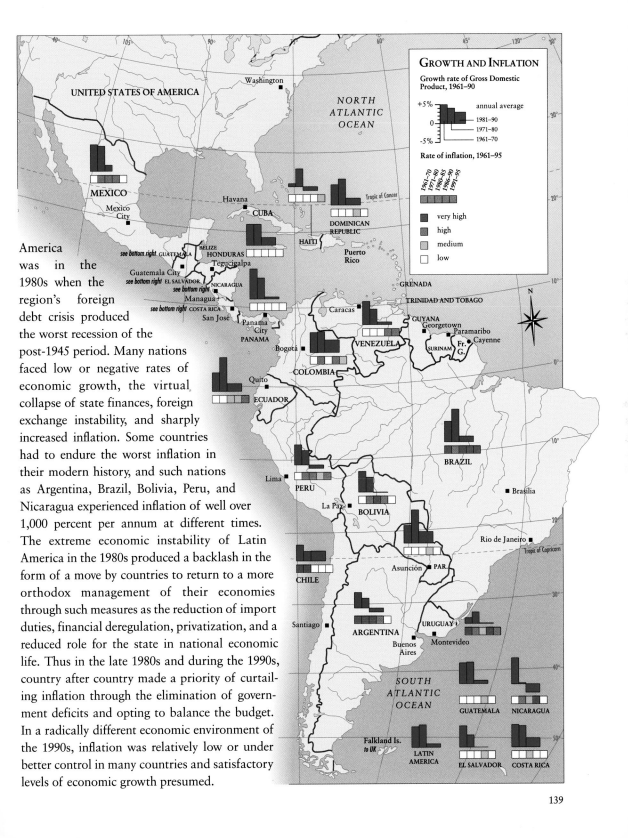

America was in the 1980s when the region's foreign debt crisis produced the worst recession of the post-1945 period. Many nations faced low or negative rates of economic growth, the virtual collapse of state finances, foreign exchange instability, and sharply increased inflation. Some countries had to endure the worst inflation in their modern history, and such nations as Argentina, Brazil, Bolivia, Peru, and Nicaragua experienced inflation of well over 1,000 percent per annum at different times. The extreme economic instability of Latin America in the 1980s produced a backlash in the form of a move by countries to return to a more orthodox management of their economies through such measures as the reduction of import duties, financial deregulation, privatization, and a reduced role for the state in national economic life. Thus in the late 1980s and during the 1990s, country after country made a priority of curtailing inflation through the elimination of government deficits and opting to balance the budget. In a radically different economic environment of the 1990s, inflation was relatively low or under better control in many countries and satisfactory levels of economic growth presumed.

FOREIGN INVESTMENT, FOREIGN DEBT

Foreign investment, a medium for the diffusion of not only capital but also technology, remained of critical importance to post-1945 Latin America, a region with a shortage of capital compounded at times by capital flight during moments of major political or economic uncertainties. At the same time, Latin America was never able to secure any long-term commitment of official development aid from a capital-exporting country like the United States, except for the short-lived Alliance for Progress partnership of the 1960s.

In spite of the capital shortfall, the climate of opinion in Latin America toward direct foreign investment was not uniformly favorable and was sometimes hostile. The memory of past disputes with foreigners, a rising sense of economic nationalism, and the growth of Marxist thinking in some circles all contributed to a more suspicious attitude to it in some countries. Argentina during the Perón era from 1946 to 1955 had an ideological antipathy to foreign capital that persisted long afterward in the ranks of the Perónist movement. In Mexico, the ruling Institutional Revolutionary Party sought to curb investment by foreigners in sensitive areas of the economy and, at one stage, advocated the Mexicanization of existing foreign stakes by opening up equity participation to national investors.

The more measured view of direct foreign investment did not, however, impede a substantial inflow of external investment into a fairly wide range of activities, above all into local manufacturing now receiving strong state protection. Initially, the United States was the main source of private foreign investment, and the buildup of this stake was relatively rapid, as the total U.S. direct investment in Latin America, amounting to $2.7 billion in 1943, rose to $4.4 billion by 1950 and ultimately reached $29.8 billion by 1981. Increasingly, U.S. investment tended to focus on manufacturing industry, whereas the sizable investment in petroleum activities became comparatively less important with time as oil properties in Bolivia, Venezuela, and Peru were nationalized. U.S. investment was spread fairly widely; nevertheless, more than half went to Brazil and Mexico, which received a total of $8.2 and $6.9 billion respectively by 1981. The American investment position was not unchallenged, however, as Japan, Germany, Britain, and other countries became important investors, with the bulk of their investments directed at the more industrialized nations of the region.

In the 1970s, an upheaval in the international economy triggered by a fourfold increase in world oil prices had vastly inflated the income of Third World oil-exporting nations, which deposited their windfall gains with international bankers to be recycled as loans to the world community. Loan offers were eagerly taken up by Mexico as well as numerous South American countries, and a borrowing binge ensued from 1973 to 1982. Both lenders and Third World borrowers largely threw caution to the winds as massive foreign currency loans, often with relatively short terms, were made with little thought as to how debtors could increase their exports to repay their hard-currency loans. Only in the cases of major oil-exporting nations like Mexico and Venezuela did the risk seem to be amply covered. Unfortunately for all, the loan bubble burst in 1982, when first Mexico and then other debtor countries were unable to service fully their bank

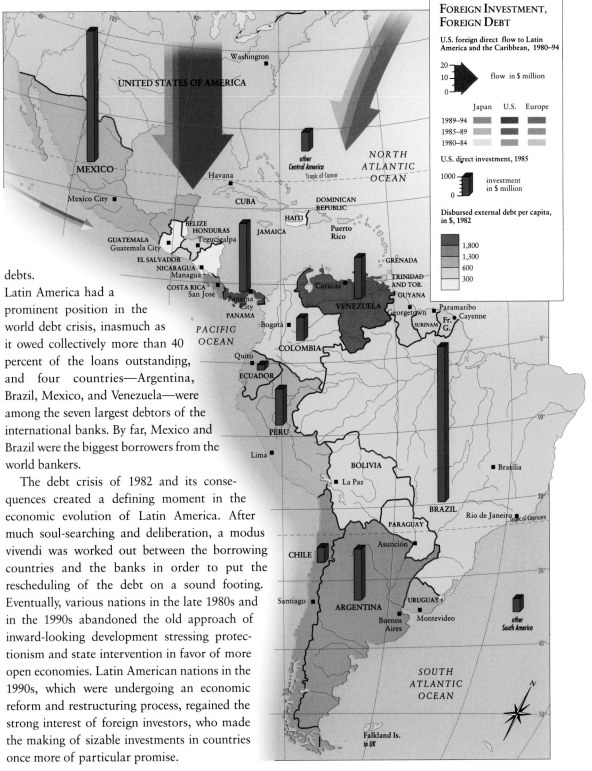

FOREIGN INVESTMENT, FOREIGN DEBT

U.S. foreign direct flow to Latin America and the Caribbean, 1980–94

flow in $ million

	Japan	U.S.	Europe
1989–94			
1985–89			
1980–84			

U.S. direct investment, 1985

investment in $ million

Disbursed external debt per capita, in $, 1982

1,800
1,300
600
300

debts.

Latin America had a prominent position in the world debt crisis, inasmuch as it owed collectively more than 40 percent of the loans outstanding, and four countries—Argentina, Brazil, Mexico, and Venezuela—were among the seven largest debtors of the international banks. By far, Mexico and Brazil were the biggest borrowers from the world bankers.

The debt crisis of 1982 and its consequences created a defining moment in the economic evolution of Latin America. After much soul-searching and deliberation, a modus vivendi was worked out between the borrowing countries and the banks in order to put the rescheduling of the debt on a sound footing. Eventually, various nations in the late 1980s and in the 1990s abandoned the old approach of inward-looking development stressing protectionism and state intervention in favor of more open economies. Latin American nations in the 1990s, which were undergoing an economic reform and restructuring process, regained the strong interest of foreign investors, who made the making of sizable investments in countries once more of particular promise.

141

REGIONAL ECONOMIC INTEGRATION

The binding together of Latin American countries into different types of political and economic unions has been a recurring issue since the 1820s, but it has recently acquired a very real importance. In the early years of independence, various federations were created, only to collapse and fragment. Simón Bolívar made a clarion call for a union of Spanish-American republics, but the Congress of Panama of 1826 that he inspired was a failure. Thereafter, the squabbling and the conflict between neighboring countries in the nineteenth century was an impediment to greater intraregional harmony; furthermore, Latin America's economic transformation from 1870 to 1930 did little to strengthen intraregional trade ties, as it expanded and oriented commerce overwhelmingly with the outside world.

In the present century, depression and war in the 1930s and 1940s began to loosen commercial ties with nations outside the region, and various neighboring countries tried to compensate for this by strengthening their trade links through bilateral agreements. But the real driving force for closer intraregional economic relations came after 1945, as countries set their sights on rapid industrialization. During the 1960s, three regional integration schemes were created. The Central American Common Market (CACM) was created in 1960, and included all nations in that geographical area except Panama. In the same year, the Latin American Free Trade Association (LAFTA) came into existence, and grouped together Mexico along with all ten of the South American republics. A more limited scheme than that of the CACM, LAFTA was still hopelessly ambitious as it included 79 percent of Latin America's landmass and 72 percent of its population; furthermore, many countries in the scheme had weak trade links with each other. In time, the organization was stymied by the lack of a political will for meaningful integration and a resistance on the part of local industrialists to the reduction of national tariffs. With LAFTA stalled, five Andean countries—Bolivia, Chile, Colombia, Ecuador, and Peru—created in 1969 the Andean Pact to work within the general confines of LAFTA but aimed at aligning their economies into a common market. Venezuela later joined the grouping in 1973, but Chile under the Pinochet regime pulled out in 1976.

In their first decades of existence, none of the three integration schemes met the hopes and expectations as countries were zealous about not surrendering their full national sovereignty and were wary of cutting their industrial tariffs. The LAFTA nations took on board the limitations of their organization, and in 1980 they reconstituted the organization of their integration scheme, narrowed its scope, and renamed the entity the Latin American Integration Association (LAIA). But disastrous economic conditions in the 1980s began to sow the seeds for closer cooperation between Latin American nations. Argentina and Brazil from 1985 onward concluded a series of agreements designed to align their economies more closely together. By the end of the 1980s, they signified their intention of creating a common market in ten years' time. When U.S. president George Bush in 1990 made his call for an Enterprise of the Americas Initiative to eventually create a Western Hemisphere free trade bloc, Argentina and Brazil

immediately decided to create a common market by 1995, and their decision drew Paraguay and Uruguay into the design. The result was the formation, in 1991, of the Common Market of the South, commonly known as the Mercosur, with the goal of creating a fully-fledged customs union. Contrary to expectations within and outside of Latin America, Mercosur not only met its deadline in creating a customs union, but it expanded to include Chile and Bolivia as associate members.

Economic integration has been given a greater impulse in other parts of Latin America. Mexico in 1994, after protracted negotiations with the United States and Canada, became a member of the North American Free Trade Association. Both the CACM and the Andean group have shown renewed interest in reinvigorating their integration schemes, and the latter is showing interest in a free trade agreement with Mercosur. Bolívar's vision of a unified Latin America is not an impossible dream after all.

REGIONAL ECONOMIC INTEGRATION

Economic organization membership

- Central American Common Market
- Andean Group
- Mercosur, founding member
- Mercosur, associate member
- North American Free Trade Association

THE DRUG TRADE

Although the cultivation and use of narcotics like the coca leaf have had a long history in the Americas, Latin America's rise as a great center in the worldwide drug trade really dates back only to the 1980s. The trafficking in illegal drugs has involved countries like Peru and Colombia as the main producers of narcotics, while many other nations serve as transshipment points in the flow of drugs to the big markets in the United States and Europe.

The sudden emergence of the drug culture in the United States during the 1960s and 1970s opened the way for the creation of the region's cocaine industry, which was able to win a big share of the U. S. market for narcotics, estimated to be between $150 and $200 billion per year. Coca leaf, the raw material for the finished product cocaine, is produced in Bolivia, Peru, and Colombia. The first two countries are the main growers of coca leaf, while Colombia has been the main refiner and distributor of cocaine to markets in the Northern Hemisphere. In the heyday of Colombia's cocaine trade, two drug cartels, one in Medellín and one in Cali, between them organized the processing of the product and also worked out the logistics of shipping a flood of drugs by air and by sea through distribution systems they initially controlled in the U.S. market.

The expanding cocaine trade in the 1980s brought about some conflict in the relations between the United States and different Latin American countries. Initially, governments in the Andean drug-producing nations took the view that the cocaine trade was demand-driven from the United States, and that it was up to the Washington authorities alone to control American drug addiction. Unsurprisingly, Washington took the line that efforts should be placed upon interdicting and destroying the supply of illegal drugs.

While the drug trade offered tangible short-term benefits to drug-producing nations, there were disturbing longer-term disadvantages in the form of an upsurge in corruption, greater intimidation and violence to those who incurred the wrath of drug barons, the expanding addiction of home populations to narcotics, and a souring of external relations with the United States. Latin American governments found it harder to maintain the line that the problem was solely demand-driven, just as the Americans, in time, were forced to acknowledge that the problem had to be attacked from the demand side as well as the supply side. In the 1990s, the fundamental character and structure of the Latin American drug trade went through some changes. No longer were the Colombian drug barons in control of the flow of cocaine through the all-important Mexican transshipment location to the U.S. market. The meteoric rise of the Mexican drug barons, who once were subservient to the Colombians, became a major development, as they controlled perhaps as much as over 70 percent of the drugs being sold in American cities. The Mexican drug barons were also thought to be financing the work of illegal Mexican migrants, who were cultivating marijuana in various areas of California and controlled much of the trade in that product.

For Latin American countries and the United States, the stakes are high in the war against the region's powerful drug traffickers.

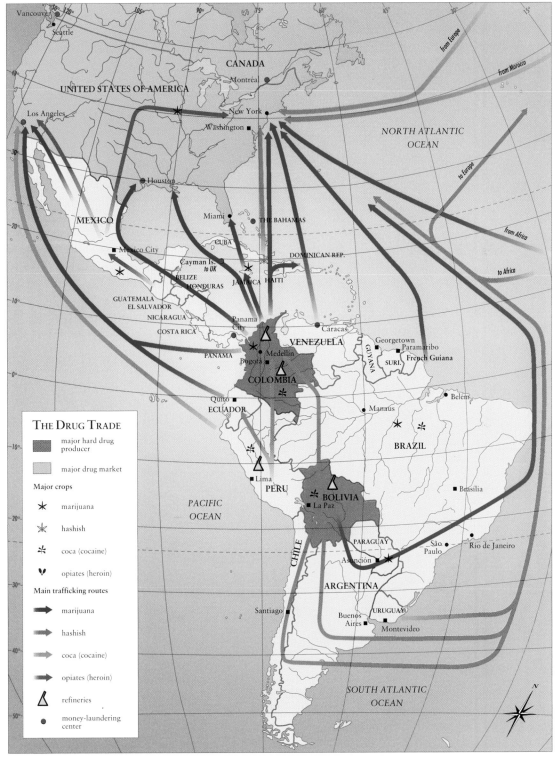

THE DRUG TRADE

- major hard drug producer
- major drug market

Major crops

- ✳ marijuana
- ✺ hashish
- ⚕ coca (cocaine)
- ❤ opiates (heroin)

Main trafficking routes

- ➡ marijuana
- ➡ hashish
- ➡ coca (cocaine)
- ➡ opiates (heroin)
- △ refineries
- ● money-laundering center

THE SOUTH ATLANTIC WAR

The brief South Atlantic War of 1982, fought over what Britain calls the Falkland Islands and Argentina calls las Islas Malvinas, was a conflict of wide international and geopolitical significance about a complex historical dispute of long standing between the two parties. In this sovereignty quarrel, Britain based its position on 150 years of uninterrupted occupation and settlement, while Argentina contended that the Malvinas stand on its continental shelf and that its legal rights stem from the fact that, as Spain was the undisputed owner at independence, lands of the Mother Country reverted to its jurisdiction.

During the twentieth century, the disputed islands have been an increasing bone of contention, especially after 1945. In the 1960s and 1970s random discussions about the problem between the two disputants and in the United Nations led nowhere. Once highly nationalistic military governments were in power, beginning in 1976, the dispute took on a sharper edge. Matters began to come to a head at the end of 1981 when a military group replaced the general occupying the presidency with a junta led by Argentine General Leopoldo Galtieri and composed of Admiral Jorge Anaya and air force brigadier Basilio Lami Dozo. No sooner had the new junta been installed than contingency plans for the invasion of the Malvinas were updated. The move showed not only nationalistic fervor but also expediency, since the ruling junta believed that its "master stroke" would neutralize mounting worker discontent with military rule and would strengthen the Galtieri government's political position. The bold initiative was based on the mistaken beliefs that the British government's commitment to the Falklands was waning and that General Galtieri's cordial contacts with Pentagon officials in Washington would ensure U.S. neutrality if not tacit support. The actual invasion electrified Argentina, Britain, and the world when the news came in that Argentine forces, on April 2, 1982, had invaded and overpowered the small British garrison on East Falkland. A day later and 800 miles to the east, the small British detachment on South Georgia was forced to surrender to the Argentines.

The resolute response of British Prime Minister Thatcher and her government in London, which dispatched a naval armada to reassert British control over islands 8,000 miles away from the United Kingdom, heightened a world crisis with serious hemispheric overtones, given the general Latin American support for Argentina. Intense diplomatic activity followed as the United States, a major player in the drama, assembled a diplomatic mission led by Secretary of State Alexander Haig to mediate between London and Buenos Aires in an effort to forestall hostilities between America's great NATO ally, Britain, and a valued hemispheric nation. From April 12 onward, the Haig mission carried out its

ARGENTINE LANDING, APRIL 2, 1982

—— road

○ British defensive positions

→ first phase of Argentine attack

➤ second phase of Argentine attack

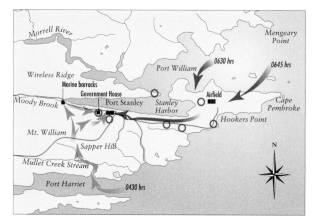

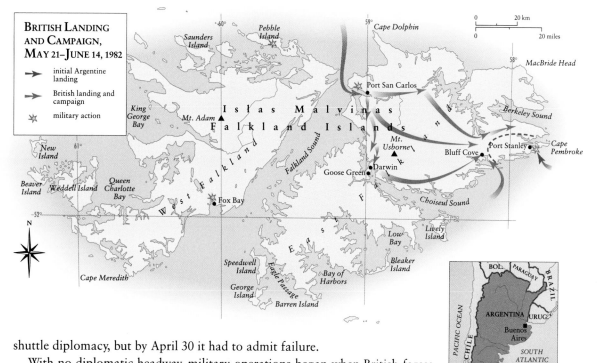

BRITISH LANDING AND CAMPAIGN, MAY 21–JUNE 14, 1982

→ initial Argentine landing

→ British landing and campaign

✦ military action

shuttle diplomacy, but by April 30 it had to admit failure.

With no diplomatic headway, military operations began when British forces on April 25 captured the island of South Georgia. The shooting war started in earnest on May 1, with British air attacks on airports at Port Stanley and Goose Green. The first three weeks of hostilities saw fighting between the air and naval units of the two belligerents and included the sinking of the Argentine cruiser *General Belgrano* and the British destroyer *HMS Sheffield*. The land war commenced on May 21 when British forces, facing fierce aerial opposition, made a successful landing at San Carlos Bay and consolidated and enlarged a bridgehead on East Falkland. British land forces then fought a three-week campaign as they drove in three movements to Port Stanley, where the Argentine commander, Mario Menéndez, was forced to surrender his occupying army on June 14, 1982. The victory by Britain was resounding, while the defeat for Argentina was a shattering blow to the armed forces, the junta government, and the Argentine public at large. Within Argentina, the repercussions were enormous, as it fatally undermined the military dictatorship and hastened the redemocratization of the country in October 1983.

The legacy of the South Atlantic War has been to make the sovereignty dispute even more intractable, as the 2,200 or so Falkland Islanders and British public opinion are more intransigent over the issue. It has not been made easier by the attention now given to the resource potential of the islands, including the possible existence of offshore petroleum deposits. On the Argentine side, the Malvinas question has become more, not less, important to the national psyche, even though a peaceful settlement, not a military one, is the overwhelming desire.

ECOLOGY: THE DEBATE HEATS UP

While green movements in Latin America struggle to make an impact on public opinion, it would appear that ecological concerns are gaining more prominence as governments reflect upon domestic and international calls for better safeguards for the environment; furthermore, the Earth Summit of 1992 in Rio de Janeiro raised the level of consciousness in the region about such problems.

Aside from the critical matter of the depletion of rain forests, Latin America is not unduly conspicuous for the severity of its environmental problems, even though the region has a full catalog of environmental maladies, such as vanishing forests, soil degradation and erosion, air and water pollution, toxic waste disposal problems, and biodiversity losses, among other things. Individual Latin American countries have greater or lesser difficulties with the different ecological problems. In comparison to other world regions, Latin America does not stack up badly. It has more of its original forest cover in percentage terms than Asia or Europe, although slightly less than Russia and North America. In addition, Latin America is only a minor contributor to the discharge of greenhouse gases. No Latin American country is on the list of the ten worst polluting countries of the world; Brazil and Mexico appear in the second-ten listing. Acid rain does not seem as extensive or as much the multicountry problem that it is in North America, Europe, or Asia, although Brazil, Venezuela, and Mexico do have an acid rain problem of their own making, primarily affecting themselves.

Still, there is no room for complacency. Since the 1960s, deforestation has accelerated, particularly in Central America and in Brazil; moreover, intensive land clearing and wood gathering in nations like Haiti and El Salvador has almost denuded these countries of all forests. In countries with major industrial belts, pollution of the air, water, and land has become serious, as in Mexico.

The one environmental area where Latin America is at the forefront of world concern is with rain forest destruction. This is understandable as the larger part of the Earth's rain forests are in Latin America. The Amazon region is the greatest rain forest preserve in the world. Because most of the photosynthesis process producing oxygen for the world is thought to occur in the canopy of rain forests, attention is very much focused on the forestry policies of Latin America in general, but more particularly upon Brazil, owner of the greatest expanse of rain forest on the Earth. Since the 1960s the Amazon territory has been seen by Brazilians as a social safety valve for landless peasants to colonize as well as a resource cornucopia for ranching, mining, and timber logging. Major road building, including the 750-mile Trans-Amazon Highway from the northeast coast to Peru, has opened up the area. Exploitation practices such as slash-and-burn agriculture and cattle ranching in leached soils have been criticized by environmentalists as unsustainable. While considerable deforestation has occurred in Brazil's Amazon area, exact figures as to the extent of the destruction are debatable, but one report estimates that approximately 11 or 12 percent of an original Amazonian forest cover of 350 million hectares has been cleared.

The future of Latin American rain forests and other environmental matters is not uniformly bleak. To protect their rain forests, Ecuador and Venezuela

A small section of the vast Amazonian rain forest. Despite its size and range, human encroachment now threatens many of its unique species of plants and animals.

SHRINKING TROPICAL FORESTS

forest destroyed or seriously degraded since 1940

extent of tropical forests, late 1980s

Tropic of Cancer

20°

MEXICO

Mexico City

Havana

CUBA

THE BAHAMAS

DOMINICAN REP.

JAMAICA

HAITI

Belmopan

BELIZE

HONDURAS

Guatemala

GUATEMALA

Salvador

SAN SALVADOR

NICARAGUA

Managua

Tegucigalpa

San José

COSTA RICA

Panama City

PANAMA

Bogotá

COLOMBIA

Quito

ECUADOR

Caracas

VENEZUELA

Georgetown

Paramaribo

French Guiana

SURI.

GUYANA

NORTH ATLANTIC OCEAN

PACIFIC OCEAN

Manaus

Belém

BRAZIL

Lima

PERU

La Paz

BOLIVIA

Brasília

PARAGUAY

Asunción

São Paulo

Rio de Janeiro

CHILE

Santiago

ARGENTINA

URUGUAY

Buenos Aires

Montevideo

SOUTH ATLANTIC OCEAN

N

have created national park reserves, which have in effect protected 38 and 22 per-cent respectively of their total land surfaces. These two countries, in percent-age terms, top the list of countries protecting land from private exploitation. Increasingly, Latin American governments have accepted the legitimacy of environmental con-cerns and have at times enacted measures to protect the environment and indigenous peoples in threatened areas. The great problem, however, lies with the implementation of environmental safeguards. The lack of political will in Brazil and some other countries to main-tain firm environmental standards is understandable given the intense inter-nal political pressure to open up unex-ploited land for short-term and often unsustainable activities. It looks increasingly likely that, if the wealthy nations of the world are not willing to offer development aid as a *quid pro quo* for the more careful management of rainforest areas, Brazil and other nations will continue to permit the progressive reduction in the size of their extensive forests.

CHRONOLOGY

Many dates approximate.

9000 BC Hunting and fishing.
8000 BC Earliest agriculture in the Andes.
6500 BC Cultivation of potatoes and manioc.
6000 BC Farming of corn and beans.
5500 BC Domestication of animals.
3000 BC Permanent settlements in Tehuacán (Mexico). Earliest pottery (Ecuador and Colombia).
2500 BC Growth of towns and cities (Central America and Peru). Emergence of religion. Cultivation of cotton. Manufacture of textiles.
2000 BC Earliest metalworking (Peru).
1600 BC First settlements at Tiahuanaco (Peru).
1200 BC Olmec civilization in Mexico. City at Chavin de Huantat (Peru).
900 BC Olmec capital at La Venta. Height of Chavin culture; spread of sculpture and temple-building (Peru).
500 BC Growth of Zapotec culture (Mexico). Chavin culture in decline. Growth of Paracas culture along southern coast.
350 BC Rise of the Nazca along the Peruvian coast; carving of the Nazca figures and lines.
300 BC The earliest Maya cities established (Central America).
50 BC Emergence of the Moche culture in northern Peru; advanced building techniques, ceramics, gold-working.
AD 50 Growth of Teotihuacán (Mexico); building of the Pyramid of the Sun.
AD 250 Building of Zapotec temples (Mexico). Maya civilization flourishes throughout Central America.
AD 550 Tiahuanaco, Huari, and El Tajín become major cities (Peru).
AD 650 Teotihuacán destroyed by fire (Mexico).
AD 800 Huari abandoned, Tiahuanaco expands. Growth of

Chan Chan in north (Peru). Metal-working in Mesoamerica.
AD 900 Maya civilization starts to decline; emergence of Chíchén Itzá and Uxmal (Central America).
AD 950 Growth of Toltec empire in Central America. Spread of Inca culture throughout Peru.
1100 Toltecs build capital at Tula (Mexico).
1168 Aztec ("Crane") people begin legendary pilgrimage.
1175 Toltec capital Tula destroyed by Chichimec tribe.
1200 Incas found settlement at Cuzco (Peru).
1325 Aztecs found their capital Tenochtitlán (Mexico).
1425 Aztec culture spreads throughout Central America.
1440 Incas start expanding their empire through Peru.
1470 Incas defeat Chimú; Incas' Andean empire stretches from Ecuador in the north to Chile in the south.
1492 Columbus reaches the Caribbean, claims Cuba for Spain.
1493 First Spanish settlement in Hispaniola (Haiti/Dominica).
1494 Treaty of Tordesillas divides Spanish and Portuguese possessions.
1500 Portuguese explorer Pedro Alvares Cabral lands in Brazil; Portuguese colonization begins. Aztecs control southern Mexico.
1510 Arrival of the first African slaves in West Indies.
1515 Height of Inca empire.
1519–1521 Spanish conquistador General Hernán Cortés overcomes the Aztecs (Mexico). Spanish introduce horses, oxen, guns, and the wheel.
1520 Magellan crosses the Pacific Ocean. Last Aztec emperor Moctezuma II captured by Cortés. Spanish under Alvarado subdue the Maya (Central America).
1525 Inca empire splits into civil war. Europeans discover the potato.
1532–1536 Spanish under Francisco Pizarro conquer the Incas

(Peru). Portuguese establish sugar plantations in Brazil.
1534 Spanish found Quito (Ecuador).
1535 Spanish found Lima (Peru).
1537 Spanish found Asunción (Paraguay).
1538 Spanish found Bogotá (Colombia).
1542 Spanish found Santiago (Chile).
1545 Silver discovered at Potosí (Peru/Bolivia) and at Zacatecas, New Spain (Mexico). First Spanish settlements in the Andean foothills.
1548 Spanish found La Paz (Bolivia).
1560 Portuguese start sugar plantations (Brazil).
1572 Fall of last Inca fort at Vilcabamba.
1586 English sailor Francis Drake raids Cartagena (Colombia). Jesuit missionarism and trading spreads in Paraguay.
1590 Spanish settlements in Eastern Argentina.
1627 English start settlements in West Indies.
1630 Dutch settlement in Northern Brazil.
1637 Dutch take control of sugar-growing regions.
1654 Dutch ousted from Brazil by Portuguese; found Guyana.
1655 English seize Jamaica from Spanish.
1667 British Surinam swapped with Dutch for New Amsterdam (New York).
1680 Portuguese settlement at Colonia del Sacramento (Uruguay); rivalry with Spanish begins for control of the region. Spanish establish sugar plantations in Cuba.
1693 Gold discovered in Brazil.
1719 New Granada founded (Venezuela, Colombia, Ecuador).
1721 Gold rush in Brazil.
1726 Spanish found Montevideo (Uruguay).
1741 British attempt to capture

Cartagena fails.

1763 Rio de Janeiro becomes capital of Brazil.

1766 British settle the Falkland Islands.

1776 Spanish separate Peru and Argentina (Río de la Plata), with capital at Buenos Aires.

1780 Inca uprising against Spanish in Peru.

1781 Communero uprising against Spanish in Colombia.

1786 King Carlos III appoints twelve governors of "New Spain."

1789 Uprising against Portuguese fails in Brazil.

1791 Slave uprising against French in Haiti.

1797 British seize Trinidad from Spanish.

1798 British occupy Maya territory of Belize.

1804 Haiti declares independence from France.

1806 Uprising against Spanish in Venezuela. British forces fail to capture Buenos Aires.

1807 The French under Napoleon invade Portugal; Portuguese king João VI escapes to Brazil with British help; Brazil opened to free trade.

1808 The French invade Spain. Montevideo declares independence from Buenos Aires.

1809 Simón Bolívar leads unsuccessful rebellions against Spanish at Sucre (Chuquisaca), La Paz, and Cochabamba.

1810 Uprising against Spanish in Mexico.

1811 Rebellion against Spanish rule by "New Granada" (Venezuela, Colombia, and Ecuador). Paraguay gains independence from Spain. Brazil attacks Uruguay.

1812–1820 Wars between Uruguayans, Argentines, and Brazilians. Brazil captures Montevideo.

1814 Dutch colonies of Essequibo, Demerara, and Berbice in north Brazil together become British Guiana (Guyana).

1815 Portugal recognizes Brazil's special status. Spanish suppress independence movement in Colombia.

1816 United Provinces of Río de la Plata (Argentina) declare independence; civil war follows.

1817 France claims French Guiana as overseas département.

1818 In Chile, Republican Bernardo O'Higgins defeats pro-Spanish Royalists at battles of Chacabuco and Maipú; Chile gains independence.

1819 In Colombia, Simón Bolívar defeats Spanish at battle of Boyacá; declares republic of Gran Colombia (Venezuela, Colombia, and Ecuador).

1821 Argentine José de San Martín captures Lima, declares Peru independent. Spanish defeated at battle of Carabobo (Venezuela); independence achieved. Mexico gains independence. King Joao VI returns to Portugal; son Pedro regent of Brazil. El Salvador, Nicaragua, and Guatemala gain independence from Spain; together form United Provinces of Central America.

1822 Pedro declares Brazil independent from Portugal, with himself emperor. Mexico and Ecuador gain independence from Spain.

1824 In Peru, Spanish defeated at battles of Junín and Ayacucho.

1825 Bolivia gains independence. All mainland South America free of Spanish control. Increasing influx of Americans into Mexico's Texas province. United Provinces (Argentina) fight Brazil over Uruguay.

1826 Last Spanish colonies in South America gain independence.

1827 Uruguayan–Argentinian victory over Brazil; Montevideo recaptured; Uruguay becomes a separate state.

1828 George Canning mediates and Uruguay wins independence.

1830 Gran Colombia fragments.

1831 Military rebellion in Brazil; Pedro succeeded by his son, Pedro II.

1833 Slavery abolished throughout British empire.

1835 Juan Manuel de Rosas establishes dictatorship in Argentina.

1836 Peru–Bolivia union collapses.

1838 Slaves freed in British Caribbean. Honduras gains independence from Spain. United Provinces of Central America split (El Salvador, Nicaragua, and Guatemala).

1838–1865 Internal strife in Uruguay.

1846–1848 War between Mexico and United States; Mexico cedes New Mexico, Arizona, Nevada, Utah, California, and Colorado.

1850 Importation of slaves halted in Brazil.

1853 Federal government instituted in Argentina. European settlement of the Pampas spreads; beef farming for export to Europe.

1858–1861 Civil war in Mexico; progressives win.

1861 Liberal government in Colombia.

1862 French invade Mexico, capture Mexico City.

1865–1870 Paraguay goes to war with Uruguay, Argentina, and Brazil; triple alliance victorious. Repressive regime in Bolivia under Mariano Melgarejo.

1866 War between Peru and Spain.

1867 Benito Juárez deposes and executes Maximilian I in Mexico.

1868–1878 Uprising asgainst Spanish rule in Cuba.

1878–1883 War against Indians south of the Argentina Pampas.

1879–1883 War between Chile, Bolivia, and Peru; Chile gains nitrate areas; Bolivia loses access to sea.

1888 Slavery abolished in Brazil.

1889 Fall of monarchy, Brazil now a republic, growing coffee exports.

1891 Federal constitution in Brazil.

Collapse of republic in Chile.

1895 Second uprising in Cuba.

1897 Spain grants Cuba partial autonomy; independence struggle continues.

1898 Spain defeated in war with United States; Cuba and Puerto Rico now under U.S. control.

1899 United States establishes military regime in Cuba.

1899–1903 Colombian liberal rebellion "War of 1000 days" fails.

1901 United States establishes Guantanamo naval base on Cuba. Chile–Argentina boundary dispute; British arbitrate. Oil production starts in Mexico.

1903 United States takes control of Panama from Colombia. Acre province of Bolivia ceded to Brazil. Left-liberal José Batllé president in Uruguay.

1908 Augusto Leguía y Salcedo establishes dictatorship in Peru.

1909 Liberal José Miguel Goméz president in Cuba; growth of tourism and gambling.

1910 Mexican Revolution begins; President Porfirio Diaz ousted; Emilio Zapata leads rural uprising.

1912 Military rule in Ecuador.

1914 Oil production begins in Venezuela.

1915 United States invades Haiti and Dominican Republic, intervenes in Mexican revolution, recognizes Carranza as president.

1916 Hipólito Yrigoyen president of Argentina; neutral in World War I. Death of Nicaraguan poet Dario.

1917–1923 United States occupies Cuba.

1918 Brazil declares war on Germany.

1919 Zapata killed in Mexico.

1920 Rebellion of Indians in Bolivia crushed. Carranza killed in Mexico.

1922 Oil production begins in Bolivia.

1925 Gerardo Machado establishes military dictatorship in Cuba.

1926 Catholic rebellion in Mexico. U.S. marines stationed in Nicaragua.

1930 Revolution in Brazil; Vargas president; rapid industrialization. Military coup in Argentina. Liberal Olaya Herrera elected president in Colombia. Leguía ousted by leftists in Peru. National Revolutionary Party in power in Mexico.

1932 Military dictatorship in El Salvador. U.S. marines again stationed in Nicaragua; opposed by General Sandino.

1932–1935 Bolivia–Paraguay wars over Chaco region; Paraguay gains territory.

1933 Military coup in Cuba lead by Fulgencio Batista. Military coup in Uruguay.

1935 Somoza family establish dictatorship in Nicaragua.

1936 Leftist coalition government in Chile.

1938 Death of Leopoldo Lugones, Argentine poet.

1939 Battle of the River Plate; German battleship *Graf Spee* attacked by British and scuttled off Montevideo. Right-wing regime in Peru.

1941 Peru–Ecuador war over El Oro province; Peru gains territory.

1942 Brazil and Mexico enter World War II; declare war on Germany.

1943 Further military coup in Argentina; General Juan Perón organizes trades unions. Chile supports United States in World War II.

1945 Military coup in Brazil; Vargas ousted. Military coup in Venezuela.

1946 Perón president of Argentina; wife Eva champions workers' rights. Right-wing regimes in Chile and Colombia.

1948 Assassination of Liberal Bogotá mayor Gaitán in Colombia; El Bogotazo riot; widespread violence. Military government in Peru. Elections in Venezuela;

novelist Rómulo Gallegos president; U.S.-backed military coup.

1951 In Brazil, socialist Vargas reelected; United States hostile. In Bolivia, Victor Paz Estenssoro elected president; military coup, revolution, restoration of Estenssoro, economic reforms.

1952 Death of Eva Perón.

1953 Military coup in Colombia. Fidel Castro leads abortive revolt in Cuba. Imprisoned, later exiled. Democratic elections in Guyana.

1954 General Alfredo Stroessner comes to power in Paraguay. Vargas commits suicide (Brazil). Democratic constitution in Belize. U.S.-backed coup ousts leftist regime in Guatemala.

1955 Perón ousted by military revolt in Argentina; exiled first to Paraguay. Military rule 1955–1958.

1956 Juscelino Kubitschek president in Brazil; U.S. investment grows. Fidel Castro leads guerrilla war against Batista. Civilian government restored in Peru.

1958 Free elections in Venezuela; Betancourt president.

1959 Castro ousts Batista in Cuba. Che Guevara, Castro's deputy; United States–Cuba relations deteriorate.

1960 Warming USSR–Cuba relations. Quadros president of Brazil, critical of foreign capital.

1961 New capital of Brazil inaugurated at Brasília. Abortive "Bay of Pigs" U.S. invasion of Cuba.

1962 United States begins economic blockade of Cuba. Cuban missile crisis; Russians back down. Brazilian musician Antonio Carlos Jobim's "bossa nova" Desafinado a worldwide hit; increasing popularity of Latin-American music.

1963 Military coups in Peru and Honduras. Publication of Argentine Julio Cortázar's Rayuela (Hopscotch).

1964 Military coup in Brazil; hard-line regime pursues economic expansion. Military coup in Bolivia.

Leftist government in Chile. Left-wing guerrilla movements growing in Colombia and Uruguay (the Tupamaros).

1966 Guyana gains independence from Britain. Guerrilla war in Guatemala.

1967 Death of revolutionary Che Guevara in Bolivia. Jorge Pacheco president in Uruguay. Guatemalan writer Miguel Angel Asturias awarded Nobel Prize for Literature.

1968 Military clampdown on dissent in Brazil and Peru. Olympic Games held in Mexico City; student demonstrators shot.

1969 13-day war between Honduras and El Salvador caused by World Cup qualifying match.

1970 Marxist Salvador Allende elected in Chile; radical program causes problems in economy.

1971 Death of Haitian president "Papa Doc" Duvalier; in ensuing chaos, mass-exodus of Haitians to United States. M-19 guerrilla group active in Colombia. Chilean poet Pablo Neruda awarded Nobel Prize for Literature.

1972 Guatemala prepares for invasion of Belize; Britain stations troops in Belize.

1973 General Pinochet leads military coup in Chile; Allende's suicide; repressive regime putting economy on sounder footing. Perón returns from exile, reelected president. Escalating Latin American foreign debt, Brazil the biggest debtor. Surinam gains independence from Dutch. Publication of Mexican Carlos Fuentes' *Terra Nostra*.

1974 Perón dies, new Argentine president Isabel Perón. Army in Uruguay assumes bigger security role.

1975 Right-wing junta in Peru combats Maoist guerrillas Sendero Luminoso. Escalating foreign debts (Brazil's largest in world). Surinam gains independence from Dutch. Publication of Mexican Carlos Fuentes' *Terra Nostra*.

1976 Isabel Perón ousted; Military junta outlaws political parties and disapearances occur in the "Dirty War." Cuban troops help Angola fight guerrillas supported by the United States and South Africa.

1978 Upsurge of guerrilla warfare and urban terrorism in Guatemala.

1979 Anastasis Somoza ousted by rebel coalition led by Sandinistas with a radical social program. Relations with United States worsen. Civilian rule restored in Ecuador.

1980 New Reagan government ready to provide military aid to counter the Sandinista and Marxist guerrillas in El Salvador. Coup in Surinam.

1981 Liberal wins presidency in Honduran elections. Return of democractic government in Bolivia. Rising guerrilla activity in El Salvador.

1982 Argentine general Galtieri invades Falkland Islands (Malvinas), recaptured by Britain. Leftist government elected in Bolivia. United States tightens economic blockade of Cuba. Colombian author Gabriel García Márquez awarded Nobel Prize for Literature.

1983 Argentine military regime leaves power, Alfonsíne elected president.

1984 Anti-drugs justice minister assassinated in Colombia. Elections in Uruguay; Julio Sanguinetti president.

1985 M-19 guerrilla massacre at Colombian ministry of justice; increasing power of drug cartels in Colombia and Bolivia. Tancredo Neves elected president in Brazil; dies. Leftists win elections in Peru. Earthquake in Mexico City.

1986 Collapse of Bolivian tin-mining industry. Liberal Virgilio Vargas elected president in Colombia. Civilian administration in Guatemala. Civil war in Surinam.

Death of Jorge Luis Borges, Argentine writer.

1987 Gold rush in Roraima, Brazil. Ecuador's President Febres arrested by army. Writer Mario Vargas Llosa leads Libertad movement in Peru.

1988 Contra rebels driven from Nicaragua into Honduras.

1989 Peronist Carlos Menem wins Argentine presidency. Pinochet retires after democratic elections in Chile; Patricio Aylwin president. Stroessner ousted in Paraguay. Elections in Bolivia; coalition government. Fernando Collor de Mello elected president in Brazil; inflation 1000 percent.

1990 Large areas of Amazonian rainforest are recognized as Indian territories (Bolivia, Ecuador). Increasing anarchy in Peru; Alberto Fujimori elected. Elections in Nicaragua. Mexican writer Octavio Paz awarded Nobel Prize for Literature.

1991 End of USSR's economic assistance of Cuba; widespread rationing. UN-brokered peace in El Salvador. Elections in Surinam.

1992 International Earth Summit held in Rio de Janeiro; Collor de Mello impeached for corruption. War against drug barons in Colombia.

1993 Eduardo Frei elected president in Chile. Pablo Escobar, leader of Colombian Medellín drug cartel, dies in police shoot-out. Elections in Paraguay.

1994 United States intervenes in Haiti, restores President Aristide. Chiapas unrest in Mexico.

1996 Guerrillas seize Japanese embassy in Lima, Peru; embassy successfully stormed by army.

1998 Oil-drilling starts off the Falkland Islands (Malvinas).

SELECT BIBLIOGRAPHY

The authors readily acknowledge the work of many scholars and works in publication which have been consulted in the preparation of this atlas. Following is a selected bibliography of works recommended for further reading on the topics covered in this atlas.

Alexander, Robert (editor), *Political Parties of the Americas: Canada, Latin America and the West Indies*, 2 vols., Greenwood, 1982

Anna, Timothy E., *The Fall of the Royal Government in Mexico City*, University of Nebraska Press, 1979

Anna, Timothy E., *Spain and the Loss of America*, University of Nebraska Press, 1982

Atkins, G. Pope, *Latin America in the International Political System*, 3rd ed., Westview, 1995

Bawden, Garth and Geoffrey W. Conrad, *The Andean Heritage; Masterpieces of Peruvian Art from the Collections of the Peabody Museum*, Peabody Museum Press, 1982

Benson, Elizabeth P. and Beatriz de la Fuente, *Olmec Art of Ancient Mexico*, Harry N. Abrams Inc., 1996

Bethell, Leslie (editor), *The Cambridge History of Latin America*, 10 vols., 1984–1996

Blanchard, Peter, *The Origins of the Peruvian Labor Movement, 1883–1919*, University of Pittsburg Press, 1982.

Boxer, C. R., *The Golden Age of Brazil, 1695–1750: Growing Pains of a Colonial Society*, University of California Press, 1969

Boxer, C. R., *The Portuguese Seaborne Empire*, Hutchinson, 1969

Burns, E. Bradford, *A History of Brazil*, 2nd ed., Columbia University Press, 1980

Burr, Robert, N., *By Reason or Force: Chile and the Balancing of Power in South America, 1830–1905*, University of California Press, 1965

Coe, Michael, *The Maya*, Thames and Hudson, 1984

Cubitt, Tessa, *Latin American Society*, Longman, 1991 (reprinted)

Cumberland, Charles C., *Mexico: The Struggle for Modernity*, Oxford University Press, 1968

Davis, Harold E., John J. Finan, F. Taylor Peck, *Latin American Diplomatic History: An Introduction*, Louisiana State University Press, 1977

Díaz del Castillo, Bernal, *The Conquest of New Spain* (translation), Penguin Books, 1986

Diehl, Richard A., *Tula: The Toltec Capital of Ancient Mexico*, Thames and Hudson, 1983

Dobyns, Henry F., and Paul L. Doughty, *Peru: A Cultural History*, Oxford University Press, 1979

Domínguez, Jorge I., *Cuba: Order and Revolution*, Harvard University Press, 1978

Dornbusch, Rudiger and Sebastian Edwards (editors), *The Macroeconomics of Populism in Latin America*, University of Chicago Press, 1991

Fisher, John R., Allan J. Kueth and Anthony McFarlane (editors), *Reform and Insurrection in Bourbon New Granada and Peru*, Louisiana State University Press, 1990

Freyre, Gilberto, *The Masters and the Slaves (Casa Grande e Senzala), a Study in the Development of Brazilian Civilization*, Alfred Knopf, 1946

Furtado, Celso, *Economic Development of Latin America, A Survey from Colonial Times to the Cuban Revolution*, Cambridge University Press, 1970

Gibson, Charles, *Spain in America*, Harper and Row, 1966

Gil, Frederico G., *Latin American–United States Relations*, Harcourt Brace Jovanovich, 1971

Gillespie, Richard, *Soldiers of Perón: Argentina's Montoneros*, Clarendon Press, 1982

Glade, William P., *The Latin American Economies, a study of their institutional evolution*, American Book Company, 1969

Hassig, Ross, *Mexico and the Spanish Conquest*, Longman, 1994

Hastings, Max and Simon Jenkins, *The Battle for the Falklands*, Michael Joseph, 1983

Hemming, John, *The Conquest of the Incas*, Macmillan (London), 1970

Hemming, John, *Red Gold: The Conquest of the Brazilian Indians*, Papermac, 1995

Herring, Hubert, *A History of Latin America from the Beginnings to the Present*, Alfred Knopf, 2nd ed. rev., 1967

Kendall, Ann, *Everyday Life of the Incas*, B. T. Batsford Ltd., 1973

Klein, Herbert S., *Bolivia: The Evolution of a Multi-Ethnic Society*, Oxford University Press, 2nd ed., 1992

Kline, Harvey F., *Colombia: Portrait of Unity and Diversity*, Westview, 1983

Knight, Franklin W., *The Caribbean: The Genesis of a Fragmented Nationalism*, Oxford University Press, 2nd ed., 1990

Lockhard, James and Stuart B. Schwartz, *Early Latin America: A History of Colonial Spanish America and Brazil*, Cambridge University Press, 1983

Lombardi, John V., *Venezuela: The Search for Order, the Dream of Progress*, Oxford University Press, 1982

Loveman, Brian, *Chile: The Legacy of Hispanic Capitalism*, Oxford University Press, 1979

Lynch, John, *Argentine Dictator: Juan Manuel de Rosas, 1829–1852*, Clarendon Press, 1981

Lynch, John, *The Spanish–American Revolutions, 1808–1826*, 2nd ed., Weidenfeld and Nicolson, 1973

Matos Moctezuma, Eduardo, *The Great Temple of the Aztecs*, Thames and Hudson, 1988

McFarlane, Anthony, *Colombia before Independence: Economy, Society and Politics under Bourbon Rule*, Cambridge University Press, 1994

Mörner, Magnus, *Race Mixture in the History of Latin America*, Little Brown, 1967

Parry, J. H., *The Spanish Seaborne Empire*, Hutchinson, 1966

Pérez, Louis A. Jr., *Cuba: between Reform and Revolution*, 2nd ed., Oxford University Press, 1995

Philip, George, *The Military in South American Politics*, Croom Helm, 1985

Porter Weaver, Muriel, *The Aztecs, Maya, and their Predecessors*, Academic Press, 1981

Rock, David, *Argentina, 1516–1987—From Spanish Colonization to Alfonsín*, University of California Press, 1987

Roet, Riordan and Richard S. Sacks, *Paraguay: the Personalist Legacy*, Westview 1991

Sánchez-Albornoz, Nicolás, *The Population of Latin America: A History*, University of California Press, 1974

Sanders, William T. and Barbara J. Price, *Mesoamerica: The Evolution of a Civilization*, Random House, 1968

Skidmore, Thomas E. and Peter H. Smith, *Modern Latin America*, Oxford University Press, 1984

Smith, Joseph, *Illusions of Conflict: Anglo–American Diplomacy Toward Latin America, 1865–1896*, University of Pittsburg Press, 1979

Stein, Stanley J. and Barbara H. Stein, *A Colonial History of Latin America. Essays on Economic Dependence in Perspective*, Oxford University Press, 1970

Thomas, Hugh, *The Conquest of Mexico*, Hutchinson, 1993

Walker, Thomas W., *Nicaragua, the Land of Sandino*, 3rd ed., revised and updated, 1991

Weinstein, Brian and Aaron Segal, *Haiti: Political Failures, Cultural Successes*, Praeger, 1984,

Weinstein, Martin, *Uruguay: Democracy at the Crossroads*, Westview, 1988

Wiarda, Howard J. and Michael J. Kryzanek, *The Dominican Republic, a Caribbean Crucible*, Westview, 1982

Williams, John Hoyt, *The Rise and Fall of the Paraguayan Republic, 1800–1870*, The University of Texas at Austin, 1979

Woodward, Ralph Lee, *Central America: A Nation Divided*, 2nd ed., Oxford University Press, 1985

INDEX

ACKNOWLEDGMENTS

Pictures are reproduced by permission of, or have been provided by the following:

e.t. archive: pp. 10, 11, 14, 17, 21, 25, 26, 30, 33, 36, 38, 45, 46, 48, 56, 63, 67, 69, 87, 110
Image Bank: pp. 28, 59, 79, 88, 91, 97, 148
Keystone Collection: p. 135
Peter Newarks American Pictures: p. 98
Private Collection: pp. 27, 39, 52, 74, 84, 102, 136

Illustrations: Peter A. B. Smith and M. A. Swanston

Design: Malcolm Swanston

Typesetting: Shirley Ellis, Marion M. Storz

Cartography: Peter Gamble, Elsa Gibert, Peter A. B. Smith, Malcolm Swanston, Isabelle Verpaux, Jonathan Young

Production: Joseph Johnson